EXILES UNDAUNTED

Ross Patrick began his career as a pharmacist, then graduated in Medicine from the University of Queensland. During World War II he served in the Australian Army Medical Corps in New Guinea. He joined the Queensland Health Department in 1947, and was director-general of Health and Medical Services from 1969 until his retirement in 1978. Ross Patrick is the author of *Horsewhip the Doctor* (UQP 1985); *A History of Health and Medicine in Queensland 1824–1960* (UQP 1987); and *The Royal Women's Hospital Brisbane: The First Fifty Years* (Boolarong 1988), all dealing with the history of medicine in Queensland.

Heather Patrick graduated first in Arts and then in Medicine from the University of Queensland which she represented in three sports, gaining a Blue in swimming. She was a medical officer in the Queensland Department of Maternal and Child Welfare, and rehabilitation medical officer at Concord Hospital, Sydney. She is presently industrial medical officer at the Prince Charles Hospital, Brisbane. As well as being a keen historian, Heather Patrick is an accomplished artist; her portraits of Eva and Kevin O'Doherty are reproduced here on the cover.

EXILES UNDAUNTED

The Irish Rebels
Kevin and Eva O'Doherty

ROSS & HEATHER PATRICK

Ross Patrick
Heather D. Patrick

University of Queensland Press

First published 1989 by University of Queensland Press
Box 42, St Lucia, Queensland 4067 Australia

© Ross and Heather Patrick 1989

This book is copyright. Apart from any fair dealing
for the purposes of private study, research, criticism
or review, as permitted under the Copyright Act, no
part may be reproduced by any process without written
permission. Enquiries should be made to the publisher.

Typeset by University of Queensland Press
Printed in Australia by Australian Print Group, Maryborough, Victoria

Distributed in the USA and Canada by
International Specialized Book Services, Inc.,
5602 N.E. Hassalo Street, Portland, Oregon 97213-3640

Cataloguing in Publication Data

National Library

Patrick, Ross, 1914– .
  Exiles undaunted : the Irish rebels Kevin and
Eva O'Doherty

  Bibliography.
  Includes index.

  1. O'Doherty, Kevin Izod, 1823–1905. 2. O'Doherty,
Eva, 1826–1910. 3. Irish — Queensland — Biography.
4. Nationalists — Ireland — Biography. 5. Surgeons —
Queensland — Biography. I. Patrick, Heather, 1931–
II. Title.

994'.0049162

ISBN 0 7022 2223 2

Contents

Dedication *vi*
List of Illustrations *vii*
Foreword *viii*
Acknowledgments *x*
Chronological Table *xii*
Map of Ireland *xiv*

Chapter 1 The O'Dohertys and the Kellys *1*
Chapter 2 Towards Rebellion *16*
Chapter 3 Imprisonment and Transportation *33*
Chapter 4 Exile *59*
Chapter 5 Reunion *87*
Chapter 6 Graduation and Migration *110*
Chapter 7 Member of Parliament *137*
Chapter 8 A Public Man *159*
Chapter 9 Many Irons in the Fire *176*
Chapter 10 His Expert Advice *202*
Chapter 11 Stand Up and Be Counted *223*
Chapter 12 Triumph then Tragedy *247*
Epilogue *266*

References *268*
Index *285*

This book is dedicated to the late Thomas Southern MacBride, father and father-in-law of the authors. He honoured the O'Dohertys in his sonnet, "So Much For Love", which appears below.

So Much For Love

So much for love — two spirits rare, conjoin'd, —
Emancipators, aye — glory forgone!
Life's sweets by sullen grief too oft purloin'd!
Far distant tracks and strange, to journey on!

Exponent was he of the healer's art,
Of tremendous use to his fellow man;
In other spheres he play'd an equal part,
Suchwise as only true philosophers can.

And she the sparkling light of his life
To record it all by the power of the muse,
Was ever man bless'd with a dearer wife
Than would sing his praise as the gods would choose?

Bricks both, glazed in the fires of tribulation —
Bright keystones in the building of our nation.

Illustrations

following page 130

Kevin O'Doherty's baptismal certificate
Eva O'Doherty, c. 25 years
Kevin O'Doherty, c. 25 years
"Lisdonagh", Ireland
Ivy House, Ireland
Royal College of Surgeons, Dublin
John Martin
William Smith O'Brien
Daniel O'Connell
Elm Cottage, Tasmania
Letter of conditional pardon from British Government
Queen Street, Brisbane, c. 1867
Eva O'Doherty, c. 40 years
Kevin O'Doherty aged 59
Brisbane Hospital in the 1870s
William O'Doherty, aged 23
Gertrude O'Doherty, aged 8
Dr William Hobbs
Dr John Thomson
Former St Stephen's Church and Cathedral, Brisbane
Dr Kearsey Cannan
Bishop James Quinn
Freedom of Dublin City invitation
Eva O'Doherty, c. 75 years
"Frascati", O'Doherty home, Ann Street, Brisbane
Kevin O'Doherty, c. 75 years
Cottage at Rosalie, Brisbane
O'Doherty memorial inscription, Toowong Cemetery, Brisbane
Caroline Nesbitt

Foreword

When my "adopted cousins" Ross and Heather Patrick invited me to write the foreword to their wonderful work on my great-great-grandparents Kevin and Eva O'Doherty, I was immensely flattered. What could be easier, I thought, or more fun? So I sat down at my typewriter, all set to bang it out, only to find that it wasn't going to be quite so simple after all. My mind kept running on two entirely different tracks.

On one level there is my enormous personal gratitude to Ross and Heather for returning a part of a family history which had only partially survived moves from Brisbane to London, London to Washington, DC, and thence eventually to New Hampshire. Remaining were an outline of the romantic story; a few news clippings and largely unidentified photographs (the ones of Kevin himself so like my father that they might have been twins); and Eva's engagement ring, which miraculously survived my grandmother's occasional tendency to pawn or lose things to wind up with me.

Ross and Heather identified the photographs, filled in the blanks, and brought from Colleen Melhuish the generous presents of a volume of Eva's poetry, and Kevin's signet ring. Reunited across a century and half the world, the rings now rest together again.

But their gifts then transcended the temporal, for in following the story I began to see that the O'Dohertys left far more than a strong physical resemblance and assorted "stuff" to their few descendants. There was that indomitable spirit shining through my enormously strongwilled grandmother. There was the intense idealism and innate sense of justice that existed in my father and led to his active support of causes like the Civil Rights Movement in his own adopted country, the United States. And I suppose it's no accident that I became among other things a writer. (A dreamer, too, I might add!)

But this is all personal, and small, as the cosmic scale goes. On a much higher level, the Patricks have given *all* of us back our families; the ones that voluntarily or by force left home, hearth and relatives with no idea of what awaited them, endured hardship, loss and separation, and finally built new (and it is hoped, better) lives in the vast, unexplored and unfettered territories of Australia, Canada and the US. Astounding to think how much of what we are, we owe to them. Humbling to think that we are the heirs of such amazing people.

So there's a lot of the human spirit here, as well as a lot of history and adventure and romance. All the elements that stir our souls, give us mirrors in which to see ourselves, remind us of what's gone before and what has yet to be done.

Come to think of it, these are also all the elements that make for great pictures. If you sell the film rights, Ross, you must arrange for me to play Eva of the Nation!

And may all of you get as much pleasure from reading this book as I have.

Caroline Nesbitt
North Sandwich, NH, USA
January 12, 1989

Acknowledgments

We are greatly indebted to many people — some acting in a private capacity, others as members of institutions — for their generous help as we sought material from which to compile this book.

In Ireland, Monica Carroll, a descendant of John Doherty, Kevin O'Doherty's brother, gave us free access to all information recorded in the family bible, obtained photocopies of appropriate entries in O'Doherty's journal written in Richmond Jail and had photographs prepared of Kevin and other family members from daguerreotypes in her possession. In 1978 Patrick Moran drove us from Galway city to Headford to view Ivy House, in which Eva was born and to Lisdonagh, the manor where she spent much of her childhood with her grandparents, the O'Flahertys. He more recently engaged a photographer, David Brown, to take valuable photographs, and, after reading the manuscript, supplied very much appreciated constructive criticism. Without the help of Anne Brennan of Dublin the ancestry of Kevin O'Doherty and Eva Kelly would have remained a mystery. From Brother Allen of the Daniel O'Connell School, Dublin, came a generous gift of a volume of Eva's poems and through the Old Dublin Society we obtained the services of one of its esteemed members, Kevin O'Rorke, as a further check of what we had written. The officers of the National Library of Ireland gave us courteous assistance while we studied the O'Doherty papers and other pertinent manuscripts during our many visits. We are indebted to the Deputy Keeper of Records, Public Record Office of Northern Ireland, Belfast, and the late Mrs R. Atkinson for permission to quote from correspondence in the John Martin papers.

In England, every co-operation was afforded us when we searched the newspapers held at the British Museum's Press Library at Colinton, while the Public Records Office at Kew, Surrey readily supplied us with copies of relevant manuscripts.

One of the highlights of our research was a visit in 1982 to New Hampshire, USA to meet Caroline and Vivian Nesbitt, great-great-granddaughters of Kevin and Eva O'Doherty. In addition to giving us important material at the time of our visit, Caroline later read our manuscript, provided family photographs and allowed us to use all the O'Doherty material.

Australian sources were found at the Archives Office of Tasmania, Hobart; the Latrobe Library, Melbourne; the National Library, Canberra; the Mitchell Library, Sydney; and in Brisbane at the Queensland Parliamentary Library, the Queensland State Archives and the John Oxley Library. The late Alan Queale supplied numerous volumes of Irish history from his extensive collection. We owe much to Colleen Melhuish and her mother, the late Mrs A.G. Melhuish of East Brisbane, stepdaughter of Gertrude O'Sullivan, nee O'Doherty, the only child who survived her parents, Kevin and Eva. We were given free access to letters, newspaper cuttings, certificates and photographs held by them. Further photographic help came from Jack Dale, Glen Oldham and John Warner. Historian Denis Martin receives our special thanks for his generous help on church matters.

Chronological Table

1823   Birth of Kevin Izod O'Doherty, 7 Sep.
1830   Birth of Mary Anne Kelly (Eva of the *Nation*), 15 Feb.
1842   O'Doherty began study of medicine.
1848   Arrest and conviction of O'Doherty.
1849   O'Doherty transported to Van Diemen's Land (Tasmania).
1854   O'Doherty left Van Diemen's Land for Melbourne, Victoria after being granted conditional pardon.
1855   O'Doherty left Victoria for England, 12 Mar.; O'Doherty and Eva Kelly married, 23 Aug. and moved to Paris.
1856   O'Doherty granted full pardon; couple returned to Dublin; birth of first son (William), 26 May.
1857   O'Doherty graduated in medicine.
1858   Birth of second son (Edward), 3 Apr.
1859   Birth of third son (Vincent), 23 Aug.
1860   O'Doherty and family migrated to Australia; birth of fourth son (Kevin jun.) at Geelong, Victoria, 8 Nov.; family moved to Sydney.
1862   O'Doherty family moved to Ipswich, Queensland; birth of fifth son (John), 30 Jun. — died 30 Jan. 1863.
1864   Birth of first daughter (Jeanette), 22 Feb. — died 8 Sep.
1865   Family moved to Brisbane, Queensland.
1866   O'Doherty appointed visiting surgeon Brisbane Hospital; birth of second daughter (Eva), 9 Mar. — died 11 Aug.
1867   O'Doherty elected to Queensland Legislative Assembly.
1869   Birth of Gertrude, only surviving daughter, 15 Nov.
1872   O'Doherty introduced first Health Act passed in Queensland Parliament.
1873   O'Doherty resigned his seat in parliament.
1874   O'Doherty played important role in opening St Stephen's Cathedral.
1875   O'Doherty delivered the O'Connell Oration.
1877   O'Doherty appointed a member of the Queensland Legislative Council; Eva travelled to America and Ireland with William, Edward and Gertrude; Eva's poems published in San Francisco.
1881   Death of Bishop Quinn.
1882   O'Doherty elected president of the Queensland Medical Society.
1883   O'Doherty chaired the Irish National Convention in Melbourne.

1885	O'Doherty elected member for Meath, Ireland in House of Commons.
1886	O'Doherty returned to Brisbane and transferred to Sydney.
1867	O'Doherty appointed government medical officer at Croydon, North Queensland.
1889	O'Doherty returned to Brisbane from Croydon.
1890	Death of Vincent O'Doherty, 3 Nov.; O'Doherty elected president of the Queensland Medico-Ethical Society.
1892	O'Doherty appointed to part-time government positions.
1893	Death of William O'Doherty, 9 Oct.
1900	Death of Kevin (jun.) O'Doherty, 15 Feb.; death of Edward, 4 Jul.
1905	Death of Kevin Izod O'Doherty, 15 Jul.
1909	Another volume of Eva's poems published in Dublin.
1910	Death of Eva O'Doherty, 21 May.
1912	Unveiling of O'Doherty monument, Toowong cemetery.
1949	Death of Gertrude O'Sullivan (nee O'Doherty), 26 Apr.

IRELAND. Showing places mentioned in the text.

CHAPTER 1

The O'Dohertys and the Kellys

"Put forward Kevin Izod O'Doherty."

As Mr Justice Crampton waited for the order to be obeyed, he looked around the courtroom at Green Street, Dublin. It was 3 November 1848 and he and Mr Justice Torrens, sitting beside him on the bench, were the presiding judges of the October commission constituted to hear charges under the Treason Felony Act. Below the bench sat the officers of the court, busy with papers and exhibits. In front of them stood the tables for the bar. At one sat the counsel for the Crown led by the Right Honourable J.J. Monahan, attorney-general. At the other, the judge saw Isaac Butt, QC, and his assistant counsel whose combined efforts had failed to save the prisoner. The judge noted the eager reporters poised to write the notes which would be the basis of their reports in the papers next day. On the right of the bench in the petit jury gallery sat the men who, two days before, had returned a verdict of guilty on one of the counts of which the prisoner had been accused. The judge lifted his eyes to the crowded public gallery in which were seated friends of the prisoner and sympathisers of the movement to which he belonged. For a moment his gaze centred on the two women in the front row of the gallery, where they had sat every day since the trial began. He had learnt that the younger of the two, a beautiful raven-haired Irish colleen, was Eva Kelly and rumour had it that she was secretly betrothed to O'Doherty. His eye finally came to rest on the raised dock, where yet another Irishman would stand to hear the price to be paid for fighting for independence for his country. Many had stood there before. The judge recalled some of them.

In June 1798 the brothers, Henry and John Sheares, heard the death sentence passed on them for their part in planning an insurrection by the United Irishmen. It was from this dock that Robert Emmet in 1803 heard Lord Norbury pronounce the death sentence on him for his leadership in an unsuccessful insurrection, in which it had been planned to attack Dublin Castle, the centre of government. It was here, also, that only a few months before the present trial, John Mitchel, a leader of the Young Ireland movement, to which O'Doherty belonged, had so dominated the courtroom that he gave the appearance of a director managing a play. He ended an eloquent post-sentence speech with the following oft-to-be-quoted words: "The cause in which I have been engaged has only commenced, and, as the Roman patriot said when the tyrant had his hand thrust into the fire, and when that hand was shrivelled and burnt to ashes, 'I can promise for one hundred, two hundred, three hundred to be of my opinion.' So say I: one — yes, two — yes, three hundred are ready to follow my course." In this Green Street Court dock, John Martin, another eminent Young Irelander, faced the August commission after his arrest on the same day as O'Doherty. Found guilty of a charge of treason felony arising from articles in his paper, the *Irish Felon*, Martin was sentenced to transportation for fourteen years.

With a start, Judge Crampton returned to the present. As the well-built, good-looking young prisoner entered the dock, he glanced quickly to the public gallery where Eva Kelly sat and a silent message passed between them. Turning to the bench, he displayed the same composure and dignity which had marked his conduct throughout the entire course of the three trials to which he had been subjected. Judge Crampton then began his pre-sentencing harangue:

> Kevin Izod O'Doherty, you were indicted for compassing the deposition of Her Majesty the Queen, and also for compassing to levy war against Her Majesty, in order by force and constraint to compel her to change her measures and counsels. You have been acquitted on all counts charging the former intent, and have been found guilty of compassing to levy war against Her Majesty the Queen, for the purpose of compelling her by force and constraint to change her measures and counsels. Your crime is one which is founded upon a statute passed so lately as the 22nd of April last. Before the passing of that statute, your crime, in England, would have been that of high treason, and in Ireland, at least a high misdemeanour; but, whether in one country or the other, before that statute, and since, a crime of great enormity. It is a felony according to the enactment to which I have just referred. Now of that felony you have been found guilty by a jury of your country, and, I must add, upon evidence sufficient, not only to satisfy the requirements of the laws, but to satisfy the mind of every impartial person who heard the trial. You were connected, I think it appears in the evidence, with the medical profession; and you seem to have abandoned that honourable and useful walk of life for the purpose of becoming a politician and a journalist. You became the publisher and proprietor of a newspaper called the *Irish Tribune*; and it is for the publications in that journal that you now stand, I am sorry to add, a convicted felon at that bar. Your offence is emphatically one of intention. Now what was that intention as found by your jury? It was an intention to raise an insurrection against the Government of the kingdom; to embark the masses of the country in a civil war, with all its attendant horrors; and your view was, no doubt, to bring a revolution, and to establish a republic in Ireland.

The judge continued to speak of O'Doherty's defiance of the laws for some time. He mentioned the fate of John Mitchel, then went on:

> In your desperate purpose, happily for yourself and for your country, you have been defeated, and you have now to abide the penalty of the law. I grieve, I do lament indeed, to see a person of your education, character and condition in life, placed in the painful position in which you now stand at that bar; and that position, I must say again, the result of your voluntary and deliberate act. But, painful as the duty is, the Court has a solemn and stern duty to

discharge, and it must be done. The intelligent and respectable jury who found you guilty have recommended you to mercy, on the ground of your youth, and on the ground of the excitement which existed in the public mind at the time when your pernicious publications issued from the *Tribune* press. But much as we desire to yield to the recommendation of the jury, and we always pay the greatest attention to such recommendations, yet, in this instance, we can follow it but in a qualified manner. What was it, let me ask, that caused the excitement truly stated in the recommendation of the jury? Was it not the long-laboured and long-continued preparation and training, and the poisoning of the public mind, under the name of constitutional agitation, which created this excitement? And was not the press, a portion of it, a chief instrument in the course of that agitation? I fear I must add, that I cannot conceive, I have never read any publications more dangerous, more wicked, more clearly designed to excite insurrection, rebellion and revolution, than those publications which have emanated from your press, and of which you have been ascertained, by the verdict of your jury, to be the guilty publisher. Under these circumstances, the Court feels called on to pronounce upon you the sentence, that you be transported for ten years.

A murmur of sympathy could be heard from the public gallery when the sentence was announced. But, O'Doherty, quite unperturbed, asked in a calm voice whether he could be permitted to speak. His request was granted but his opening remarks met with the strong disapproval of Judge Crampton. O'Doherty said that he had hoped that upon being placed in the dock a third time, after two juries had refused to find a verdict against him, that his prosecutors "would have been scrupulous and taken care that in attempting to uphold their law, they would have not violated every principle of justice". He then claimed that during the trial the attorney-general stated that there were but three Roman Catholics set aside on the jury. These statements brought stern rebukes from the judge and a warning that the court would not listen if the convicted man continued in such a vein. Changing the tenor of his comments, O'Doherty then explained the motives and feelings which influenced his actions leading up to his arrest:

> I may with perfect truth say that I was influenced but by one feeling, and had but one object in view. I did feel deeply for the sufferings and privations endured by my fellow countrymen. I desired, I

confess, by every means consistent with a manly and honourable resistance to put an end to those sufferings .... My lords, with respect to myself, I fear not. I trust I shall be enabled to bear my sentence with all the forebearance due to what I believe to be the opinions of twelve conscientious enemies to me; and that I shall endure the wrath of the Government, whose mouthpiece they were, with all due patience. But certainly I will never cease to deplore the unhappy destiny which gave me birth in this wretched country; and compelled me, as an Irishman, here in this dock, to receive at your hands a felon's doom, for discharging what I conceived to be, and still conceive to be, my duty. My lord, the matter of fact that I was about to mention I brought here in writing. Inquiries have been made by my friends, and the result of them was handed to me; and it was in consequence of that that I felt it my duty to mention this, as well in justice to myself as to my Roman Catholic fellow countrymen. The names of the jurors set aside by the Attorney-General are mentioned in it; and instead of three, I find there are thirteen; and I hold in my hand a list of their names; and out of twelve jurors he permitted to be sworn there was not one Roman Catholic. I merely wished to mention that fact my lord.

Mr Justice Crampton. That is a matter utterly unconnected with the proceedings in this place.

The judge waited and when he saw that O'Doherty had no more to say, gave the order for the prisoner to be removed. The convicted man, still holding himself proudly, bowed slightly to the bench and turned to descend the steps from the dock. On the threshold of the court the Irish colleen, Eva Kelly, was waiting for the prisoner to pass. "Have faith, I'll wait," she whispered to him. The turnkeys took up their position of escort and he strode, head held high, down the vaulted passage that connected the court to Newgate jail, back to his cell.

The large and powerful O'Doherty clan had their origin in Donegal. From the eighth century they possessed Inishowen, the most northern part of Ireland. They ruled there until King James I came to the throne of England in 1603. Sir Cahir O'Doherty attacked the English at Londonderry but he was overwhelmed by superior numbers and lost his life. Other clan leaders fled to the European continent and Inishowen was granted by the king to Arthur Chichester, Baron Belfast.

In Irish, the name is spelt O'Dochartaigh and means

"obstructive". On the shield of the O'Doherty coat of arms three white five-pointed stars on a green background surmount a red springing deer. The motto reads, "Ar nDuthchas" — "Our heritage". Variations in the English spelling of the name include O'Docharty, Dougherty, Dorrity and O'Dogherty. During the submergence of Catholic and Gaelic Ireland, which began when English and Scottish settlers were granted lands confiscated by James I, the prefixes of "Mac" and "O" to Irish names were dropped in many areas.

The convicted man's forebears were among those who had dropped the prefix "O". Records in the family bible reveal that his great-grandfather was George Doherty of Dublin. It is not known how long he had lived in the city. He had two sons, Kevin Izod and William Izod, of whom the first became our subject's grandfather. Catholics who wished to trade were obliged to make appropriate application and records reveal that grandfather Kevin was granted permission to set up a grocer's shop at 53 Abbey Street, Dublin, in the 1780s. In 1799 he is listed as porter and ale brewer at the corner of Bonham and Watling Streets in the area where the great Guinness complex stands today.

The grocer and brewer married Mary Knabbs and before she died in 1795, she had borne him five children: George (1786), William Izod (1787), Elizabeth (1789), Amelia (1790) and John (1794). The Dublin in which Kevin and Mary Doherty lived was a city of distinction with approximately 180,000 people. The English architect, James Gandon, had seen his planning brought to fruition in the magnificent buildings of the Four Courts and Customs House, both overlooking the Liffey quays. On both sides of the Liffey, elegant squares and Georgian houses were built to add to the splendour. The Irish parliament (completely Protestant) still met in Dublin and there was evidence of prosperity, even though it was a prosperity confined mostly to a minority — the Anglo-Irish ascendancy.

But the elegance of the city hid the memories of the oppression that had been imposed on the majority of the Irish people during the two preceding centuries. In addition to the plantation of English and Scottish settlers on confiscated lands in northern Ireland, they had suffered Cromwell's brutal sacking of Drogheda in 1649 in revenge for the atrocities committed against Protestants during Sir Phelim O'Neill's rebellion a few years previously and then the English leader's subjugation of the whole of Ireland. The Catholic hopes had been dashed with the defeat of the armies of James II by William of Orange at the Battle of the Boyne in 1690 and next came the introduction of the harsh Penal Laws which placed heavy restrictions on the Catholic population.

Under these measures Catholics were excluded from parliament, the magistracy, the services, the bar and juries, as well as being deprived of voting rights at political elections. No Catholic was allowed to purchase or inherit land. Harsh provisions relating to their religion and education were introduced. The Catholic church hierarchy was banished from the country with a reduced number of registered priests being allowed to attend their religious duties. No Catholic could keep a school nor send his children abroad for education.

Towards the end of the eighteenth century, the government, influenced by the American War of Independence and the French Revolution, reduced the harshness of the Penal Laws. Catholics were allowed to hold land, priests were not required to register and Catholic school masters could teach. By 1790 eligibility to practise law and the franchise were restored but Catholics were still excluded from parliament, the higher civil service posts and the bench.

Despite the relaxation of the Penal Laws many Irishmen were unhappy with conditions in their country and in the closing years of the eighteenth century, Wolfe Tone, with his United Irishmen, strove to throw off the English yoke and have Ireland follow France and become a republic. His rebellion ended in disaster with Tone and the rebel military leader, Lord Edward Fitzgerald, dying in prison. Pitt, the English prime minister, considered these events had produced an opportune time to proceed with plans of a legislative union between England and Ireland.

If the decision, which would be made in the Irish parliament, favoured the union, that parliament would be voted out of existence and Ireland would be governed by the British parliament to which Ireland would send representatives. Although the Catholics, excluded from parliament, would have no say in the decision-making, they did have opinions on such a vital proposal. Some, believing that the union would be coupled with Catholic emancipation, favoured the move. Others, led by a young barrister, Daniel O'Connell, believed Ireland needed an independent parliament. In the Irish parliament opposition to the union was led by Henry Grattan but a majority, many of whom were influenced by the promise of favours, in the way of "pensions, places and peerages", voted at a second debate on the subject in favour of the union. It came into force at the beginning of 1801. Catholic emancipation was not part of the settlement.

Doherty, the brewer, stood aloof from all these political and rebellious activities. He took advantage of the opportunity offered in trade and commerce to better himself financially. In addition to a successful brewing business he acquired considerable property in Milltown, Dublin. His second son, William Izod, also took advantage of the relaxation of the Penal Laws and entered the legal profession, a vocation denied Catholics before 1790. He was admitted to Kings Inn in 1804 to commence the necessary study and graduated in 1809. Like his father, he went quietly about his profession and became successful.

On 31 July 1816, the young solicitor married Anne, daughter of Timothy McEvoy, a prosperous Dublin builder, and his wife, also Anne. The newly-married couple lived at 5 Gloucester Street, Dublin, where four children were born — William Izod (1819), Anne Eliza (1820), Jane Annette (1822) and Kevin Izod (1823). It was this second son who was destined to stand in the Green Street dock in 1848. In the 1820s William Doherty was permitted to place the letters, KCE, after his name, indicating that he could now plead before the King's Bench, Common Pleas and the Exchequer. Not long after the birth of their fourth child, Kevin Izod, the attorney and his family moved to 34 Upper Westmoreland Street, where another son was born and christened John Timothy. In 1831, the family was saddened by the death of their father when he had reached forty-four years. Anne Doherty was left with a young family to rear, ranging from five to twelve years. She lived on in the city for a few years and then, in 1840, moved to Frascati, near Blackrock, further from the city. The area took its name from Frascati House, the home of Lord Edward Fitzgerald, the ill-fated military commander of the United Irishmen.

The Doherty family bible gives the date of the birth of convict Doherty — later O'Doherty — as 7 September 1823 and baptismal records of St Andrew's Catholic Church, Westland Row, Dublin, show that he was baptised on 21 September. The surname in the records is spelt "Dougherty", probably recorded in error as such by the priest as the father had always used the spelling of "Doherty". The baptism was conducted by Father William McCabe at a church in Townsend Street, the records being transferred to St Andrew's after the latter was built in 1834. The day after the ceremony, the baby boy was taken by Wet Nurse Kinsella to Ashford, a village in County Wicklow, and it was not until 11 July 1824 that the nurse and the child returned to his parents' home.

Research did not reveal why the name, "Izod", appears so often among members of the Doherty family. Burke's *The Landed Gentry* includes a family of "Izod" of Chapel Izod House, County Kilkenny. The entry states that "the name appears to be an old Irish one; mention is made in Harris's *History of Dublin*, of 'Izod Tower' demolished by the Earl of Essex to make room for Essex Gate, and also of 'Izod's Fort in the Park' ". Burke makes special mention of Kevin Izod and William Izod of the Kilkenny Izods — christian names which appear in the Doherty lineage. However, research revealed no connection between the Dohertys and the Izods nor any reason for the frequent use of the name by the Doherty family.

Despite the early loss of her husband, Anne Doherty had no apparent difficulty in providing a sound education for her sons nor in making arrangements for their entry to professions. Kevin was educated privately by Reverend Dr Cahill and also attended Dr Wall's school in Hume Street, Dublin. In 1842, when he was nearing his nineteenth birthday, he was enrolled as a medical student when Ireland was enjoying a golden era in medicine.

The leading Irish medical practitioners were not only foremost in the British Isles but also were highly respected on the European continent. Much of their work was original and future generations of medical students were to learn of diseases and clinical signs which were first described by Irish doctors and referred to in the future by their names. "Colles fracture" of the wrist, first described in 1814 by Abraham Colles, professor of anatomy at the Royal College of Surgeons, Ireland, bears his name and "Cheyne-Stokes breathing", a type of respiratory distress indicative of a particular heart condition, is named after two famous Irish physicians of that era, John Cheyne and William Stokes. Another eminent physician of this period, Robert Graves, professor of medicine at Trinity College, Dublin, gave his name to a disease of the thyroid gland. Another leading Irish physician, Dominic Corrigan, is remembered by a clinical sign — Corrigan's pulse — which, when present in a patient, is evidence of an inadequate heart valve.

The Irish leaders of medicine were not only famous for their clinical expertise. They were also renowned for their teaching of students. Dr Graves was appointed to the Meath Hospital in 1821 and introduced a new method of bedside teaching which soon made himself and the hospital famous. Previously medical students had followed the physicians as they did their rounds and picked up information as best they could. Under Graves' method, a student was allotted a patient and obliged to study all aspects of the disease and its treatment under the physician's supervision.

In all records of our subject's medical course that have been preserved his name is spelt, "O'Doherty". Edward Maclysaght, the esteemed authority on Irish names, states that during a resurgence of Irish nationalism in the latter half of the nineteenth century, many Irishmen resumed the prefix. Kevin O'Doherty had embraced this nationalism and shown his hand by the new spelling of his name before many of his fellow countrymen. He was the only member of his family to do so. While he was studying medicine, his brothers were also preparing to enter professions. His elder brother, William, became a dentist and John, two years Kevin's junior, entered the legal profession. At no time, either in their student days or later in life, did Kevin's brothers use the prefix in the spelling of the surname.

Kevin O'Doherty commenced his medical course by becoming apprenticed to Michael Donovan, an apothecary, who, unlike some of his colleagues, believed he should stay in his shop and not endeavour to usurp the place of physicians. However, Donovan was more than a pharmacist. He was a distinguished physicist and chemist and contributed erudite papers to scientific journals. After attending the Ledwich, formerly the Original School of Medicine, Peter Street, one of a number of private medical schools in Dublin, O'Doherty transferred to the medical school of the Royal College of Surgeons, St Stephen's Green. For two years he was a resident student at St Mark's Hospital for Diseases of the Eye and Ear, which had been opened in Park Street by Sir William Wilde, the father of Oscar Wilde. Later, O'Doherty gained clinical experience at St Vincent's Hospital, St Stephen's Green and finally at Meath Hospital. The latter hospital was then situated on land once known as Jonathan Swift's vineyard. It had commenced functioning in the Earl of Meath's Liberties in the Coombe. At the Meath Hospital, O'Doherty was fortunate to have as his clinical teachers the famous William Stokes and Robert Graves.

Certificates issued by teachers throughout his course show that O'Doherty was a keen student. J. Moore Negligan, who lectured in Materia Medica and Therapeutics, certified that Kevin Izod O'Doherty very diligently attended a course of lectures in those subjects from 1 November 1842 to 29 April 1843. He endorsed the certificate with these words: "Mr O'Doherty was much distinguished whilst my pupil for digilence and talent. He obtained this certificate by distinguished answering at an examination at the termination of the session and I formed a high opinion of his medical attainments." Evidence of Kevin's attendance at Meath Hospital was given by William Stokes and Cathcart Lee, visiting physicians. They stated that:

> Mr Kevin I. O'Doherty filled the situation of Clinical Practising Assistant in the Medical Department of the Meath Hospital and County of Dublin Infirmary from October 1847 to May 1848. During this time Mr K.I. O'Doherty had a considerable number of cases of chronic and acute disease including fevers under his immediate care. He also studied the use of the stethoscope and the General Diagnosis of the Chest. We recommend him as a gentleman whose experience and practical knowledge of his profession and intimacy with the details of an hospital fully qualify him to undertake the charge of a public medical institution.

The certificate also carries the statement that such are only given to gentlemen who have practised for a certain period of time under the daily observation of physicians to the hospital. With this experience O'Doherty had completed a medical course of high standard and was well equipped to sit for his final examination in medicine a few weeks later.

Unlike Kevin O'Doherty, who had lived all his life in Dublin, Eva Kelly had arrived in the city only a few months before the young medical student was arrested. Imbued with a burning desire to be at the centre of the campaign against the British domination of her country, she left the family home of Killeen House, near Portumna, County Galway, to travel to the capital. Killeen House is situated close to the eastern boundary of the lands once called Ui Maine, which included the southern part of the present County Roscommon and the eastern portion of County Galway. It was here that the greatest of all the O'Kelly clans held sway in the centuries gone by. The O'Kellys were one of a number of Irish clans living in the countryside around Galway city, known as the City of the Tribes. The tribes were the aristocratic merchant families of Anglo-Norman blood, who ruled the city in mediaeval times and included the Lynches, the Blakes and the Joyces. These city dwellers listed the O'Kellys among their traditional foes. A Galway City order made in the sixteenth century directed that "neither O nor Mac shall strut or swagger through the streets of Galway". A more specific instruction forbade the citizens of the city to admit to their houses the Burkes, MacWilliams, O'Kellys or any other sept. In notes that Eva Kelly made in her later life when preparing to write her memoirs, she claimed direct descent from the rebel stock of Ui Maine.

Eva's paternal grandfather was Hyacinth Kelly of Killeen who married Ally Skerrit of Eyre's Court, County Galway, daughter of Patrick Skerrit. An indentured deed of marriage settlement between bride and bridegroom dated 3 March 1793 shows that a dowry of £1,000 ($2,000) would be provided. A son of this union, Edward Kelly, became Eva's father. Griffith's Primary Valuation for 1853 shows that Edward Kelly's 68 acres (28 hectares) at Killeen with house, land and mills had an annual rateable value of £68 ($136) and the church tithe book for Tynagh parish indicates that he paid tithes of £6.2.8 ($13.28) in 1826 for 94 acres (38 hectares). This branch of the Kellys were peaceful farmers and had dropped the prefix "O" from the surname borne by their ancestors.

When Edward Kelly sought a bride, he went a little further west in County Galway and found her in Mary O'Flaherty, in Headford, some seventeen miles (twenty-seven kilometres) north of Galway city. Like other country clans in this area, the early O'Flahertys had been a bane to the inhabitants of that city. An inscription carved over the west gate of the city in 1549 read, "This gate was erected to protect us from the fury of the ferocious O'Flahertys". Mary O'Flaherty was the daughter of John O'Flaherty who lived in Ivy House in the village of Headford itself. Later he moved to Lisdonagh, two miles from the village. Lisdonagh House in which the O'Flahertys lived is described in Burke's *Guide to Country Houses* as a two-storey house, probably built in the 1790s with a front of two bays on either side of a curved bow. The main entry leads through rustic fanlighted doorways in the bow into an oval hall, the walls of which are decorated with classical figures painted in grisaille by J. Ryan. *Slater's Directory for 1846* lists Eva's maternal grandfather amongst the nobility and gentry. While John O'Flaherty lived a law-abiding existence, the family, who had not dropped the prefix "O", contained some members who were active in the politics of the time. Eva's grand-uncle, Francis O'Flaherty, joined the ranks of the United Irishmen and her uncle, Martin O'Flaherty, was a Young Ireland sympathiser.

Edward Kelly took his bride back to live in Killeen House and she bore him seven children — six girls and one son. The girl to be known as Eva for most of her life was christened Mary Anne. Before she was born, her mother returned to the O'Flaherty home in Headford for the confinement which took place on 15 February 1830. It was at Headford and later at Lisdonagh that Eva spent much of her childhood. Like most children of the gentry, Eva was educated at home by governesses. One of these, Miss Gormley, recognised early literary talents in the young girl. She encouraged her ability to write verse, which she was composing at a very tender age. Two of her first poems were "The Banshee" and "The Leprechaun". The former was based on a legend of an eerie spirit whose wailing heralded the death of members of leading Irish families including her own. Eva was delighted when it appeared in the *Nation*, the best known of a number of newspapers published by members of the Young Ireland movement. "The Leprechaun" catches the spirit of the delightful legend of the fairy shoemaker which the world associates with Ireland. One stanza reads:

> There, when the sun is low,
> A tapping noise doth come and go;
> 'Tis the Leprechaun at his last
> At which he raps away so fast.
> He wears a cocked hat on his head,
> And a tiny coat of scarlet red.

At this stage of her writing the young poetess submitted her verse under various signatures. In a short time she adopted the name "Eva", and retained it for all future contributions. Her poems appeared so regularly in the *Nation* that she became known as "Eva of the Nation". When the identity of "Eva" became known to her friends they began using her pseudonym when they addressed her. She then adopted it herself as though it were her given name.

It was not long before Eva's poems began to express an

intense sympathy with the national movement for freedom which was being espoused by the Young Irelanders. In later years she explained the influences which were pressing her in this direction when she wrote in her notebook, "By ancestry, I came of rebel stock, and I early developed the traits of my ancestors, not long after having learned to read. No one, it appears to me, could be other than an Irish rebel, who had a heart to feel or a brain to think." This trend was encouraged by her uncle, Martin O'Flaherty. It is not surprising that soon she was writing poems directed against the British, as is seen in "Down Brittannia":

Down Britannia
Down, Britannia, brigand down
No more to rule with sceptred hand:
Truth raises o'er thy throne and crown
Her exorcising wand.
I see the "writing on the wall"
The proud, the thrice-accursed shall fall
    Down, Britannia, down.

While Eva was writing nationalistic poems for the Young Ireland newspapers, two of her sisters, Bedelia and Annie, entered convents, becoming Mother de Sales in the Presentation Order, Galway, and Mother Brigid in the Sisters of Mercy, Ballinasloe, respectively. Another sister became the wife of a bank manager in Loughrea. Her brother, named Edward after his father, was, according to Eva, a ne'er-do-well and left the area. On the deaths of their parents, two more girls, Izmina and Eleanor, ran the mill at Killeen. In their later years they were often seen driving a phaeton into Portumna. With their deaths, the property passed out of the Kelly name.

CHAPTER 2

Towards Rebellion

During Kevin O'Doherty's early childhood the most important political goal in the minds of the Irish Catholics was to win emancipation, which did not, as many had hoped, accompany the legislative union of Britain and Ireland. Although constituting over eighty per cent of the population, they were still denied equal opportunity in the civil and political life of their country. Catholics could not enter parliament nor occupy high civil posts. Their champion in this cause was Daniel O'Connell, the solicitor who had opposed the union. O'Connell came from County Kerry in south-west Ireland where his Uncle Maurice had made him heir to his house of Derrynane and its surrounding land near the shores of Cahirdonnel Bay.

It was to be well into the nineteenth century before O'Connell initiated the movement which finally brought success. During the first two decades there had been a number of attempts to achieve emancipation but all had come to nought. The British government had been willing to grant emancipation under certain conditions. It promised legislation which, while satisfying the Catholic aims, would include state control over the appointment of Catholic bishops and state contribution to the payment of Catholic clergy. Some Irish Catholics, including a number of their bishops, saw no problems in these "wings", as they were called, but O'Connell opposed them.

One of the most important events in the campaign for emancipation took place in 1823, the year of Kevin O'Doherty's birth. It was the formation of the Catholic Association in which O'Connell played a leading role. After a slow start O'Connell sponsored a programme involving the whole of the Catholic population. Associate members were enrolled at a subscription of a penny a month. A fighting fund was thus built up and the Catholic peasantry joined the middle class and the Church in the campaign. The Catholic aristocracy, while not actually participating in the operations, contributed to the funds. O'Connell, the dominant figure in the association, turned his efforts to mass agitation. However, it was a disciplined agitation as O'Connell, who had a horror of violence and bloodshed, always controlled the large meetings with his honeyed oratory. In the 1826 general election, the forty-shilling freeholders, who had previously voted as directed by their landlords, now, urged on by their priests, voted for pro-emancipation candidates in Waterford and other electorates. These actions dismayed the British government and Wellington and Peel formed a new ministry opposed to emancipation. In Ireland, O'Connell held large meetings of the Catholic Association in various parts of the country and in 1828 he decided to stand at the Clare election against a member of Wellington's cabinet. There was nothing illegal in a Catholic standing at an election although there would be difficulties when he went to take his place in the Commons should he win. O'Connell won easily due to another disciplined campaign amongst the forty-shilling freeholders. Wellington and Peel, fearing rebellion in Ireland, advised an unwilling King George IV to grant Catholic emancipation and he reluctantly assented to the legislation. Catholics could now take a seat in parliament and be appointed to all public offices with the exception of regent, lord chancellor of Ireland or England or lord lieutenant of Ireland. For his tremendous efforts in obtaining emancipation, O'Connell received the appellation of the Great Liberator.

After the Emancipation Act was passed by the British parliament in 1829, O'Connell made a triumphant return from London to Dublin. O'Doherty, then aged five years, was taken by his father to witness the event. The following is part of a description of the incident which he wrote later in life:

> How vividly has the scene I then beheld been ever since impressed on my mind. The observed of all observers, he was borne along to the capital amidst the plaudits of tens of thousands of his grateful countrymen — his figure, his bearing, his noble countenance, beyond comparison the finest on which I ever rested my eyes. A giant in stature, as in intellect, with sparkling blue eyes and the most winning smile, it was no wonder if, in common with numbers of my young countrymen, I received on the great occasion an impression that served to shape the whole course of my future life.

Catholics believed that emancipation would give them equality with the Protestant establishment but such was not to be. They still had many grievances. The continuation of the payment of tithes was one which caused much hostility. It is easy to understand the resentment felt by Catholics who had to contribute to the maintenance of Protestant clergy who gave them no spiritual services. The refusal to pay tithes became quite common and the collectors were given police and sometimes army protection. Legislation in 1838 provided for the inclusion of tithes as part of the rent. While this reduced the violence which had accompanied the collection of tithes, it did not erase the grievance felt about having to pay.

In October 1842, an event occurred which, though not as spectacular as O'Connell's return to Dublin after emancipation had been granted, was to influence O'Doherty's future far more than the memory of the Liberator's great hour of triumph. This was the foundation of the newspaper, the *Nation*, by Charles Gavan Duffy, Thomas Osborne Davis and John Blake Dillon. All three in their twenties and from middle class families, Duffy and Dillon were Catholics and Davis, probably the leading light in propounding the paper's policy, was a Protestant. "They shared certain views on the subject of patriotism, the identity of Ireland, the destiny of the Irish nation, and the duties all Irishmen owed to the nation." Their aim was to create an Irish nationalism to which the whole population, irrespective of creed, could subscribe. The new paper encouraged all efforts which might lead to the creation of the nationalism which its proprietors so earnestly sought. Its pages included biographies of the country's past heroes in all aspects of life. It published the poems of current writers while retention of the native language was high on its list of ideals.

O'Doherty, unhampered by the conservatism of a father now dead over ten years, and living in Dublin city away from any influence his mother and elder brother, William, may have had, was one of the many young Irishmen attracted by the policy of the *Nation*. The paper had commenced publication at the same time as he started his medical course and although he pursued his studies assiduously he could still find time to set about arousing enthusiasm for a national spirit among his fellow students. He found a colleague in Dalton Williams, another medical student, who was soon contributing verse to the *Nation* under the pseudonym of "Shamrock". The two played a leading role in the founding of the Student and Polytechnic clubs which the *Freeman's Journal* described as being "associated in the cause of liberty in this city". It was at this time that O'Doherty added the prefix "O" to his name.

Meanwhile Daniel O'Connell had turned his energy to having the union of Britain and Ireland repealed. In 1834, as a member of the House of Commons, he urged its members to appoint a committee to inquire into the legality of the union, its effect on Ireland and the probable consequences of its continuation. He claimed that for twenty of the thirty-four years since the beginning of the nation, England had shut Ireland out from the light of liberty, with the enforcement of Insurrection Acts, Martial and Coercion Laws and the suspension of the Habeas Corpus Act. The absentee landlords had acquired new power under the union — "a power that has done much to increase agrarian violence . . . a power of seizing the growing crops of the tenants and a law to eject these unfortunate people". His proposal was strongly opposed with Peel claiming that repeal "must lead to dismemberment of the empire, must make England a fourth-rate power in Europe and Ireland a savage wilderness". O'Connell's recommendation was overwhelmingly defeated.

O'Connell revived the campaign for repeal of the union in 1840 with an organisation which became known as the Loyal National Repeal Association. It followed the lines of the earlier Catholic Association with a similar penny per month subscription for associate membership — the repeal rent. The movement fared poorly at first with meetings at the Corn Exchange in Dublin being sparsely attended. However, with the support of Duffy, Davis and Dillon of the *Nation* as well as the Catholic church, the association grew rapidly and the repeal rent reached handsome proportions. The campaign developed along a familiar pattern with monster meetings being held at places selected for their historic significance such as Tara, the seat of prehistoric Irish kings. At these open air meetings O'Connell addressed disciplined crowds often running into hundreds of thousands. The Liberator reaffirmed his hatred of violence to achieve his objectives and expressed his loyalty to the Crown, sentiments with which the *Nation*, at first, agreed.

O'Doherty and Williams, too junior to be full members of the Repeal Association, attended meetings at the Corn Exchange open to associate members. They were delighted with the occasional invitations to join the *Nation* writers at their homes where, over supper, enthusiastic informal discussions were held on various subjects dear to their hearts. An English journalist, who suggested the trio at the *Nation* and their supporters were aping a group in his own country called Young England, derisively labelled them Young Ireland. It was a name which they first resented but later accepted proudly. The two medical students attended the monster meetings when distance permitted and, with thousands of other Irishmen, were looking forward expectantly to a monster meeting scheduled to be held in October 1843 at Clontarf on the shores near Dublin where Brian Boru, the undisputed high king of Ireland, defeated the Vikings in 1014, but met his death while doing so. They were to be disappointed. The British government, now greatly concerned with O'Connell's repeal campaign, prohibited the meeting by a proclamation the day before it was to be held. O'Connell, fearing violent confrontation between his huge array of followers and the British troops, took urgent steps to cancel the meeting — a decision with which the *Nation* agreed. O'Connell and Duffy were prosecuted and sentenced to twelve months in Richmond Prison. They spent their sentence in the luxurious surroundings of the prison governor's house where they held frequent dinner parties and from where they kept in easy contact with their supporters. The House of Lords later reversed the verdict and they were released.

The actions of the British government brought the repeal movement an important recruit. He was William Smith O'Brien, a distinguished Protestant landlord and MP for Limerick for many years. When a number of magistrates were dismissed for attending repeal meetings, he resigned his own commission of peace. The prohibition of the Clontarf meeting and the prosecution of O'Connell further dismayed Smith O'Brien and with a complete reversal of attitude from his former pro-union stance he joined the Repeal Association and actually chaired meetings during O'Connell's absence in prison.

In 1844, the strong support of the Young Irelanders for O'Connell began to weaken. These literary idealists could not understand the negotiations of O'Connell, the practical politician, with outside factions, particularly the British Whigs. The *Nation* group feared that such activities would compromise the campaign for repeal. The split widened when British Prime Minister Peel, in a programme of appeasement, proposed three regional university colleges at Belfast, Cork and Galway, open to Catholics and Protestants alike. The Young Irelanders saw the proposal as an opportunity for nationalism to be promoted in young Irishmen of all creeds. O'Connell, following the line of the Catholic hierarchy, called the proposed institutions, "Godless Colleges". The debate developed into a display of sectarian differences.

In September 1845, Davis died from scarlet fever and there was a short truce while both sides mourned the loss of the most imaginative and generous mind among the Young Irelanders. His death prompted the young poetess from Killeen to write a "Lament for Thomas Davis". This was the first poem she contributed under the pseudonym of "Eva". She was fifteen years old at the time. A stanza reads:

> Oh! how can I believe it? — it can't be as they say,
> That all the gifts so near to heav'n are quenched within
>   the clay;
> It cannot be, it cannot be, that all the noble dower
> Of Truth, and Love, and Genius high, on earth no more
>   has power.
> Thomas Davis! Thomas Davis! — is that a phantom name —
> An empty, silent, churchyard word, so full of life and fame?

The Irish autumn of 1845 also saw the beginning of a national calamity of tremendous proportions which devastated the country for over five years — famine. By the 1840s, the potato was the only food of a third of the Irish population and the main component of their diet for thousands more. Potato blight which had attacked the crop in America spread to Ireland in September. The disease reduced a healthy crop almost overnight to a mess of evil-smelling rottenness. For five years the potato rot returned, attacking each annual crop in varying degrees, with "black 1847" being probably the worst year. The effect on the people was disastrous. During the famine years, the Irish population, which till then had been increasing quite rapidly, decreased by over two millions. A little less than half of the reduction was due to deaths from starvation and the fevers that accompanied the famine, mainly typhus and relapsing fever. Over a million of the frightened populace emigrated, most to America.

The west and the south-west of Ireland suffered most severely from the famine and the accompanying fevers but the epidemics occurred in practically every area. Refugees from famine, seeking food, brought the fevers to Dublin at the beginning of 1847. Tents and fever sheds were used to nurse the sufferers and it was here that O'Doherty in the clinical years of his course saw the havoc that the diseases were wreaking on the sufferers. Many of the medical attendants contracted the fever and died as a result. O'Doherty fortunately escaped this fate.

The Young Irelanders wrote vividly of the sufferings of those in the grip of the famine and with vitriolic pens laid the blame for the disaster at Britain's door. Of the many articles written, one by John Mitchel stands out. Mitchel, a young Protestant solicitor and son of a Unitarian parson, had replaced Davis on the *Nation*. Mitchel wrote of his experience when revisiting a hamlet in western Ireland where he had been hospitably received two years before but which was now completely decimated by the famine:

> There is a horrible silence; grass grows before the doors; we fear to look into any door, though they are all open or off the hinges, for we fear to see yellow chapless skeletons grinning there; but our footfalls rouse two lean dogs that run from us with doleful howling, and we know by the felon-gleam in the wolfish eyes how they lived after their masters died. We stop before the threshold of our host of two years ago, put our head, with our eyes shut, inside the door-jamb, and say, with shaking voice, "God save all here!" — No answer — ghastly silence, and mouldy stench, as from the mouth of burial vaults. Ah! they are dead! the strong man and the fair dark-eyed woman and the little ones, with their liquid Gaelic accents that melted into music two years ago; they shrank and withered together until their voices dwindled to a rueful gibbering, and they hardly knew one another's faces; but their horrid eyes scowled on each other with a cannibal glare.

To some, Mitchel's colourful language might suggest exaggeration of the position. But there were many other accounts recording similar scenes during the calamity. N.M. Cummins, a magistrate from County Cork, wrote to the Duke of Wellington. His letter published in *The Times* of 24 December 1846 contained an account of what he found at Skibbereen during an official visit:

> I entered some of the hovels to ascertain the cause and the scenes that presented themselves were such as no tongue or pen can convey the slightest idea of. In the first, six famished and ghastly skeletons, to all appearance dead, were huddled in a corner on some filthy straw, their sole covering what seemed a ragged horsecloth, their wretched legs hanging about, naked above the knees. I approached with horror, and found by a low moaning they

were alive — they were in fever, four children, a woman and what once had been a man. It is impossible to go through detail. Suffice it to say, that in a few minutes I was surrounded by at least two hundred of such phantoms, such frightful spectres as no words can describe.

Duffy claimed that the famine was "a fearful murder committed on the mass of the people". Mitchel, too, considered that the British used the famine to commit genocide. This extreme view arose from the knowledge that for most of the famine years food was actually being exported from Ireland while hundreds of thousands were starving to death. One can understand the anger of the Young Irelanders when they saw ships leaving Irish ports with oats, wheat, butter and eggs while so many had no food. Peel has been praised for his role in the earlier years of the famine, but in 1846 Russell became prime minister and he led a party which was committed to a policy of free trade and private enterprise. It was probably this policy which was the reason why the workhouses in Ireland were crowded and why the attempts to provide relief by public works, soup kitchens and imported Indian meal failed to prevent so many from dying from starvation. The famine was not "man-made" and was probably inevitable but its disastrous effects could have been lessened by more determined action.

Now to return to the repeal movement. The bickering between the two factions continued and in the middle of 1846 came to a head. A debate on the use of physical force to achieve their objectives extended over several meetings. Although, at this stage, the Young Irelanders still had no plans for violence, they could not accept the abstract principle that force was never justified. Thomas Francis Meagher, son of a Catholic mayor of Waterford and a new recruit to the Repeal Association, delivered what O'Doherty described as "the celebrated apostrophe to the patriot's sword, in language that flashed, smote and conquered like the weapon he invoked". From this time on he was "Meagher of the Sword". Bitter wrangling followed Meagher's speech and Smith O'Brien, who for several months had steered a middle course between the two groups, left the meeting followed by Meagher, Mitchel,

Duffy and several other Young Irelanders including O'Doherty. The breach was never healed, and with the death of O'Connell in May 1847, while travelling to the south of Europe for his health's sake, the Repeal Association never recovered its prestige.

The Young Irelanders formed their own association — the Irish Confederation — but their charter, published after several months, differed very little from that of the Repeal Association. Confederate clubs were formed throughout the country but the movement lacked vitality, as the people were most concerned with staying alive during the famine — and the Young Irelanders had nothing to offer the starving millions.

At this time, letters, suggesting a different approach, began to appear in the *Nation*. They came from James Fintan Lalor whose father had been active in the anti-tithe campaign. His younger brother, Peter, was destined to migrate to Australia where in the colony of Victoria in 1854 he would become the hero of the Eureka Stockade on the Ballarat goldfield in Australia in the culmination of the miners' battle against a stringent licensing system. James Lalor pointed out to Duffy that repeal was not something that mattered to the Irish peasants. Land was the only subject which would rouse them. He urged the tenants to refuse to pay rents unless the landlords acknowledged that the people who worked the land had co-equal rights. Lalor's proposals were too radical for most of the Young Ireland leaders with the exception of John Mitchel and junior members such as O'Doherty and Dalton Williams. Duffy offered an alternative plan to hold up business in the House of Commons by filibustering. In the event of this failing to force the British government to listen to Irish demands for a separate parliament, there would be a withdrawal from Westminster and a council of three hundred would be formed to run Irish affairs. Mitchel left the *Nation* and began publishing his own paper, the *United Irishman*, in which he advocated rebellion and addressed Clarendon, Ireland's lord lieutenant, as "Her Majesty's Executioner-General". With their leaders going in different directions the affairs of the Young Irelanders were in the doldrums.

However, enthusiasm returned in February 1848 when reports of events in Europe were received.

An almost bloodless revolution occurred in France overthrowing Louis Phillippe. This was followed by similar events in Vienna, Berlin and Budapest. Now, even the moderate Young Irelanders began to speak of revolution. The lord lieutenant became worried at the reports of plans for an armed rebellion and called for assistance in the way of military aid and legislation. The British garrison in Ireland was reinforced and after a little hesitation the British parliament passed a new Treason Felony Act. It was purposely aimed at curbing the speeches of Mitchel, Duffy, Meagher and other Young Irelanders, providing as it did a new offence of felony. Any person found guilty of compassing or plotting, by publishing, printing, writing or by open and advised speaking, the deposition of the Queen or the levying of war against her was subject to transportation for not less than seven years. The British government now had the means of sending the Young Ireland leaders to Van Diemen's Land. It was under this law that Mitchel was tried in May 1848. An allegedly packed jury found him guilty and the government, fearing an attempt to rescue him, quickly removed him from Dublin to Spike Island in Cork Harbour, to wait transportation for the ten years meted out to him by the judge.

Mitchel's conviction was followed by the first real planning of a conspiracy to overthrow the British in Ireland. Duffy and his supporters, urged on by Father Kenyon from Tipperary, one of the few Catholic priests among the Young Ireland sympathisers, talked seriously of an armed rebellion. For the first time, action to obtain money, arms and officers from outside Ireland was planned. The conspirators hoped their fellow countrymen in America would give generous aid. Although the French government had rejected an earlier approach, help was expected from the revolutionary clubs in Paris. It was also believed that the British Chartists would lend a hand. An insurrection was planned for August after the harvest. The Young Irelander thirty confederate clubs in Dublin and the country would be key units in the formation of a national guard.

O'Doherty, unlike in the days when he had to be satisfied with associate membership of the Repeal Association, was now a fully-fledged member of the confederation. He was president of the Hugh O'Donnell Club, established for the Merrion ward of Dublin.

On the night of John Mitchel's conviction, a group of students including O'Doherty and fellow militant, Dalton Williams, met in Dublin, discussing the events of the day. The possible rescue of Mitchel was the first topic but this was something for their leaders to organise. The discussion then turned to Mitchel's speech and his impassioned claims that hundreds would take his place. All eagerly expressed a burning desire to take up the challenge. What could they do? The answer was staring them in the face. With Mitchel's arrest, his newspaper had been suppressed. Here lay the answer. The students would replace the *United Irishman* with a publication of their own. Next came a debate on who should edit the projected paper. Many students sought the position. Finally, O'Doherty and Williams won the coveted task. Both had already earned a literary reputation. In later life, Kevin's brother John was to express the opinion that, "Kevin's writings were always clever and I fully expected that his career would have been a literary one, at which he would I think have done much better than the mechanical one which cost him so much time and labour and money." Williams' reputation had come from his contributions to the *Nation* under the pseudonym of "Shamrock".

The two young embryo publishers went to work with great enthusiasm. They obtained premises at No. 11 Trinity Street, and Denis Hoban was engaged to print the paper. Advertisements were vigorously canvassed. The first issue of the *Irish Tribune*, the name chosen for the new journal, appeared on Saturday, 10 June 1848, only fourteen days after the students' decision was made. The amount of organisation in those two weeks was amazing. In that time, the proprietors had been able to attract advertising from shippers, merchants and retailers of shoes and hats, and, significantly, promises of articles from literary circles in which members of the Young

Ireland movement were active. The first issue announced the names of agents from as far away as Glasgow in Scotland, and Manchester and Newcastle-on-Tyne in England and over fifty centres from all over Ireland. The paper contained sixteen pages in tabloid form, its format complying with the accepted appearance of contemporary newspapers. The *Tribune* presented the case for Ireland in long editorials and articles. These were written with vehemence and flamboyance, and like Mitchel's paper, which the *Tribune* replaced, inviting action and almost asking for its own demise. Dalton Williams took ill soon after the commencement of the paper and the burden of editing rested on O'Doherty. How many of the editorials and the numerous articles aimed at the British came from O'Doherty's pen is not known but when several were used by the prosecution in his trials he denied authorship of only one.

The first issue included a profile of John Mitchel, an account of the revolution in France, a Poets' Corner, and an announcement that yet another reactionary journal would soon appear. It would be published by John Martin, another of the Young Ireland leaders. The policy of the paper was quite obvious from the outset. Britain was to blame for most if not all of Ireland's troubles, and action to right this must be taken immediately. In the first editorial Britain was accused of creating a "state of slavery" in Ireland for which there was only one answer — repeal of the union. Extracts read:

> Ireland may practically be said not to be under any other rule than that of military sway, for never did a government rule less in the hearts of the people than that of Ireland this day — a reign of terror, of police inspectors and dragoons of "detectives and light infantry"; . . .. Sunk in the low state of education — her wealth drained off in such large, yearly draughts, that she has sunk almost exhausted under her losses; her actual existence imperilled by long-continued famine and disease, till the dogs not only licked her sores, but have eaten of her flesh, and her political existence almost annihilated by the improper administration of the law in jury packing. What remains of freedom or life?
> "You do take away the life
> When you remove the means to live."

> She is the plague-spot of Europe — the leper among nations.
> from whom all turn aside and avoid . . ..
>   Repeal — the bright, the morning star, which is to guide us in this valley of the shadow of death through which our country passes — the talismanic word which no longer dwells confined to the mouths of Conciliation Hall or Confederate orators, but has diffused itself among the the Protestant middle class, among the shopocracy, and even to the clubs, to whom it has become a lamp and light to their paths. Repeal, no longer the shibboleth of Saxon and Celt but the acknowledged and the only mode of raising Ireland up to the condition of a nation, and to make her dying and disheartened people happy, healthy and prosperous.

In an editorial entitled "Our Harvest Prospects", the paper deplored the practice of the past years by which much of the harvest was used by the tenant farmers to pay the rent and most of the grain was exported to England. In eloquent and picturesque language it was urged that this should cease:

> Shall we, with folded arms, and a patience that is, in truth, a spectacle to the world, for the finger of scorn and derision to be pointed at, witness our jackal foe drive from our fields, and from before our very eyes, our sheep and our oxen, and the corn thereof to thrive and fatten upon, whilst they torture their hellish minds for inventions to aid the gallows, extermination, emigration, the prison, or the fever-shed to rid themselves by wholesale of their serfs, and nourish the next crop with the marrow and the bones of the widow and the orphan?
>   Forbid it Heaven. No; the strong men of this land . . . whose hearts have not yet withered into decay under the blighting influence of the sickness, and whose blood quickens with long pent-up fire of revenge, will gladden our eyes by saving the coming harvest and easing their longing thirst deep, deep in the blood of the English foe.

The editor of the *Tribune* followed the lead of Duffy and Mitchel in laying the blame for the famine on the British in a stirring article, "Blood for Blood":

> Our souls are daily harrowed with accounts of the wholesale assassination of our rapidly-disappearing peasantry. Men have heard the story of "extermination" so often, that it palls upon the ear. The famine — not sent by heaven but deliberately made by our English tyrants and their landlord slave-drivers — and plague, the sister of famine, left a wretched remnant on the desolated plains; but these, too, apparently must perish. Every ditch has its corpse,

and every lordling Moloch his hetacomb of murdered tenantry . . . .

Clearly we are guilty if we turn not our hand against the foes of our race — clearly we are imbecile if we fail in striking to the earth, yet reeking with the blood of their victims, crying aloud to heaven for vengeance, those enemies of God and those destroyers of men! Shall not the wicked and the evil doer be overcome? Shall not the God of battles prosper our arms? Yes, there is might in a righteous cause, and ours is holy. Then, "scourge the spoiler from our coasts", exterminate the English despots, and crush with them the anti-Irish aristocracy for ever!

Another editorial called on the Young Irelanders for action and failing that for the citizens themselves to move against the British crown. However in an explanation under the heading of "Courage", the citizens were warned that the struggle would be "no bright and glittering pageant for mere holiday folk, but a desperate, life-and-death encounter". The appeal to the people read:

We call upon the people of Dublin, as they value their lives, their liberties and the happiness of their homes, and would desire to see famine and pestilence banished forever from their soil, to take this matter into their own hands, and, if their leaders will not move, to take the lead themselves and prepare, in a fitting manner, through the mouths of their representatives in this council, to tell this royal lady who we are told is about to visit this ill-fated shore, by blandishments to soothe us into contented obedience to British rule that the crown, which will stand in the way of the Irish people righting and ruling themselves, and saving the harvest of this year of 1848 for their own use and benefit, must perish.

The verses in the poets' corner section of the paper, were, as to be expected, for the most part patriotic in theme. However, Eva Kelly, whose relationship with O'Doherty had not yet begun, contributed a poem which, perhaps with Irish premonition, predicted what was in store for herself and her lover-to-be. A stanza of "Parting Words" reads:

> You came to win my heart,
> You stayed to win my troth,
> I never dreamed a parting hour
> So woeful for us both.
> Oh, bitter, bitter are my tears,
> Adieu, my darling one,

> What shall I do this weary hour
> When I feel that you are gone?

The Young Irelanders made no great effort to keep their plans secret and with provocative articles like those appearing in the *Irish Tribune*, Clarendon, who had not relished the idea of going to Ireland as lord lieutenant, believed that a rebellion was definitely being planned. Spies, who easily penetrated meetings of the Irish Confederation and its clubs, provided Dublin Castle with information. Clarendon persuaded the British government to act before the harvest as he knew that the Young Irelanders planned to delay any rising until after that event. Early in July, the government struck by arresting some of the leaders under the Treason Felony Act. Gavan Duffy, proprietor of the *Nation*, and John Martin, who had begun publishing the *Irish Felon*, were arrested on Saturday 8 July and charged in relation to articles which had appeared in their respective papers. Then the police pounced on O'Doherty about 10 p.m. on the same day and he was taken to the College Street police station where he spent the night with his printer Denis Hoban who had met a similar fate about the same time. The next morning the two were joined by Dalton Williams whom the police had found with Dr Antisell in Richmond Street.

The three appeared before a police magistrate, Tyndal, at 2.30 p.m. on the Sunday on charges of having intended to compass the deposition of Her Majesty, the Queen, from her royal name and title of the Crown of the United Kingdom, and to levy war against her in that part of the United Kingdom called Ireland, for the purpose of forcing her by constraint to change her measures and counsels. The magistrate was satisfied that there was a case for committing them for trial before the commission. The following account from the *Freeman's Journal* on 10 July 1848, shows the next step in the drama:

> The warrants of committal having been completed, Messrs O'Dogherty and Williams were conveyed in a covered car (which was followed by an outside car with an escort of police) and taken off to Newgate Prison. The facts of these gentlemen's arrest not being publicly known, few, save some friends and gentlemen con-

nected with the press, were present at the committal. There was no crowd around the office, nor any manifestation of public feeling, the people doubtless not being aware that the Sabbath day had been selected for the exercise of the law, and to uphold the government authority. The vehicles drove off rapidly, conveying the "Felons" to Newgate Prison. Thus far they follow the path and fulfil the promise of John Mitchel.

Kevin O'Doherty, who had expected to be passing through the portals of the College of Surgeons in a few weeks for his final examination in medicine, heard the gates of the prison close behind him.

CHAPTER 3

Imprisonment and Transportation

Newgate prison, built in 1781 on the Little Green of Dublin, was a rectangular stone building fronting Green Street. Its three stories above the basement contained sixty-two cells in addition to storerooms, infirmaries, kitchens, a chapel and a parlour. From the entrance a passage led through the building to the governor's quarters opening on to Halston Street. The passage served as a dividing line between the state side and the felons' side. The state side provided accommodation not only for political prisoners but also for debtors. Under the harsh laws existing at the time the Dublin prisons were full with persons imprisoned for failing to pay debts as small as ten shillings. Over the front steps of the jail a platform extended as a balcony from which criminals were hanged.

The shocking conditions of the felons' side of the prison were in keeping with those found in many such institutions of the period. The windows had iron bars but no glazing. There were no fireplaces and no means of warming the premises in winter. The dungeons in which refractory prisoners were confined were totally dark with no ventilation other than an opening over the door leading into the corridor. The accommodation in the debtors' section was much better and it was in this area that the Young Irelanders were placed. The prison was controlled by the Dublin corporation and, at first, they were treated quite leniently. When O'Doherty and Williams arrived they were greeted by Duffy and Martin. Duffy's arrival the night before had drawn the attention of a large crowd. After he was committed by Magistrate Tyndal at the College Street police station he was escorted by detectives to Newgate. Many of his friends, who had been present during the hearing, accompanied the covered cab in which Duffy and the detectives made the journey. As the procession drew nearer to Green Street, a crowd, increasing every minute, followed on foot. By the time Newgate was reached the crowd was estimated to be between 1,200 and 1,500. The horse drawing the cab was held and there was cries of "Take him out; take him out!". For a time it appeared that he would be rescued. It was only after Duffy appealed to the crowd that the cab could be driven into the prison courtyard.

The Young Ireland leader was taken to a cell containing an iron bedstead and a straw palliasse. However, he was permitted to send for his upholsterer, Mr Dillon of Henry Street, who provided a comfortable bed for him. O'Doherty, too, arranged for his own bed of French maple to be brought to the twelve feet (3.6 metres) square cell which he shared with Williams. Not far away, Denis Hoban, the printer, occupied a cell down the corridor. The four Young Irelanders dined together in Duffy's cell at night. Their dinner was supplied from a hotel, and plenty of cigars and a copious supply of wines, spirits and ale were also provided. Permission was obtained to use a large room during the day and here they met the numerous visitors who were allowed in the early days after their arrest. The number of visitors became so great that Duffy requested through the press that no person visit after 3 p.m.

After 8 p.m. the political prisoners were obliged to return to their own cells and here they suffered from the poor conditions existing in the jail generally and Duffy wrote later: "State prisoners got the best accommodation the place afforded, yet my friends reported that the wall of their bedchamber was honeycombed with the nests of spiders and cockroaches, which fall upon them in bed and into the basins in which they were washing, and the glasses from which they were drinking."

Duffy and Martin continued to write for their papers, but the *Irish Tribune*, published by O'Doherty and Williams, was suppressed. However, they planned to start another from their cell in Newgate prison and impudently call it the *Newgate Calendar*. Part of the advertisement in the *Irish Felon* of 22 July 1848 in which they announced their plan read:

> ON TUESDAY NEXT
> AND on every future THURSDAY and TUESDAY
> will be published
> "THE NEWGATE CALENDAR"
> successor to
> "THE IRISH TRIBUNE"
> A Political, Military, and Felonious Journal,
> edited by
> R.D. Williams
> and
> Kevin I. O'Doherty
> at present prisoners in Newgate Gaol
> Price — TWOPENCE

The *Newgate Calendar* did not appear. It is debatable how serious O'Doherty and Williams were with their proposal. Perhaps they were being deliberately provocative. There would have been great difficulty in recommencing publication. Other printers, knowing the fate of Denis Hoban, would have been unlikely to volunteer for the position and the Young Irelanders who, it was claimed in another part of the advertisement, would contribute articles on "city fighting, guerilla war, military engineering and munitions of war", had soon other subjects to occupy their minds. The prisoners themselves were also shortly engaged otherwise. They learnt that they could expect to face their trials before a commission which would commence sitting on 8 August. Discussions with their defending counsels — Isaac Butt for O'Doherty and Samuel Ferguson for Williams — took up much of their time.

Meanwhile outside Newgate the tempo of events began to

quicken. The arrests triggered off a public debate on jury-packing — the exclusion of Roman Catholics from juries as occurred in John Mitchel's trial. The *Freeman's Journal* claimed that a recent pamphlet paved the way for inevitable conviction by insisting on total exclusion from the jury-box of every Roman Catholic, and other pro-Catholic papers took up the cry. From the other side came support for the exclusion with the pro-government paper, the *Evening Mail*, maintaining that, "The statement of juries of being packed, is always the cry of the convicted and to refute this alleged grievance must become the duty of all who administer or are anxious to sustain the law."

The British continued to send troops to Ireland and disperse them in Dublin and other strategic points throughout the country. The second battalion of the 60th Royal Rifles arrived in Dublin from Liverpool on 25 July and marched into the Royal Barracks. Two more regiments were waiting to leave England — the 4th Royal Irish Dragoons and the 9th Regiment. Three regiments were encamped in Phoenix Park in the capital city and similar encampments were a common sight on the edge of several southern cities. The 3rd Buffs were sent from Belfast to Waterford. Four pieces of artillery and a mortar gun were added to the military force at Cork, escorted by the 12th Lancers. The Lancers were hooted and spat at by the crowd which gathered. The *Limerick Chronicle* reported that the batteries on the lower Shannon as well as those at the head of the river were in a most perfect state, complete in every department, and ready for service at any moment. The *Evening Mail* reported that the army in Ireland amounted to 45,000 men.

The Young Ireland leaders, for a time, still believed that they had ample time to finalise arrangements and retained their plans to initiate the rebellion after the August harvest. Smith O'Brien left for a tour of southern Ireland to estimate the support for the movement. In Dublin, a meeting of the confederation elected an executive council of war with five members — Thomas Meagher, John Dillon, Richard O'Gorman, Devin Reilly and Darcy McGee. Some reports include the name of Father Kenyon, one of the few priests who gave enthusiastic support for the proposed rebellion, but it seems doubtful that he was included. The confederates miscalculated the speed of the British who moved more quickly than they expected. On 20 July, the government proclaimed the Crime and Outrage Act in Dublin, Cork, Waterford and Drogheda. Persons possessing arms were obliged to surrender them on penalty of imprisonment. Then came a serious blow, the possibility of which the Young Irelanders had surprisingly overlooked. Lord Clarendon, the lord lieutenant, not satisfied with the measures already taken, consistently implored the government to suspend the Habeas Corpus Act. It finally agreed and an extraordinary government gazette suppressed the confederate clubs and proclaimed the Act. Names of the wanted leaders were published in a *Hue and Cry*. They could be arrested on sight. There were three courses open to them — submit to arrest quietly, flee to America or Europe, or fight. At a hurriedly called meeting the last option was considered the most honourable. The same meeting decided that the strength of the British troops precluded striking the first blow in the capital and favoured Kilkenny, the site of earlier historic government, as the place to begin. McGee volunteered to go to Glasgow in Scotland to lead the Irish population there in an attack on the British troops stationed in that city. Vessels would be seized and he would return with two thousand men. Dillon and Meagher went south to consult Smith O'Brien. When they found him at Wexford, he surprised them by throwing away his usual caution and expressing a desire to fight.

When news of Smith O'Brien's determination to commence a rebellion reached Duffy in Newgate, he longed to join him, and raised with the other prisoners the possibility of an escape. They excitedly agreed to join him in an attempt. A rope ladder was smuggled into the prison and hidden in Duffy's cell. With the assistance of accomplices from outside, the prisoners planned to climb down the rope ladder to an ill-lit and unguarded courtyard. They hoped to escape through the prison entrance and make their way out of Dublin and join the leaders in the south. But, where in the south would they go? There was no regular news of Smith O'Brien. The Young Irelanders had no headquarters and no intelligence section. Duffy and his fellow prisoners waited impatiently for news which did not come. The plan was reluctantly deferred.

After making his decision to fight, Smith O'Brien soon realised the difficulty of his task. The Young Irelanders had no detailed plans; they had no military command, very few arms and no food for the thousands they hoped would join them. In fact, men, weakened by famine and discouraged by their priests, had little heart to fight the British troops encamped on the outskirts of many cities. The first disappointment came at Wexford. Smith O'Brien decided it would be foolish to start an insurrection there with British warships lying in the harbour. The leaders moved on to Kilkenny which the Dublin meeting had considered to be a likely spot to initiate the rising. Here, too, the Young Ireland leaders had a discouraging reception. Dr Cane, the mayor and a Young Ireland sympathiser, told them there was no hope of defeating the British troops encamped on the outskirts of the city unless help came from elsewhere. The story of lack of enthusiasm for their cause continued. Even in Templederry, Father Kenyon's stronghold, the previously optimistic priest was loath to help them. This was a severe blow indeed.

Dillon was sent to Mayo County to start a rebellion there but support for the campaign was negligible. The leaders continued their efforts in Tipperary, Cashel, Carrick and Clonmel. At times, promising crowds of supporters rallied but when the Young Irelanders had no food and no arms to give them, they dwindled away. Reports of arrests of prominent members in other parts of the country reached them and news came that Darcy McGee's hopeful visit to Glasgow had resulted in far fewer recruits than anticipated.

Finally, a number of leaders came together at Ballingarry, a small town in Tipperary County. At a council of war on the night of 28 July, most of them, who included two new arrivals Terrance McManus, a prosperous young Liverpool merchant, and Patrick O'Donohue, a Dublin law clerk, were in favour of going into hiding with a view to making a bid at a later date. O'Brien refused to accept this opinion and was determined to continue in the hope that he would raise sufficient support to attack the British forces. McManus stayed with O'Brien while other leaders left to make further attempts to rouse the countryside. Next morning, McManus was inspecting the "troops" — about forty in all, some armed with hunting guns and pistols, others with pikes. There were some hangers-on, prepared to throw stones. While the inspection was in progress, word came that Inspector Trant of the Callan police, with a body of men, was on his way to arrest Smith O'Brien. Trant saw the O'Brien "forces" and mistakenly believing he was outnumbered, took his men across the fields to take refuge in a two-storied house surrounded by a cabbage-patch, belonging to a widow, Mrs MacCormack. The widow was absent in Ballingarry and the police, amidst the cries of five of her children whom she had left at home, barricaded themselves in her house. O'Brien's motley crowd, taking their leaders reluctantly with them, chased the police. McManus began to pile hay at the back door to smoke out the police. At this juncture the widow returned and pleaded with both sides. O'Brien ordered McManus to cease his attempt and crept up to a window to parley with the police. Some of his followers began to throw stones and the police retaliated by opening fire, killing one of O'Brien's men and wounding another. The rest of the Young Ireland "army" fled and O'Brien was persuaded to follow suit on a borrowed police horse. The 1848 rebellion was over with no shots exchanged between the rebels and the British troops. O'Doherty, who had strongly urged the rising, had been in Newgate prison while the attempt was being made.

The leaders were now all on the run and many failed to elude capture. Smith O'Brien, after a week dodging from place to place, decided to attempt to see his family in Limerick. He calmly walked through the town of Thurles to the railway station where he bought a ticket to his home town. He was recognised by a railway guard and arrested. Meagher and O'Donohue suffered the same fate while walking between

Cashel and Holycross. Terrance McManus had boarded an emigrant ship bound for America but was detained before it left Ireland.

Some of the Young Irelanders were more fortunate and escaped to Europe or America. Dillon, who had gone to Western Ireland, made for Galway city in an attempt to flee the country. Among the many who sheltered him was Eva Kelly's family at Killeen. Eva, who had returned home from Dublin for a short visit, was present at the time. Writing later, she said that, "The only sensation we had at Killeen House was the arrival one evening as a fugitive, after the Ballingarry fiasco, of John Dillon . . . . He had only gone off a short time when we were that night invaded by police and the magistrate. Our house was ransacked from top to bottom." Dillon escaped to America disguised as a priest. Given a missal by a clerical friend, he read or pretended to read the masses with a devotion seldom observed by true ministers of the church.

Smith O'Brien was ridiculed over his "cabbage-patch" rebellion. The *Illustrated London News* reported that, "The silly dupe of his own vanity — poor self-deluded Smith O'Brien — found himself deserted by his 'forces' on the very first ground he had chosen for making a stand against the authorities . . . .. A more comical, yet more humiliating, spectacle history does not offer than the Irish Rebellion of 1848, under the guidance of Mr Smith O'Brien of the Pike (nine feet long) and Mr Meagher of the Sword."

But not all accounts have ridiculed Smith O'Brien. Analyses by more recent historians have suggested that the Young Irelanders influenced Irish nationalism. Writing 120 years after the rising, Gearoit O'Tuathaigh said that, "Though in practical terms it achieved little, the Young Ireland movement left a legacy of ideas which were to have a propelling influence on the thought and activities of later generations of Irish Nationalists."

With all hope of a rebellion gone, O'Doherty and his fellow prisoners waited for their trials with rather dejected spirits. But it was not all dejection for Kevin. Among the many visitors to the Young Irelanders in Newgate was Miss Bruton, an ardent sympathiser. Her visits commenced soon after the arrests and towards the end of July she took with her the young poetess, Eva Kelly. In the large common-room in which the prisoners were permitted to spend most of the day, Eva found herself conversing mainly with O'Doherty and Williams. She continued to visit and then spent most of the time with Kevin. Mutual attraction developed into a love that was to last nearly sixty years. P.J. Smyth, a prominent member of the movement, referred to the romance in his memoirs with these words, "Like many members of the party Kevin was visited by Miss Bruton. On one occasion she took with her a young girl, Miss Kelly, who at that time was charming everyone by the sweetness of her poems . . .. Tall, with dark dreamy eyes and wonderful black hair reaching to her knees, poor O'Doherty fell a victim to her charms."

Lord Chief Baron Pigot and Baron Pennefather were selected to form the August commission to hear the charges against the four Young Irelanders. (Baron was a title given to judges of the Court of the Exchequer.) When the two judges, accompanied by the lord mayor of Dublin, took their places on the bench shortly after 11 a.m. on 8 August, the Green Street court was packed. The approaches to the court were guarded by police who were stationed at both ends of Green Street. Several more were placed at strategic points in the courtroom. The first action was the swearing in of eighteen eminent citizens to comprise the grand jury whose task it would be to decide whether the four prisoners had a case to answer. After an address of some length by the chief baron they retired, to return later when their foreman announced that a true bill for treason felony had been found against all four prisoners.

O'Doherty was the first to be tried. The long indictment was read and he was charged with both offences under the Treason Felony Act. They were based on articles appearing in the *Irish Tribune* on 1 and 8 July 1848 under the headings of "Our Harvest Prospects", "Our War Department — Cannon Courage" and "A Lesson from the Insurrection in Paris". Prosecuting for the Crown, Attorney-general J.J. Monahan took the jury through all the articles. In concluding his address, he said:

> I only say that the question you will have to try is simply this — what I have ascribed to him were the object and intention of this man. Did he really wish and intend, and desire to bring about these objects? If I have not deceived myself he has expressed it so plainly that no human can doubt. If, however, you can put any other meaning on these articles of course you will do so, and it will be your duty to acquit the prisoner. But, as I said before, it does not occur to me that in due discharge of your duty you will have any other question to consider.

In leading the defence for O'Doherty, thirty-five-year-old Queen's Counsel, Isaac Butt, demonstrated the brilliance which had already won him acclaim at the bar. He admitted the articles might be seditious, but his client was not being tried for sedition. The charge was that he offended certain provisions of an Act of parliament. To find him guilty, if he had indeed written the articles, the jury would have to be satisfied firstly that the prisoner in his inmost heart and soul intended either to depose the Queen or to levy war against her in order by force and constraint to compel her to change her measures and counsels and secondly that he expressed those intentions in those articles. Butt claimed that the crux of his argument was that the jury, before they could find O'Doherty guilty, must be certain that "in his inmost soul and in those secret thoughts which are alone known to the Great Searcher of all hearts" there was the treasonable intention mentioned in the indictment.

The prosecution, the counsel said, had only produced evidence that O'Doherty was one of the registered proprietors of the *Irish Tribune*. No manuscript in O'Doherty's handwriting had been produced to support the claim that the articles were his. In the concluding part of his address to the jury the barrister referred to the part O'Doherty had played during the typhus fever epidemic in Dublin, for which he had been praised by the medical profession and the community. A French physician, M. Henry De Musny, had come to Dublin to study the epidemic but contracted the fever himself. He was attended by an eminent Dublin doctor, John Curran, who, in turn, became infected with the disease. There was some difficulty in obtaining a medical attendant for Dr Curran in view of the desperately contagious nature of the infection. O'Doherty, despising contagion, volunteered and attended the Irish physician until he unfortunately died from the affliction. "Was this the kind of man", Butt asked the jury, "who would sanction pillage or plunder?"

In exercising the prosecution's right of reply, Solicitor-General John Hatchell claimed that the prisoner "had evinced his intention unambiguously, and had announced it, triumphantly and without disguise". After an impartial summing-up by Baron Pennefather, the jury retired in the mid-afternoon of 11 August. When no word had been heard from the jury by 10 p.m., the lord chief baron called the jury into the courtroom to be informed that no agreement had been reached and there seemed not the slightest chance of agreement. He directed the jury to retire for the night, and as was the practice of the times, an order for the deprivation of food and warmth was given. When there was still no agreement on a verdict the next morning the jury was discharged and the proceedings concluded.

It was by no means over for O'Doherty and he had to face a new trial almost immediately. When the second trial commenced on 17 August, Sir Colman O'Loghlen, O'Doherty's junior counsel, challenged the array of jurors on the grounds that Roman Catholics had been improperly excluded and O'Doherty, as a Catholic, would be prejudiced. Of 4,000 citizens available for jury service, 3,000 were Catholics but in the panel of one hundred and fifty selected for the case only thirty were Catholics. In the legal argument which followed none of Sir Colman's statements was denied but the Crown argued that religion was not a ground on which jurors would be challenged. Two members of the grand jury, appointed to adjudicate on the matter, announced that the jury panel had been fairly and impartially selected.

This time, the Crown produced a copy of a handwritten manuscript of "Our Harvest", one of the articles on which the charges were based. It had been found by the police when they ransacked the *Irish Tribune* office on the day that O'Doherty had been arrested. Francis McKeever, who had worked with O'Doherty during the latter's apprenticeship with Dr Donovan, gave evidence that the writing was O'Doherty's. In a three-hour address to the jury, Isaac Butt used the same arguments which he had used in the first trial. Unless the jury was completely certain that there had been intent in O'Doherty's heart and soul, he must be acquitted. When referring to McKeever's evidence relating to the handwriting the counsel asked why had not some respectable person been produced who would testify that the handwriting was that of his client? Why had not Dr Donovan been produced as a witness? He had been O'Doherty's master, and, of course well acquainted with the defendant's handwriting. He did not say that McKeever was bribed; but did the jury believe him when he said he expected no reward? What took him to Dublin Castle? He received an invitation and went to betray a friend. The jury must discount McKeever's evidence.

Butt then went on to explain how his client came to establish his paper — the *Irish Tribune*. Mr O'Doherty was a medical student and it had been his lot to attend the poor people who, during the late famine, were stricken with fever. They were admitted into fever sheds especially erected for their accommodation. There his nerves were shocked with sights he witnessed and the misery of the people; the idea haunted him, unsettled his judgment, and made him do that which it was hoped in God he regretted having done. The barrister asked the jury if they could not believe that when O'Doherty went among abodes of the poor and saw their squalid and famine-stricken countenances in the long and sleepless nights he spent at their bedsides, that the idea haunted his mind that in a few short months the peasantry would see the land covered with an abundance of golden grain, and that in the midst of that abundance their children should die of starvation. Could the jury not believe that these considerations influenced him enough to give the advice that the people ought not to permit that harvest to be carried away to another country?

Once again a jury retired to decide O'Doherty's fate. After

five hours they were recalled to report progress. Again a foreman advised that agreement was unlikely and further, two jurors were seriously ill. When a physician testified that further confinement would be injurious to the ill jurors, O'Doherty once more heard a jury discharged without a verdict being reached. An application to release him on bail was emphatically refused and he returned to his cell in Newgate prison.

Immediately O'Doherty's trial was terminated, John Martin, who had been found guilty, was brought into the court to be sentenced. He was to be transported beyond the seas for ten years. Denis Hoban, the printer, was sentenced to one month's jail from the time of his committal. As he had already been in prison for six weeks he was discharged. The commission closed on 19 August with O'Doherty, Duffy and Williams waiting for the next sittings to begin on 2 October.

As quiet descended on Green Street, the battle was resumed in the newspapers. The *Freeman's Journal* claimed that "the press of both countries is ringing with discussion upon the memorable struggle of which the Court in Green Street was the scene last week . . . . The attention that has been turned by almost all the newspapers to the memorable argument of Mr Butt is sufficient to prove the importance of the principles attached to it." The *London Times* believed O'Doherty's case was one of the clearest for conviction that was ever considered by a jury and that trial by jury was not the proper procedure in such cases. "Trial by jury implies the tranquillity of the country in which it is appealed to . . . . It implies that men's minds are undisturbed by apprehension, or suspicions, or hopes." The *Dublin Post* accused Butt of having used craft and iniquity in his addresses to the jury. The *Pilot* attacked the editor of its contemporary for this "flagrant and revolting conduct . . . . The *craft* being the extraordinary talent evinced by Mr Butt and the *iniquity*, the successful application of it in vindicating his client."

While O'Doherty and his fellow prisoners waited in Newgate for the October commission, attention was focussed on the Tipperary County court at Clonmel where Smith O'Brien, Meagher, McManus and O'Donohue stood on charges of treason, for which the penalty was death, before a special commission of Lord Chief Justice John Doherty and Judge Blackburne. The evidence was so strong that the ability and eloquence of the defence team of Mr Whiteside, QC, Isaac Butt, Sir Colman O'Loghlen and Francis Fitzgerald proved of no avail. When Smith O'Brien stood in the dock to be sentenced, he heard the chief justice pronounce as follows: "That you, William Smith O'Brien, be taken from hence to the place from whence you came and be thence drawn on a hurdle to the place of execution, and there be hanged by the neck until you be dead; that afterwards your head shall be severed from your body and your body be divided into four quarters, to be disposed of as Her Majesty shall please." His three fellow prisoners heard the judge mete out to them the same harsh sentence.

The British government was worried at such a sentence. The *Illustrated London News* reflected this concern in an editorial which said, "The living Smith O'Brien will never more cause disquietude; his name will never more be used to stir people to revolt . . .. But, Smith O'Brien dead upon the scaffold will be exalted into a martyr; his name will stir the blood of an excitable people, and will be used as the war cry of rebellion." However, there was a legal difficulty in commuting the death penalty to a lesser one of transportation. The legislation demanded that the convicted men agree to such commutation. When the Young Irelanders were approached, they treated the suggestion with scorn. They preferred to die for their cause. The government's way out of this dilemma would be to pass legislation which would make the change.

A few weeks after the August commission ended, O'Doherty and Williams were visited by Father Ennis, a priest well known to them. He had come from Dublin Castle with a message from the government. Lord Clarendon, the lord lieutenant, would come to certain arrangements if they would plead guilty. Williams in writing to Martin who had been transferred to Richmond prison said they were to go "scot-free" and Duffy, writing later of O'Doherty, said that, "Lord Clarendon was willing to let him off, providing he would set the example of debasing himself. If he would plead guilty, he would not be called up for judgment." It appears that the government was fearful of a third failure to convict O'Doherty.

O'Doherty's first reaction was to reject the offer — to take nothing from the British. But he began to have second thoughts. The Young Ireland movement was in disarray. The leaders were either condemned to death or transportation or had successfully fled the country. Only Duffy was waiting trial. Being free would mean he could complete his medical course and further his suit with Eva Kelly. On her next visit the two discussed the proposition. The young Irish girl had no doubt about the course he should adopt. He must be true to Ireland. Eva gave Kevin some hope that she would also be true to him. The British offer was rejected. Williams also rejected the offer but for different reasons. He was optimistic of an acquittal. Due to his illness he had taken little part in the publication of the *Irish Tribune* but there was one manuscript in his handwriting among the papers seized from the *Tribune* office. Count Dalton, Williams' father was friendly with Crown Solicitor Kempes who promised that the papers would be so arranged that the damaging manuscript would not be seen when the Crown was preparing its case against Williams.

As the October commission neared, Duffy again raised the idea of escape — this time to America. The rope ladder was still hidden in Duffy's cell and news of the successful escapes of Dillon and others had filtered through to the prisoners. With Martin no longer in Newgate, Duffy discussed the proposal with O'Doherty and Williams. Williams, believing that he would be acquitted, declined but O'Doherty was enthusiastic to join Duffy in any attempt. Contact was made with friends outside the prison and arrangements were made for a small vessel to be ready to take them to a harbour to board a ship to America. But escape would not be easy. "It was from armed gaolers, through armed sentinels and over high walls which the eye grows dizzy to look upon that the attempt was to be made." Plans were finalised and a night set for the escape. The first move would be to lower themselves by the rope ladder into a courtyard left unguarded. During the day preceding the night planned, O'Doherty made an alarming discovery. The hitherto unguarded courtyard was now under the watchful eye of a policeman stationed on a platform. Duffy went to investigate and engaged the guard in conversation. He was Peter Hutchison who had written to Duffy as proprietor of the *Nation*. He also confided to Duffy that his brother was a member of a confederate club. Further discussion gave Duffy the impression that it would be safe to confide in Hutchison. The young policeman promised to help but the attempt would have to be postponed until he was on guard at night. Friends outside were advised of the change of plans and Duffy and O'Doherty waited for Hutchison to come on duty the next day to hear of a new date for the attempt. When O'Doherty was looking for the policeman the following morning he was amazed to see him conferring in the courtyard with the governor of the prison, John Smith. Minutes later, while the two prisoners were discussing the disturbing discovery in Duffy's cell, the governor entered with a retinue of prison officers. Hutchison had turned informer. Duffy, O'Doherty and Williams were immediately transferred to the criminal side of the prison. All privileges were lost; their cells were guarded and all visitors prohibited. Kevin's only sight of Eva over the next two weeks was in the Green Street courtroom.

O'Doherty's third trial began on 30 October 1848 before a new commission of Judge Crampton and Judge Torrens. The proceedings began with numerous challenges from both sides in the selection of a jury. The Crown succeeded in having a completely Protestant jury empanelled. When O'Doherty entered the dock, he appeared in good health and spirits, despite the restrictions that had been placed on him after the plan to escape had been discovered. He nodded cheerfully to friends in the public gallery and to his counsel. His pulse quickened as Eva smiled back to him from the front of the gallery. The Crown put forward the same case as in the second trial and once again Isaac Butt addressed the jury with his brilliant oratory. On the third day, Judge Crampton's summing-up suggested a verdict of guilty. He believed that Butt had gone too far with his claim that it was possible that

O'Doherty had not even read the articles, much less approved and adopted them before publication. He pointed out that the defence had produced no witnesses to oppose McKeever's evidence that it was O'Doherty's handwriting on the manuscript tendered in court. Such witnesses were surely easily available. The jury deliberated for three hours and returned a verdict of guilty on the count of intent to levy war against Her Majesty, the Queen. It was accompanied with a recommendation of mercy on account of O'Doherty's youth and the excited state of public feeling at the time of publication of the articles for which he had been indicted.

O'Doherty heard the verdict unmoved. When the judge announced that he would be brought up for sentence on another day he left the dock with a firm step, smiling to Eva and other friends. The next day Williams faced his trial. His belief in his acquittal proved to be correct and he left the court a free man. Immediately after Williams' trial ended, O'Doherty was brought up to hear his sentence of transportation for ten years. A week later he was transferred to Richmond prison. The Crown was still not ready to proceed with Duffy's trial and the October commission closed while he still waited in Newgate. Finally, after nine months, during which there were five separate indictments and two trials, Duffy gained his liberty in April 1849 when another jury disagreed.

Richmond penitentiary, a little further south of Newgate prison over the Liffey River, was built in 1813 on the site of Greenwoods' nurseries. It was bounded by South Circular Road to the north, Clanbrassil Street on the east, and the Grand Canal to the south. A church and a school were built on its western boundary. In 1848, it was known as a bridewell or a house of correction and over its entrance was inscribed a message for those who were incarcerated there — "Cease to do Evil, Learn to do Well". To many it was known as the "Cease to do Evil Hotel". Later it was used for army purposes when it was first called the Wellington Barracks, then the Griffiths Barracks. Like Newgate, Richmond prison had two sections in which conditions differed. A small section had quite reasonable accommodation but in a large convict wing conditions were much worse. When John Martin arrived at Richmond, he was privileged to occupy a separate room in the former section. O'Doherty was placed in a cell in the convict wing with O'Brien, McManus, Meagher and O'Donohue who had been transferred there after their trials at Clonmel. When Martin learnt where O'Doherty had been placed, he remonstrated with the prison governor who defended the decision by claiming O'Doherty had broken trust by attempting to escape from Newgate. In reply Martin was emphatic that O'Doherty had not given a pledge not to escape. He added that O'Doherty would never break a pledge of any kind. When O'Doherty gave his word that he would not attempt to escape from Richmond he was transferred to the more privileged area. Smith O'Brien and his Ballingarry companions were gradually granted similar approval.

The Young Ireland prisoners were mostly men of letters and were allowed extensive libraries of their own in Richmond. Martin wrote that by the end of October, two months after his transfer from Newgate, he had read Scott's *Heart of Midlothian* and *Marmion*, several of Shakespeare's plays, two chapters of Gibbon's *The Rise and Fall of the Roman Empire* and nine chapters of Smollett's *England*. He was also attempting to translate Homer's *Iliad*. O'Doherty decided to divide his time between the study of medicine and literature and a turnkey gave him permission to use his parlour during the day for his studies. His journal, written while he was an inmate at Richmond, contains selections from well-known poets as well as verse composed in the prison. A study of these reveals the different emotions the prisoner was experiencing. Bitterness towards the British is reflected in his own composition of a verse, based on the inscription over the entrance of the prison.

> "Cease to do Evil! Learn to do Well!"
> Cease to do Evil! Aye — ye madmen cease!
> Cease to love Ireland, cease to serve her well.
> Make with her foes a foul and fatal peace,
> And quick will ope your darkest, dreariest cell.
> "Learn to do Well!" Aye! learn to betray,
> Learn to revile the land in which you dwell.

England will bless you on your altered way.
"Cease to do Evil, Learn to do Well!".

Patriotism stirred as he penned those well-known lines from Walter Scott:

> Breathes there a man with soul so dead
> Who never to himself hath said,
> "This is my own, my native land".

At times he took solace by thinking of others in the same plight as himself. This was his mood when he recalled the following from Byron's "The Prisoner of Chillon":

> Eternal Spirit of the chainless mind!
> Brightest in dungeons, Liberty! thou art:
> For there thy habitation is the heart —
> The heart which love of thee alone can bind.

At times O'Doherty felt depressed, and sombre thoughts prevailed. It was on one such occasion that he copied the following lesser known prose from Dickens:

> When death strikes down the innocent and young, for every fragile form from which he lets the passing spirit free a hundred virtues rise, in shapes of mercy, charity and love to walk the world and bless it. Of every tear that sorrowing mortals shed on such green graves some good is born — some gentler nature comes. In the Destroyer's steps there spring up bright creations that defy his Power and his dark path becomes a way of light to Heaven.

It must have been in similar mood that he wrote verse to which he assigned no author but under which he signed his own name. Three stanzas read:

One by One Love's Links are Broken

> One by one love's links are broken,
> One by one our friends depart,
> Voices that have kindly spoken,
> Heart that throbbed to kindred heart.
>
> Some are resting in the ocean,
> Hidden mid its secrets deep,

> Heedless of its wild commotion,
> Sleeping there a dreamless sleep.
>
> Some have wandered o'er the billow,
> Prayers, nor tears their lives could save,
> Deep they rest beneath the willow,
> In some distant churchyard grave.

O'Doherty consoled himself with other poems and he was in more optimistic frame of mind when he recorded in his journal those famous lines of Pope:

> Hope springs eternal in the human breast.
> Man never is but always to be blest.

It was in Richmond prison that the romance between Kevin and Eva blossomed and it was no doubt because of this that he adopted a hopeful outlook towards the future. When he was deprived of visitors in Newgate after the plan to escape was discovered there was no firm agreement as to his relationship with Eva. Her whispered promise of "Have faith! I'll wait", as Kevin stepped from the dock on the day he was sentenced came somewhat as a surprise but lifted his spirits tremendously.

Richmond prison, like Newgate, was conducted by the Dublin Corporation and many privileges were restored. Among these was an almost unrestricted number of visitors. Kevin waited for Eva's first visit with mixed thoughts. Would she really wait ten years for him? Was it fair to expect this of her? He soon found there was no indecision on Eva's part and so it was that in Richmond the romance was sealed by betrothal. Arrangements were made for an engagement ring — diamonds in a cluster setting — to be purchased. But the ring would not be worn in public yet. Their engagement was to be kept a secret.

The weeks passed and still the six Young Irelanders remained in Richmond prison. The British government had decided to send them to Van Diemen's Land, the island convict settlement south of New South Wales, 12,000 miles (19,000 kilometres) away in the southern hemisphere. Two convict ships, *Maria II* and *Hyderabad*, left Ireland in April and May

1849 respectively, but the state prisoners were not on board. The government had not yet introduced the legislation in the House of Commons which would commute the death sentences of O'Brien, Meagher, McManus and O'Donohue to transportation. Then a decision was made for them all to be transported by the *Mount Stewart Elphinstone*, which was expected to call at Cork in June 1849. There was still delay in passing the necessary Act and finally only O'Doherty and Martin were taken from Richmond on 16 June 1849. They were aroused at 5 a.m. and ordered to get themselves ready. Approximately one hour later they said farewell to their four companions and entered the prison van. An extract from a press article recorded the events which followed:

> After some difficulty in getting fixed the two articles of baggage belonging to the prisoners, the van, with its escort, issued from the prison gates, where it was met by a nearly complete regiment of dragoons — the advance guard with loaded carbines, and the rest with swords drawn. Mr O'Farrell, inspector of police was present. The cortege set off at a gallop along Circular road, skirting the city, and struck in on the Kingston highway at Baggot Street bridge, and thus at a rapid pace proceeded to Kingston, where, we understand the *Trident* war steamer was awaiting the arrival of the prisoners, with orders to proceed, having received them on board, to Cork harbour, where she will land the prisoners on Spike Island.

When the *Trident* reached Cork harbour the next morning, the two prisoners were not landed at the convict settlement on Spike Island, where twelve months before John Mitchel had languished for four days before he was transported on the *Scourge* to Bermuda. They were taken aboard the *Mount Stewart Elphinstone*, the convict ship, which had called at Cork for Irish prisoners. She already had on board 163 prisoners from Pentonville, Milbank and Waterfield prisons and the hulks at Woolwich in England. Another 70 would be added at Cork. These men were being transported to Moreton Bay settlement in New South Wales. At Moreton Bay, no longer a convict settlement, they would be given the opportunity of finding honest employment with free settlers who were clamouring for labour.

The *Mount Stewart Elphinstone* had arrived at Cork on 7

June and there, according to Reverend J.R. Walpole, who had been appointed chaplain of religious instruction on the ship, "made a tedious stay for Smith O'Brien and the others". Although the necessary Act to commute their sentences to transportation had been passed, the necessary documentation had not been completed and so the convict ship left Cork on 28 June 1849 about 11 a.m. without Smith O'Brien and his three fellow prisoners.

The delay had some compensation for O'Doherty. The suddenness of the departure from Richmond prison had prevented a farewell meeting with Eva but the days at Cork gave her time to send him a letter to the ship. She wrote also to John Martin who, in reply, assured her that Kevin was in good health and spirits. Back in Richmond, McManus wrote to a friend at St Stephen's Green, Dublin, advising that permission had arrived for Eva to visit the other prisoners, but he supposed that "she would not be able to muster heart to come now that her two favourites are gone!" The betrothal was still a secret.

The *Mount Stewart Elphinstone* of 611 tons was built at Bombay in 1826. She was one of a number of long-lived Indian ships which were used for the transportation of convicts and of which Charles Bateson, well-known maritime historian, said, "After years of arduous service, the Indian vessels, particularly those built of the finest teak, were still thoroughly seaworthy and capable of making good passages." Her classification of AE1 at Lloyds meant that she fell into a group of vessels which formed a second description of those in first-class condition. She had passed the prescribed age for A1 classification and had not been sufficiently repaired to secure a continuation of A1 but was well-found in equipment. Commanded by Henry Loney, she was making her third trip as a convict transport. Before the *Mount Stewart Elphinstone* left England, artificers came aboard at Portsmouth to fit up special cabins for the state prisoners. O'Doherty and Martin thus had comfortable quarters for the voyage, made more spacious because the four other Young Irelanders had not joined the ship. During the voyage, Reverend Walpole "sent away the old bed place from his cabin and had in its stead one of the mahogany sofas, which were sent aboard for the state prisoners".

Captain Loney's orders were to sail direct to Port Jackson in New South Wales, where he would receive further orders for the disposal of his 230 "exiles" and two state prisoners. The course would take the vessel south through the Atlantic Ocean until the Cape of Good Hope could be rounded. Then, turning eastwards and veering southwards to catch the "roaring forties" she would cross the Indian Ocean, pass to the south of Van Diemen's Land and then turn northwards for the run to Port Jackson. As the vessel was clearing Cork harbour, guns from the British navy ships and Fort Westmoreland on Spike Island were firing salutes in honour of the anniversary of the coronation of Queen Victoria. Reverend Walpole wrote in his journal that, "It appeared a striking coincidence to see the state prisoners standing on deck seeing the rejoicings of the salute etc. in token of the Queen's supremacy while they were just leaving their native land to enter on their long voyage and exile." There is no record of what O'Doherty was thinking of the gracious lady against whom he had been convicted of intent to levy war.

Being allowed on deck during the day was one of the privileges the two prisoners enjoyed during the voyage. But there were restrictions. They were forbidden to have any communication with any of the ship's crew except the captain and the surgeon and were obliged to retire to their cabin by nine o'clock at night. A guard was on watch continuously whether they were in their quarters or on deck. Their conditions, however, were a deep contrast to those being experienced by the 230 convicts below decks and who, at all times, were under the close guard of Lieutenant Roney, Ensign Osborne, two corporals and forty-five rank and file. Allowed on deck in groups occasionally for exercise and divine service, they were often confined below decks for long periods.

O'Doherty and Martin spent time reading and discussing a wide range of subjects — literature, the future of Ireland and their own future in Van Diemen's Land. They had heard of the infamous station at Macquarie Harbour on the west coast where irreclaimables and the worst offenders had been sent. They heard also of Port Arthur which had replaced Macquarie Harbour and which was joined to the rest of the island by a narrow neck of land where dogs were chained at intervals to prevent escape. But the two prisoners also knew that convicts in Van Diemen's land were graded into classes with varying degrees of privileges. Their favourable treatment on board the *Mount Stewart Elphinstone* generated an optimism that they would be given a classification in which some leniency would be shown. That a deep friendship developed between O'Doherty and Martin during the voyage is confirmed in a letter that Martin wrote to Eva from Van Diemen's Land. Speaking of his former shipboard companion he said:

> May God soon grant him and you a happy meeting never more to part for a long and happy life! He and I were comrades in Newgate and Richmond jails. In the *Mount Stewart* convict ship we became friends. And for his sake I am exceeding glad to learn your secret. I cordially agree with him that it was his guardian angel that placed him, a convicted felon, in Richmond jail. I must not envy him, the happy dog! But he must labour hard to make himself in some degree worthy of the happy destiny that Heaven and your grace bestows upon him.

The voyage was regarded as quite normal. As expected, the temperature rose as the vessel neared the equator and Reverend Walpole recorded that he "commenced to wear cotton drawers, leaving off worsted — commenced thin shoes". The weather worsened across the Indian Ocean and on 4 September the vessel was struck by a "most tremendous sea abeam" while she was hove to. The prison below, the soldiers' barracks and the hospital were flooded but were cleared by pumping without further mishap. Two days later, an emigrant ship, the *Mahommed Shah*, was sighted. She had been dismasted in the same area and eight seamen lost. But repairs were made and she reached her destination, Port Phillip, without further trouble.

On 2 October 1849, the *Mount Stewart Elphinstone* anchored in Port Jackson after 97 days at sea, on some of which the ship had been becalmed and on others she had made good runs of up to 247 miles (395 kilometres) with the "roaring forties" blowing her along. For the most part, the health of the prisoners below decks had been good. There had been seven deaths — a small number compared with similar voyages in the earlier years of transportation to New South Wales. Surgeon Superintendent George Moxey reported that O'Doherty and Martin had maintained excellent health throughout the voyage despite the forebodings felt about the fate of Martin by his friends in Ireland before his departure. The *Mount Stewart Elphinstone* stayed in Port Jackson for seventeen days before she left for Moreton Bay. During this time a meeting of Irishmen in Sydney was held in the Long Room at Mr Gray's Lighthouse Hotel at the corner of Sussex and Bathurst Streets. Many of the 400 present had to stand outside in the streets. Most agreed that O'Doherty and Martin were national heroes and not criminals and enthusiastically supported a decision to appoint a committee which would consider the means by which the government of New South Wales would be forced to ensure that the condition of the state prisoners be ameliorated. There were one or two present who considered that the matter was not one in which the New South Wales government had any jurisdiction. This latter opinion was overwhelmingly discounted by the meeting but was found to be correct when the approach was made. Permission for representatives for the Irish community to board the convict ship and converse with O'Doherty and Martin was also refused but a gift of 94 sovereigns reached them. On 20 October O'Doherty and Martin were transferred to the brig *Emma*, a vessel of 139 tons, under the command of Captain Pockley. Whilst the two Irishmen appreciated the offer of accommodation in the ladies' cabin, the presence of Lieutenant Goode's guard reminded them of their prisoner status. On 22 October, the brig lifted anchor and passing through the heads, turned south to convey them to Van Diemen's Land.

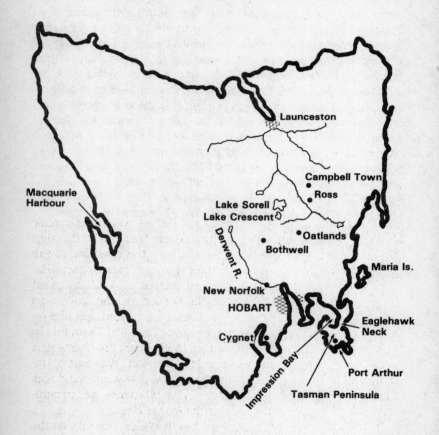

VAN DIEMEN'S LAND (TASMANIA). Showing places mentioned in the text.

CHAPTER 4

Exile

As the *Emma* sailed southwards in the last week of October 1849, O'Doherty and Martin, granted the freedom of the ship by Lieutenant Goode, saw in the distance the coastline of the land in which they would serve their sentence of transportation — Van Diemen's Land. It was so named in 1642 by Abel Tasman, the Dutch navigator, in honour of the governor-general of Batavia, Anthony Van Diemen, who had sent him on a voyage of discovery. The name was changed to Tasmania in honour of the navigator himself in 1855. From his charts it is seen that the Dutchman presumed the new land was part of the mainland to the north. The discovery that it was an island was made by Matthew Flinders in 1798–99 when he circumnavigated Van Diemen's Land with George Bass.

In 1803, Governor King of New South Wales, fearful that the French would take possession of the island and wishing to divide his convicts and procure timber there, sent young Lieutenant Bowen with a handful of convicts and a few soldiers to guard them, as well as a small number of free men, to establish a settlement on the Derwent River in the south. Bowen commenced his task at Risdon on the east bank but he was superseded by David Collins who had abandoned a proposal to settle at Port Phillip on the mainland. Collins transferred the tiny settlement to Sullivan's Cove on the west bank and called it Hobart Town, which became the centre of government for the island. Collins was the first of a line of lieutenant-governors who grappled with many problems as the number of convicts transported to Van Diemen's Land increased — the threat of famine, bushrangers (mostly escaped convicts), marauding Aborigines until they were all eliminated, and the settlers who demanded more land, representative government and an end to transportation.

When the Irish exiles arrived in Van Diemen's Land, Sir William Denison had been lieutenant-governor for nearly three years. He believed that the purpose of punishment was to deter, not to reform, and that as idleness was the cause of most crimes, all convicts should spend their sentences carrying out hard labour. When he received a memorandum from Earl Grey, secretary of state for the Colonies, in respect to the treatment that O'Doherty and his companions were to receive on their arrival, Denison was appalled. An extract reads:

> At the same time the difficulty of suitably regulating the punishment to be undergone by convicts of education and who belong to a Superior Class in Society appears to have been felt in the Colonies to which offenders are transported. To subject them to the same hard labour as persons accustomed to manual toil has been found scarcely practicable, nor would it really be placing them on an equality as regards the severity of their punishment with those to whom in appearance their condition was thus assimilated. On the other hand banishment and the foreefeiture of fortune and station is in their own case a far heavier infliction than in that of offenders in a humbler grade of Society . . . . Much will depend on their conduct during the voyage and on the spirit in which they may reach the Colony under your government. If they shall manifest a refractory disposition or one in the least inimical to good order it may be necessary that you should confine them in the Prison you may consider the most appropriate for the purpose. But if there should be no reason of this kind for additional severity, I should wish you to grant them Tickets-of-Leave, placing them as far as you can in separate Districts at a distance from the Capital.

A ticket-of-leave was an indulgence which Denison granted to other convicts only after several years of hard labour and good conduct. He told his wife if he had been able to have his way, he would put these new Irish prisoners "into grey jackets and send them to wheel barrows on the wharf or break stones on the roads like ordinary convicts". But Denison knew that Grey's instruction could not be modified.

During the morning of 30 October the *Emma* rounded the Tasman peninsula in the south-east of the island and later entered the wide estuary of the Derwent River. In mid-afternoon they came in sight of Hobart and Lieutenant Goode pointed out to them Mount Wellington; its peak, covered in low cloud, rose 4,000 feet (1,220 metres). Between its slopes and the western banks of the river lay the town, now a busy capital with 25,000 inhabitants. The *Emma* nosed into the harbour at Sullivan's Cove after threading her way through numerous ships riding at anchor. About a hundred yards away lay a British war-sloop. Lieutenant Goode said it was the *Swift* which had left Dublin on 10 July on a special mission to bring their fellow rebels, Smith O'Brien, Meagher, McManus and O'Donohue to Van Diemen's Land and had arrived two days previously. On hearing this exciting piece of news O'Doherty and Martin scanned the decks of the *Swift* for signs of their fellow exiles. At first disappointed, they later saw McManus "strutting about the *Swift* with a telescope in his hand and sending great demonstrations of friendly salutations across the water".

Soon afterwards, the Catholic vicar general, Reverend Mr Hall, came aboard to greet O'Doherty and Martin. He told them that, like themselves, their four fellow exiles had been treated well on the voyage from Ireland. William Nairn, assistant comptroller-general of convicts, had visited the *Swift* and offered them tickets-of-leave in separate districts, after receiving written promises that the comparative liberty would not be used to attempt an escape. O'Brien declined as he stated that he had no intention of pledging his word to an arrangement which would deprive him of any opportunity to escape which might occur. McManus at first followed O'Brien's lead but later accepted the offer, while Meagher and O'Donohue accepted immediately. Meagher had left that morning to travel to Campbelltown, eighty miles (one hundred and twenty-eight kilometres) north of Hobart, in the district to which he was assigned. O'Brien and O'Donohue had been put ashore, with the former, dressed in convict garb, being marched to a wharf to travel by ship to Maria Island off the east coast to serve his time at Darlington Probation Station. As O'Donohue had claimed that he had no chance of obtaining employment outside the capital he was permitted to remain in Hobart, contrary to the instructions from England. McManus was waiting instructions to proceed to New Norfolk on the Derwent River, twenty-five miles (forty kilometres) west of Hobart. O'Doherty and Martin were handed a letter from Meagher, written hastily before he had left the *Swift*. He told of the short notice they were given on leaving Dublin and how, at the Cape of Good Hope, the vessel carrying Mitchel from Bermuda had not been sighted. Their friends in Ireland were all well but there was no special message for Kevin from Eva.

The next morning O'Doherty and Martin met the assistant comptroller-general of convicts in the captain's cabin. He announced the lieutenant-governor's intention to extend the same offer as their fellow rebels had received — tickets-of-leave on receipt of favourable reports of their behaviour from the captains of the *Mount Stewart Elphinstone* and the *Emma* and provided they gave a written promise that they would not use the comparative liberty to escape. He added that both captains had submitted favourable reports and left them to forward their replies within twenty-four hours. Soon afterwards they were summoned to the captain's cabin again where the assistant registrar of convicts diffidently explained it was his duty to obtain a description of their physical appearance. The record which he made of O'Doherty reads as follows:-"Height, 5'11½"; age, 26; complexion, fresh; head, medium; hair, brown; whiskers, ditto; visage, oval; forehead, broad; eyebrows, brown; eyes, ditto; nose, medium; mouth, ditto; chin, small".

During the morning Martin wrote to Mr Coveney of Sydney

regarding the 94 sovereigns presented to them there. Believing that 50 sovereigns were a gift and the remainder a loan, he was sending back 22 sovereigns with Captain Pockley of the *Emma* to return to the donors. O'Doherty would keep his 22 sovereigns for the time being but would return them when he obtained employment. Coming on deck again they were hailed by a man in a dinghy. It was O'Donohue, to whom Lieutenant Goode gave permission to approach within speaking distance. He looked well, and O'Doherty and Martin gathered that his relations with his three fellow rebels during the voyage from Ireland had been cordial. They were pleased at this, for the former clerk had a reputation of being quarrelsome. When he left they went below to read the Hobart newspapers which had come aboard. The *Hobart Town Courier* had comment and advice to give to the rebels:

> They must be contented, therefore, to suffer not only the stigma of treason but the sorrows of exile. It becomes them now to yield with submission to an inevitable lot. On calm reflection they will be thankful it is the British nation whose captives they are; and that, since another race must rule their country, that race is Anglo-Saxon . . .. We are not unaware that some dangers may arise from another quarter. There are men in all communities who buzz like flies about a distinguished stranger, and extract all the honey he may bring; and then sting like wasps . . .. If these gentlemen [the Irish rebels] are wise, we say, they will study botany, poetry, metaphysics — anything but colonial factions.

O'Doherty and Martin agreed to accept tickets-of-leave and early next morning sent their written promise to the convict department. A further visit from the vicar general and from Mr Moore, editor of the pro-Irish paper, the *Hobart Guardian*, indicated they would have many friends in their land of exile. At midday came the instructions from the comptroller-general of convicts. O'Doherty was to proceed to Oatlands, fifty-three miles (eighty-five kilometres) to the north of Hobart and Martin to Bothwell, forty-five miles (seventy-two kilometres) to the north-west. They would catch the Launceston night coach leaving that afternoon and could travel together to Oatlands. Martin was to find his own way to his district the next day. Before leaving the ship, O'Doherty gave the steward and Corporal O'Connor a half-sovereign each — generosity with which Martin did not altogether agree. At 3 p.m. they stood on the wharf — the first land their feet had touched for over four months. A few sympathisers watched them enter a cab arranged for them by Mr Moore of the *Hobart Guardian* with a dray taking their luggage. They drove to the police station to collect the regulations governing their tickets-of-leave. When O'Doherty opened the document he read:

Regulations

to be observed by the undersigned holder of a ticket-of-leave.
Kevin Izod O'Doherty

(1) Not to proceed out of the District within which your residence has been limited.
(2) To report your residence to the Police Magistrate and every change of residence you desire to make.
(3) To report yourself personally to the Police Magistrate of the District once a month.
(4) Not to be absent from your registered place of residence after 10 o'clock at night.
(5) Not to enter any theatre or billiard room.

Next stop was the post office to give directions for their mail and then to Albion Inn, the terminal of the New Norfolk coach, hoping to see McManus before he left for his district. In a few minutes McManus arrived accompanied by O'Donohue. A small crowd of sympathisers and onlookers gathered and the meeting was transferred to a room in the inn where many emotional speeches were made. From there O'Doherty and Martin drove to the Ship Inn in Collins Street to catch their coach. After shaking hands with a score or more of well-wishers they took their seat on the front of the coach. The guard blew his bugle; the coachman cracked his long whip, and amid shouts from the rebels' new friends the hard-bitten greys began the fifteen hours' journey to Launceston, of which the two exiles would travel less than half. There was still enough light for O'Doherty and Martin to notice that for much of their journey they were passing through sheep country with flocks grazing in the fields and an occasional bullock driver unyoking his team from a dray laden with wool to spend the night on the road before moving on towards Hobart the next morning.

Towards 10 p.m. the dim lights of Oatlands came into view and the coach came to a stop outside Oatlands Inn where a man came to unharness the horses and mine host stood in the doorway to welcome any guests. An Irish voice asked the guard for the mailbag and then inquired if Mr O'Doherty was among the travellers. It was John Ryan, the Oatlands postmaster, who hailed from Tipperary. Would Mr O'Doherty care to be his guest at his home just down the street on the opposite side of the highway? If so, he was welcome to stay the night and as long as he cared to do so. Kevin accepted this offer of hospitality and, with Martin settled in the inn, went off with another new friend to eat an enjoyable supper prepared by Mrs Ryan and to spend a comfortable night in Elm Cottage where he was to stay for the remainder of his time in Oatlands.

Next morning Kevin set out with Martin for the courthouse in Campbell Street where he was obliged to report to the magistrate, John Whiteford. Erected in 1829 to become one of the first public buildings in the town, the courthouse was a solid masonry structure with a shingle roof. Like many other buildings in Oatlands, the stone used in its erection was quarried from the edge of nearby Lake Dulverton. It served not only for the magistrate but also to accommodate the Supreme Court which had been held there since 1841, making the small town an important centre outside Hobart and Launceston. Kevin's duty completed, the two Irishmen walked down the street almost opposite, passing the high stone walls of the large jail which housed male and female convicts including those whom the judge had declared should suffer the extreme penalty on the scaffold.

As the two exiles returned to the inn they discussed their future. They agreed that for the time being they would endeavour to serve their sentences without attempting an escape. In these interchanges they occasionally used the names they had given each other on the voyage on the *Mount Stewart Elphinstone*. Martin, admiring so many fine characteristics in O'Doherty, called him Saint Kevin, after Saint Kevin of Glendalough who had become one of the special patrons of Dublin and Wicklow. In return Martin was dubbed John Knox, after the Scottish religious reformer who was responsible for the final triumph of Protestantism in Scotland. They shook hands in front of the inn and Martin took his seat in the gig of a settler travelling south. He would go back over the road they had travelled the day before hoping to obtain another lift to Bothwell.

After Martin's departure, O'Doherty continued an inspection of the small town, noting other solidly constructed public buildings and houses, more inns, and the two-storied Holyrood House erected a few years before for John Whiteford, the police magistrate. Most people he passed in the street greeted him cordially but there was one person who avoided his gaze. He was Solomon Bleay, the colony's hangman, who lived at Oatlands. He was so unpopular that when he had a job to do in Hobart or Launceston, he was forced to walk all the way, for no coachman would carry him.

In the afternoon O'Doherty met Dr Edward Hall, the assistant colonial surgeon, and discussed the possibility of employment. The friendly doctor could offer no prospect in the medical field but promised to help the young exile keep up with his medical studies, an offer which was gladly accepted. That night he wrote a letter to Eva by candlelight. He had much to tell her and tried to hide from her the feeling of despondency that was creeping over him. When he finished writing he pondered his position. He was already missing Martin's companionship and hopes of employment were dim. Completion of his medical course and a subsequent professional career seemed far away. Above all, he wanted desperately to be back in Ireland with Eva. He thought of escape only to dismiss it. Escape meant escape to America and probably never returning to his own country. His stack of sovereigns was already reduced and he wrote another letter to Ireland for funds.

On Sunday Father Bond came to Ryan's cottage to say mass. William Bond had arrived in Van Diemen's Land in 1844 with

Bishop Willson who had appointed him "religious instructor to penal stations". He arrived in Oatlands earlier in 1849 to carry out his duties among male convicts working on the roads in the district. After mass, discussion centred on the erection of a Catholic church at Oatlands. The lieutenant-governor had granted the Catholics land but declined to give any financial aid for the building. Undaunted by the refusal, a small band of Catholics, who had met in the courthouse the preceding April, had decided to proceed with the project. They raised £300 ($600) by subscriptions, sufficient to commence building. O'Doherty met the men who, with Father Bond, were trustees of the land — John Bacon, Henry Anstey and Daniel O'Connor.

Henry Anstey, approximately O'Doherty's age, was to be a regular companion in the days ahead. He was the son of Thomas Anstey, the respected pioneer magistrate of Oatlands, now living at Anstey Barton on 20,000 acres (8,000 hectares) to the west of the town. Anstey Barton was maintained in the style of an old English manor — butlers, maids, grooms and gardeners and forty men clearing the land and attending the sheep. Kevin and Henry Anstey often took horses from the stables there and rode the countryside.

When O'Doherty commented on the absence of Aborigines, Henry Anstey explained how many had died at the hands of the early settlers. When the natives became aggressive Lieutenant-Governor Arthur was persuaded to mount the "Black Line", by which the military and volunteers proposed to drive the Aborigines into the south-east corner of the island. The operation resulted in the capture of one Aboriginal man and a boy. Then George Robinson, the conciliator, had spent years walking around the island persuading the remaining natives to live on Flinders Island in Bass Street where most pined and died. Two years before O'Doherty arrived the sad remnants of a once 4,000 strong race, now reduced to forty-four, were removed to Oyster Cove, south of Hobart.

The Irish exiles wrote frequently to each other in the first few months, with O'Doherty receiving more than he sent, an omission for which he was often criticised. The first letter O'Doherty received came from Martin who had written the first night he arrived at Bothwell. He, too, had been well received in his district, with even the police magistrate, Captain King, being well disposed towards him. When Martin raised the difficulty he anticipated in determining the boundary between their two districts, King said that "there would be no annoyance offered us by requiring a nice determination of such geographical questions; and proposed Mr Jones' red brick house as a convenient meeting place", and gave detailed directions as to how it could be reached. Not long afterwards O'Doherty heard from Meagher, whose district bordered on the Oatlands district to the north. Meagher had very quickly shifted from Campbelltown to Ross, a town seven miles (eleven kilometres) closer to Oatlands but still in his original district. He, too, had discussed the boundaries of the respective districts with his magistrate and invited O'Doherty to meet him at a bridge over Blackman's River which formed the boundary near a convict station called Tunbridge. Kevin borrowed a horse from the Anstey stables and rode the fourteen miles (twenty-two kilometres) to Tunbridge. Deciding that the exact line of the boundary would be in the middle of the bridge the pair set up a table there and ate a meal delivered from the nearby inn, with each sitting in his respective district. Meagher in a letter to Duffy in Dublin said that:

> To be sure, the passage through the air, for upwards of five hundred yards or so, solidified the gravy somewhat; but the old salmon-coloured inn was not to blame for that. In all these cases the Home Office spoiled the cooking. One very hot day — the bed of the river being almost quite dry — we dined under the bridge; having first of all erected something like a Druid's altar on the top of which we laid a cloth. The seats were constructed much after the same fashion; and the hamper which brought the ale, the plates, and cheese, being emptied, kicked over and turned upside-down served in the capacity of a very respectable dumb waiter.

Then Martin wrote that he had been told of a point where the borders of their districts met. It lay 2,500 feet (760 metres) up on the edge of the western tier between Lakes Sorrell and Crescent. It was approximately twenty miles (thirty-two kilometres) riding from each of their places of residence, O'Doherty and Meagher having to travel in a westerly direction and Martin, north-easterly.

After guides had taken them on the first visit, the three arranged to meet there weekly at a set time at the hut of a shepherd, Stephen Cooper, employed by Mr G.C. Clarke, the owner of the land. Meagher wrote of these meetings as follows:

> Here we dine, and spend the evening up to half past five o'clock, when we descend the "Tier" and betake ourselves to our respective houses. Whilst the preparations for the dinner are going on, whilst Mr Cooper is splitting chops, shelling peas, washing onions, and melting himself away in a variety of labours by the log fire, we are rambling along the shores of the lake, talking of old times, singing the old songs, weaving fresh hopes among the old ones that have ceased to bloom.

In addition to the weekly meetings there were special days, and Meagher bought a boat which he called *Speranza*, after Jane Elgee, one of the writers for the *Nation*. The boat was hauled by bullock-team from Hobart and O'Doherty received instructions for the supervision of its transport through his district and particularly along the track up the "Tier". Meagher planned to launch it in Lake Sorrell on St Patrick's Day 1850. This event would be celebrated by a two-day visit to which John Ryan and John Bacon were also invited, bringing guns to fire a grand salute at the launching.

But O'Doherty did not always make the journey and Martin expressed concern at his absences in a letter:

> I am afraid you are sick or suffering from some accident. So is Meagher. He and I met at the lakes on Thursday the 6th and again on Monday last, and we were looking eagerly and anxiously for your arrival. We don't know how to account for your failure to keep the appointments unless by supposing you are unable to leave the house. Why have you not written or employed some one to write to us? If you are little worse than lazy I ought to be angry at you for giving us causeless alarm, though the fact is I will be heartily glad to learn that you are well. If you are ill, you ought to let us know; and some of us would endeavour to get permission to visit you.

Then Meagher learnt that O'Doherty would not be attending the launching of his boat and wrote begging him to come.

O'Doherty had some excuse for not attending the launching on St Patrick's Day. It fell on a Sunday and Father Bond would be saying a special mass and being a devout Catholic, he felt obliged to attend. He may have felt as Martin did about celebrations for their patron saint. In a letter he told O'Doherty that, "Our great national anniversary should be celebrated with sackcloth and ashes and shame and lamentation, rather than with gaiety and joy."

While these explanations may be submitted for O'Doherty's failure to attend the special celebrations at the lakes, there is no palpable excuse for his absence at other times. He had no employment which prohibited leaving Oatlands; he was helping to lay the foundations for the new church but was not obliged to attend every day; neither was there need for continuous study of medical subjects and he was finding time to ride with Henry Anstey. The only answer must lie in the return of the feeling of dejection which came over him the night he wrote his first letter to Eva. At such times he wished no communication with his fellow exiles.

The lakes were not the only rendezvous for the Irishmen. They often met surreptitiously in the homes of sympathetic settlers. One home that welcomed them frequently was that of Mr and Mrs Connell at Glenconnel, near the Sugarloaf at Ross. Their son became the first Australian Benedictine monk and Father Maurus, as he was called, was a favourite with the exiles during his visits home from his studies in Sydney. A letter written by Martin to Mrs Connell when he was leaving Van Diemen's Land, begins with these words: "I shall never forget the true heartiness of the hospitality with which you, Mr Connell, your daughters and your son received my 'rebel' comrades and myself, that moonlight night when we cantered over the marsh, to visit the Irish family at the foot of the Sugarloaf. It was both very sad and very delightful to me to find in a forest at the Antipodes the warm Irish feelings and the grace and intelligent nature of the Irish character, and to think that all that is fast being extirpated at home."

In the early weeks at Oatlands O'Doherty also received letters from O'Donohue and Smith O'Brien. O'Donohue's letter came in reply to one Kevin had written mentioning his hope to be recognised in some way as a medical practitioner and offering O'Donohue a loan. O'Donohue was somewhat of an outcast with his fellow rebels but O'Doherty always treated him kindly. Later he was to write that, "O'Donohue's trials and suffering were such that his execution would have been a great mercy". In his letter O'Donohue expressed his view that Dr McNamara, a Hobart doctor, and the vicar general, Reverend Hall, "believed O'Doherty's prospects of practising medicine were bright". Smith O'Brien, writing from Maria Island, presumed that O'Doherty had "no desire to dabble in colonial politics" and that he was "preparing to take out a medical degree at Hobart Town". O'Brien also complained that he had "been consigned to an isolation from mankind nearly as complete as the will of Sir William Denison, aided by Dr John Hampton, could create". (Dr Hampton was the comptroller-general of convicts.) Sympathisers in Van Diemen's Land and Ireland made much of the alleged ill-treatment of Smith O'Brien. There were others, no doubt, who agreed with Sir William Denison when he wrote, "How little they appreciate that lenity which not only spared their lives but has placed them in a position of comparative freedom, to which others have to struggle through many years of labour and difficulty." It was O'Brien's own choice that he was at Maria Island and not enjoying the "comparative freedom" of a ticket-of-leave as his fellow exiles were.

The letter for which O'Doherty had been so anxiously waiting arrived in February 1850. Eva had written on 11 September 1849 whilst he was on the high seas in the *Mount Stewart Elphinstone*.

Back with her family at Killeen House in Galway, she had not picked up her pen nor strummed her harp since Kevin's departure. She was spending many hours walking in the country, thinking always of her loved one. Letters from Gavan Duffy and Dalton Williams had cheered her a little. Duffy, travelling with Thomas Carlyle, the Scottish historian and essayist, in western Ireland, not far away from Killeen, wrote, "You who are unquenchable, what will you do for the cause?

Do you still with verse interpret the heart of to-day?" Dalton Williams, finding Kevin's old rooms in Dublin vacant, had taken them. He said that he felt "a melancholy pleasure in being surrounded by the objects which were so familiar to him, and recalling the conversations they had had when their hopes were high". He advised Eva to pay no attention to newspaper reports about the state prisoners, saying he was convinced that they would never spend half the time in exile mentioned in court. O'Doherty shared his letter with Martin when he made a special effort to go to the lakes and "John Knox" responded by rewarding Eva with a long letter telling her much of the activities of the exiles. Writing on 6 June 1850 he also expressed his disappointment at not hearing from his brothers or sisters or from his friends. He had received newspapers featuring the state of the Queen of England's health and the Prince Consort's occupation with his guns and with literary, artistic and charitable engagements; but now after nearly twelve months since he and O'Doherty had left Cork he had not received one letter from Ireland.

Meanwhile, in Hobart, O'Donohue began a paper, the *Irish Exile and Freedom's Advocate*, much to the surprise and concern of the other exiles who tried to dissuade him from the project as they believed they should not mix with politics. It was also surprising that the lieutenant-governor permitted its publication, which continued for fifteen months before it was suppressed. Many of the articles in O'Donohue's paper were criticisms of Denison's treatment of the exiles voiced in extravagant language. However, he recorded the arrival of John Mitchel in the convict ship, *Neptune*, in April 1850 in rather gracious terms:

> The entire community of these colonies will, no doubt, feel thankful to Sir William Denison's Government for their discretionary exercise of leniency in permitting Mr Mitchel to select the residence of his oldest and most cherished friend, John Martin, who so steadily walked in the footprints of his old school-fellow, Mitchel, the GREAT IRISH POLITICAL REFORMER.

O'Donohue also reported Smith O'Brien's foiled attempt to escape from Maria Island in August 1850. A Catholic priest had conveyed to O'Brien a plan in which a ship would hover off the island. One of its boats would be despatched to the shore within wading distance to rescue O'Brien. However, when O'Brien reached the boat no help was given and a constable, following the rebel out, arrested him. It was believed that the ship's master had informed the authorities of the plan. Shortly afterwards Smith O'Brien was transferred to Port Arthur. During a court inquiry into the incident, Allan Stonor, the solicitor-general, claimed that Smith O'Brien had been shown mercy. O'Donohue, in a verbose report couched in extravagant language, endeavoured to convince his readers that neither generally nor individually had the rebels been treated mercifully. Of the treatment O'Doherty had received, the *Irish Exile* had this to say:

> Was it "mercy" to seize upon and cut off in his professional career the ardent and enthusiastic youth, Kevin Izod O'Dogherty, because he called upon the people, through the Press, — on which he wasted his patrimony to establish — not to permit themselves to be further reduced to starvation, but to keep, and to subsist upon the plenteous food, which the bounty of heaven had blessed our soil with? . . . Was it "mercy" to fetter this young man for his utterance of language which proved his innate virtue, his sympathy for human woe, and his longing for its alleviation? . . . The young patriot was transported to Van Diemen's Land for his humanity — yet Mr Stonor calls his treatment merciful.

The failure to obtain employment and the lack of money was a worry to nearly all the exiles. Early in January 1850 Martin wrote to O'Doherty advising him that all his money had gone and "if you can spare me a loan, be so good as to bring four or five sovereigns in your pocket when you come to our rendezvous next Monday and I will be your humble debtor". But the generous O'Doherty himself was in financial straits and Meagher sent him a £5 note drawn on the Van Diemen's Land Commercial Bank. A few months later he could not find twelve shillings ($1.20) for freight on packages of food which came to him to forward on to Mitchel. When no funds came from home and no permission was granted for him to practise medicine, he decided to forego his ticket-of-leave and go to a convict station where he would at least be housed and fed. He advised

Martin that, "On Tuesday I sent a letter to the second jailer in command, Hampton, resigning my ticket-of-leave. I could stand it no longer not even long enough to consult with any of you. When I found another vessel in with nothing for me I sent a letter through Whiteford [the police magistrate] who urged me, very strongly and kindly against it."

A prompt reply came from the convict department giving approval for his application and advising that "the Lieutenant-Governor has approved of his being stationed at Salt Water River in Tasman's Peninsula, where he will be employed as Dispenser and allowed pay at the rate of 1s. a day with quarters and the usual ration". O'Doherty's friends acted quickly in an endeavour to persuade him not to take this step. Bishop Willson, whom the Irish rebel had met when the bishop had come to Oatlands on 9 April earlier in the year to lay the foundation stone of St Paul's Catholic Church, wrote two letters advising strongly against giving up his ticket-of-leave and "eating the Government bread". The bishop suggested that O'Doherty apply for a transfer to another district. Perhaps he could transfer to Ross and work with Dr Hall who was now stationed there or to Hobart or Launceston where he could dispense medicines in a druggist's establishment. The pleas of his friends prevailed and O'Doherty stayed in Oatlands for the time being. In a few days a second letter from Eva came in reply to his own written on his second night in Oatlands. She welcomed the news of his safe arrival and his accommodation with the Ryan family. She was strumming her harp again and hoped to send a new poem with her next letter. Dalton Williams had spent Christmas "among the lakes, the mountains and the venerable ruins of Glendalough". He hoped to visit Eva to convey to her his impressions of the "antiquities of the Seven Churches in person". (The Seven Churches were established in the seventh century by Saint Kevin whose name Martin gave O'Doherty.)

A few weeks later O'Doherty heard of the possibility of working in Dr William Crooke's Tasmanian Dispensary in Hobart. Besides being a prominent physician, Dr Crooke was a magistrate and strong supporter of the Total Abstinence Society. Kevin wrote to Dr McCarthy, another Hobart physician, to plead his cause but unfortunately the doctors were not on speaking terms. It was O'Donohue who came to the rescue. When Bishop Willson learnt from O'Donohue the need for support, quick action was taken to convince Crooke that O'Doherty would bring the custom of the Catholic Irish to the dispensary. Approval to transfer from Oatlands was granted by the lieutenant-governor and on 7 December 1850 the *Hobart Town Courier* announced his new position as follows: "Mr O'Dogherty. We are happy to inform our countrymen and the public generally that the abovenamed Exiled Patriot is now in Hobart Town, managing the Tasmanian Dispensary opposite Saint Joseph's Church. We wish him every success and we doubt not our countrymen will render all aid in their power by patronising the above dispensary as Mr O'Dogherty is a most amiable and deserving gentleman."

Shortly after O'Doherty commenced duty at the dispensary McManus, then located at Launceston, sought permission to visit Hobart. Although this was refused he made the visit and called on O'Doherty and O'Donohue. The three decided to risk visiting Smith O'Brien who, persuaded by friends to accept a ticket-of-leave, was living at New Norfolk. The journey was made on 3 December 1850 but a joyful reunion had serious consequences. Their appearance in New Norfolk was reported to the authorities and they were summoned to appear before magistrates on charges of being absent from their places of residence without permission. O'Doherty appeared before Police Magistrate Mason at New Norfolk who said he was prepared to take the same action as was taken when McManus faced a similar charge at Launceston. On pledging that in future he would not leave Launceston without first seeking permission, McManus was admonished and discharged. O'Doherty stated he was willing to take such a pledge but he could not undertake to say that, if permission were not granted, he would not leave his district if he felt justified. On hearing this Mr Mason said: "I hope if you determine upon leaving your district, permission having been refused, and you elect to do so, you will select some other locality than New Norfolk, as it is, I assure you, very painful to me to be compelled to deal anything approaching to even apparent harshness with a gentleman of your character." O'Doherty was then admonished and discharged.

The light penalty of admonishment of the exiles — it included O'Donohue also — shocked Sir William Denison who had not changed his opinion that they were being treated too lightly by having been granted tickets-of-leave. He overruled the magistrates' sentences and gave instructions that O'Doherty, McManus and O'Donohue were to spend three months at convict stations on the Tasman Peninsula. The *government gazette* of 4 January 1851 contained the sober message that the lieutenant-governor had revoked the tickets-of-leave of McManus, O'Doherty and O'Donohue. O'Doherty was arrested immediately and taken to the Hobart penitentiary. Two mornings later he was dressed in convict grey and marched with other convicts to the wharf to board the *Lady Franklin* to be conveyed to Impression Bay probation station. A few days later, McManus found himself at the Cascade station, a few miles away but O'Donohue was indisposed and too weak to be moved immediately.

The *Hobart Town Courier* of 4 January 1851 criticised Denison's action in these words:

> The attempt to attach an infamous penalty to a mere infraction of a petty regulation will only awaken a more determined resolution to refuse that moral countenance without which the whole fabric of penal government must soon fall to the ground. All men feel degraded by living in a country where persons, treated as political offenders, are, for some error of judgment in reference to their letters of licence, dragged from the intimacies of social life by a convict authority, and, without a hearing, thrown among thieves and murderers . . . .

Impression Bay probation station, one of several convict centres on Tasman Peninsula, was situated on its northern coast on Norfolk Bay (now called Premaydena). Convicts were occupied mainly in the timber industry. In its heyday it provided much of the wooden requirements for the convict department — furniture, carts, barrows and a good deal of sawn timber, especially for the convict coal mines a few miles further west on the peninsula. The prisoners slept twenty to a hut at the end of which a light was kept burning to deter the practice of "unnatural acts".

The *Hobart Advertiser* claimed that O'Doherty was given special treatment and kept apart from other convicts. Hugh Magorian, Catholic chaplain at Impression Bay, strongly denied this in a letter to the press: "He [O'Doherty] was obliged to attend the daily muster, march with his gang to and from work, associate with them whilst at work, and to attend medical inspection with them each week." In a letter to Martin, smuggled out by the priest, O'Doherty described his assignment to a road gang:

> So far from any distinction being made in my favour as compared with the ordinary convicts, I was treated with more vigour and harshness than the worst amongst them having been put into the hardest labouring gang on the station; and refused the poor privilege of obtaining credit (i.e. shortening my time by increased industry) — which was afforded all the rest. Finding after the first few days my health was being improved by the labour I resolved to tackle my work with energy in order completely to restore it and being sent with my gang to clear a road through a very thick part of the bush — I astonished my overseer by the zeal with which I swept down the scrub with my pioneer axe and handled the crosscutting saw in getting through the great logs that obstructed our way . . ..

From road making O'Doherty was placed in a team splitting shingles. From a pile of swamp gum logs, all hauled by manpower only, two prisoners poled a log into position for a pair of convicts to cut into fifteen-inch (thirty-eight-centimetre) lengths. Each block was then quartered and the pieces were carried to a gang of shingle splitters of whom O'Doherty was one. Using an implement called a froe the quarter was split into shingles. O'Doherty, who had no previous experience at such an occupation, wrote of his work as follows:

> Upon finishing our road work I was turned to shingle splitting at which it was supposed I could make no hand — but having determined to put the rascally old superintendent in the wrong on account of his refusal to give me credit — I worked like a trojan and

speedily became a professional hand at the art, accomplishing my government stack and more, greatly to the chagrin of the old super who is likely to get into a serious scrape as I am informed, by his overzealous prosecution . . . .

In addition to the press criticism over the lieutenant-governor's action towards the three exiles, Bishop Willson wrote to him on behalf of O'Doherty and McManus, beseeching him "earnestly and respectfully to extend his clemency, and remit that portion of suffering that otherwise awaits them". The lieutenant-governor's reaction was to promise a remission of two-thirds of O'Doherty's sentence contingent upon his good conduct but said that McManus had no claim to any indulgence. He was distinctly refused permission to leave his district and came to Hobart in direct defiance of the government.

Another stroke of good fortune came O'Doherty's way. Contrary to his expectation that he would receive no credit for good conduct and industry, another week was deducted from O'Doherty's sentence and he was back in Hobart within three weeks and resumed duty at the dispensary.

Although O'Doherty found the hard labour at the convict station improved his health, the period, reduced as it was, was not an experience of which he later had fond memories. In a letter to Meagher, written at the convict station he implored him not to take any action which would incur similar punishment. He wrote:

> You will doubtless have heard I am at a place called Impression Bay — that I am in the "Royal Greys" and even the "commissary helmet". But all this is a trifle. I am treated as a common convict, obliged to sleep with every species of scoundrel and to work in a gang from six o'clock in the morning to six o'clock in the evening — being all the while next to starved, as I find it wholly impossible to touch their abominable skilly; which is the breakfast and supper offered me. This is an outline. The details, I am glad, I must spare you for want of room . . . . But my prayer, my fond entreaty to you, and through you to all the others, is to keep out of the hands of these men as you would out of the clutches of the very demon himself . . . .

When it was learnt that McManus and O'Donohue were to

serve the three months demanded by Denison, he was again attacked by the *Hobart Town Courier*:

> It is no concern with right-minded men whether the magistrates imposed an improper sentence; but it is clear that no confidence can be placed in a mind which descends to a vindictive exercise of power, and supersedes all the forms of enquiry and judicial arbitration. The newspaper of the Governor attempted to meet the public indignation by an exaggeration of the offence, and by intimating, with an air of authority, the vengeance of His Excellency would be speedily satisfied . . ..

McManus did not serve his three months at Cascades. Friends challenged Denison's action in the Supreme Court where McManus appeared in convict garb. The judges ruled that the lieutenant-governor had acted illegally and McManus was discharged. Denison ordered his rearrest but the Irishman had already gone into hiding. He made a brief appearance at Meagher's marriage to Catherine Bennett, governess to Dr Hall's children at Ross, and then went on to Launceston. The searching police found an allegedly sick man in McManus's bed at his lodgings. They were instructed to remove the patient to the government hospital but to their embarrassment found that the "sick man" was not McManus but his healthy friend, John Galvin. Meanwhile McManus was on a ship bound to America — the first of the exiles to escape.

When O'Donohue was well enough to leave hospital he served his sentence at Saltwater River convict station. The *Irish Exile* was published by friends during his absence but on his release Denison ordered his transfer to Oatlands and publication ceased.

O'Doherty left Dr Crooke's dispensary at the end of March 1851 for unknown reasons. Martin tried to find out when he wrote, "I am vexed to hear that your business in Hobart Town which seemed to you at first to open 'comparatively delightful prospects', is turning out a 'damned business'. How is this? Is Crooke not the right sort or are the Hobartians too healthy, or is there a prejudice against you as an Irish rebel, lately come from Probation, or does the Medical Board interfere against you or how is it?" No explanation is available.

O'Doherty then lived quietly in Hobart reading his medical textbooks. A welcome letter from Eva revealed that she was contributing to the *Nation* again and she sent a poem written especially for him.

The Path Across the Sea

My love, my hope, my longing,
    Make a path across the sea:
I can reach thee, I can clasp thee,
    Though parted we may be.
        Oh! naught can part us, dearest —
    Naught hold thee back from me.

How oft my feet have trodden
    That pathway o'er the sea,
Which from my heart I builded
    To bear me home to thee —
        Which I builded with my longing
    And my love and faith to thee!

Eva's letters brought Kevin moments of happiness but then followed a period of despondency during which the frustration of further unemployment and longing for Eva were uppermost.

In May 1851, Mitchel received permission to visit Hobart to await the arrival of his wife and family from Ireland. In his *Jail Journal* he describes how he rode with Kevin to a picnic spot south of Hobart. An extract reads:

> St Kevin is sometimes gloomy and desponding; and the mood is on him now for a few minutes. There dwells in Ireland — I should have known it well, though he never told me — a dark-eyed lady, a fair and gentle lady, with hair like blackest midnight; and in the tangle of those silken tresses she has bound my poor friend's soul; round the solid hemisphere it has held him, and he drags a lengthening chain. The potency of those dark glances, darting like electricity through the dull massive planet, shooting through crust and centre, strikes him here, and flashes on his day-dream.

Again, perhaps undeservedly, he was receiving letters of criticism from Martin for not writing. Whilst Kevin was going through another period in which he was disinclined to visit or communicate with his friends, he was at least carrying out kindly acts for Meagher who was living with his bride in a cottage on an island in Lake Sorrell where he kept a few bullocks, horses and a small flock of sheep, which were supervised by Tom Egan, a Kilkenny convict. Meagher acknowledged Kevin's good deeds in a letter of 31 July 1851: "Many, many thanks for the oranges, lemons, and raspberry vinegar — They were an exquisite treat for poor Bennie. So, like a darling true Irish boy (as you are, and as old Martin endearingly calls you) get three dozen more . . .. If you could lay your hands, too, upon some nice fish — or even a few oysters — I should thank you warmly for them."

After five months, O'Doherty's friends succeeded in obtaining for him an appointment as house surgeon at St Mary's Hospital on the corner of Davey Street and Salamanca Place, conducted by Dr E.S. Bedford. Born in Van Diemen's Land, Dr Bedford had learnt his medicine as an apprentice to James Scott, senior colonial surgeon. Later he was awarded a fellowship of the Royal College of Surgeons, England. Although an official colonial hospital was already functioning, Bedford opened St Mary's Hospital in Campbell Street in 1841 as a "self-supporting hospital, for the benefit of the labouring classes of society, to afford at a small cost, medical attention to the poor, to enable the rich to assist the destitute sick and at the same time to encourage the efforts of the working classes in procuring aid at their own expense". The accommodation in the original St Mary's was not sufficient to meet the demand and on 23 June 1847 the foundation stone of a new hospital in Davey Street was laid. When completed it was a solid stone structure of two stories. Its heating was especially notable for the times and in the hospital's sanatorium hot baths were available daily between 3 p.m. and 6 p.m. at 2s.6d. (25 cents) for a single ticket or £1.1.0 ($2.10) for twelve baths.

Dr Bedford hoped that the hospital would do more than treat the sick. He optimistically planned that it be used as a preparatory medical school for all the Australian colonies, attendance at which would be recognised by the Royal College of Surgeons, England, thus reducing the period to be spent in England by Australian students by twelve months. The advertised curriculum included not only medical subjects of anatomy, hospital practice and clinical subjects but also classical subjects of Vergil, Livy and Homer as well as Greek and English history. Dr Bedford was listed as medical instructor, with Thomas Arnold, son of the famous Dr Arnold of Rugby, as classical lecturer. Neither the other colonies nor the College of Surgeons was very receptive but by 1859 Bedford could boast that eight of his students had graduated in England, two being medal winners.

Under the high standards demanded by Dr Bedford, O'Doherty gained valuable clinical experience. The Launceston surgeon, William Pugh, used ether for anaesthesia within nine months of its first use for that purpose by Morton in America in 1846. Bedford was quick to follow and with Pugh was the recipient of an ether inhaler sent in 1847 from England by Bishop Nixon, Anglican bishop of Van Diemen's Land, who was visiting there. O'Doherty thus had experience in the use of the new agent during amputations and external surgical procedures. At this period abdominal surgery was still many years away. O'Doherty was house surgeon when the following advertisement appeared in the press: "Vaccination. Attendance is given on Mondays and Thursdays from one o'clock to two o'clock for gratuitous vaccination. That the vaccination be known to be effective the person bringing the child will be required to deposit two shillings and sixpence [25 cents] which will be returned on the child being brought on the fourth and eighth days after."

During his term at St Mary's, O'Doherty was left in charge of the hospital and thus solely responsible for treatment. A newspaper report in August 1852 of an inquest into the death of a man, who died after a dispute on the wharf during which he was stabbed with an umbrella, contained medical evidence as follows: "Kevin Izod O'Doherty, surgeon at St Mary's Hospital deposed:- 'I bled him and that gave him some apparent relief; I left him again for a little while and saw him a quarter of an hour afterwards when he was worse. I saw that he was dying and as a last chance I bled him again. He died while I was bleeding him."

In addition to excellent professional experience which he gained at St Mary's Hospital, he was far better off financially than he had been during the months at Oatlands. Hospital records show that the house surgeon's salary between 1850 and 1854 ranged from £21.18.6 ($43.86) to £92.0.3 ($184.03) per annum. In the O'Doherty papers there are duplicates of bank bills for £20 ($40) drawn on the Bank of Australasia, Hobart, and O'Doherty refers in a letter to Martin of monthly remittances from Ireland.

In his off-duty hours O'Doherty visited Catholic families and on Sunday worshipped at St Joseph's Church in Macquarie Street. A letter written during this period by J.R. Sheehy contains this passage: "My brother says that when O'Doherty would take him out to walk on the sea-shore, he thought he was some romantic being of the middle ages and not a matter-of-fact nineteenth century man." The house surgeon also visited secretly Nant Cottage outside Bothwell where Mitchel and Martin were living and in one letter Martin wrote that, "Alick Reid told me yesterday he met you one evening lately at a billiard room — Regulation No. 5 to the contrary notwithstanding". (It was a game at which O'Doherty excelled.) He was a happier man at this time.

While O'Doherty was working at St Mary's Hospital three more exiles escaped — Meagher, O'Donohue and Mitchel, all to America. Shortly after Meagher's escape, his wife gave birth to a son. Unfortunately the child lived only four months and was buried in the cemetery at John the Baptist Church at Richmond. When the cemetery was threatened by the Coal River the body was reburied nearer the church. It is frequently viewed by tourists who include the church in a visit to historic Richmond.

O'Doherty was not involved in the escapes of Meagher and O'Donohue but played a minor role in that of Mitchel in 1853. In January of that year he was surprised one day in the dispensary of St Mary's Hospital by the appearance of Patrick Smyth, a Young Irelander, who had been sent by the Irish Directorate in New York to organise the escape of at least one of the remaining rebels. The house surgeon alerted the other exiles of Smyth's arrival and it was decided that Mitchel should make an escape attempt and Mrs Mitchel would leave with him or about the same time. A number of plans went astray but in June Mitchel handed in his ticket-of-leave to a confused magistrate at Bothwell. He hid with sympathisers and finally Mrs Mitchel boarded the brig, *Emma*, at Hobart leaving on a regular voyage to Sydney. Shortly after leaving the wharf, the vessel stopped in the Derwent River to pick up Mr Wright, a late passenger — Mitchel in disguise. The family reached America safely.

During the weeks that Mitchel was on the run, O'Doherty passed on information to Mrs Mitchel at Nant Cottage which the family and Martin still occupied. When Mitchel, disguised as a priest, was coming into Hobart on the day when he was making his escape attempt, O'Doherty boarded the coach to accompany him on the last few miles. It was O'Doherty who found a suitable young woman to travel as nursemaid with Mrs Mitchel.

In September 1853, the Van Diemen's Land Board of Medical Examiners gave O'Doherty permission to practise medicine at Port Cygnet, forty miles (sixty-four kilometres) south of Hobart. The population of 100 was not sufficient to support a doctor and it is not surprising that the young Irishman told O'Brien in a letter written early in 1854 that his practice was by no means thriving. He was existing on money sent from Ireland. Martin, himself a prodigious letter writer, continued to chide O'Doherty about his infrequent correspondence. However, he took time to inform Martin of the prospects of a position supervising a timber mill in one letter and to send another, enclosing £15 ($30). Martin refused the suggestion that he supervise the mill, claiming he knew nothing about the industry and doubted his ability to control the convicts to be employed. But, on second thoughts, he asked O'Doherty for further details which were furnished after diligent inquiries. However, finally, Martin accepted a position as tutor to Mr Jackson's children at Ross. O'Brien had also transferred to another district, renting rooms at Richmond, fourteen miles (twenty-two kilometres) from Hobart.

After supervising the safe arrival of Mitchel and his family in America, Smyth returned to engineer the escape of one of the three remaining exiles, probably Smith O'Brien. He wrote to Martin from Melbourne on the Australian mainland in April 1854 advising him of his plans and went to Hobart in June. However, his help was not required. The British government, yielding to pressure, which men such as Sir Lucius O'Brien, Smith O'Brien's brother, had been applying, decided to grant O'Doherty and his two companions a conditional pardon. Lord Palmerston, secretary of state for the Colonies, conveyed the decision to Sir William Denison in a memorandum:

> Whereas William Smith O'Brien was at a commission of Assize holden at Clonmel in September, 1848, convicted of High Treason and sentenced to Death for the same, but subsequently received Our Pardon on condition of being transported beyond the seas for the term of his natural life, and whereas John Martin and Kevin Izod O'Doherty were convicted of Felony at Dublin, the said John Martin in August, 1848, and the said Kevin Izod O'Doherty in October, 1848, and sentenced respectively to ten years for transportation for the same; We, in consideration of some circumstances humbly represented unto us, are graciously pleased to extend our Grace and Mercy unto them, and to Grant them Our Pardon for the crimes for which they severally stand convicted, upon condition that they do not return to Our United Kingdom during the remainder of their said sentences.

Kevin heard the wonderful news in a letter from Eva which reached him in May 1854. The British government had briefly announced the decision and details were scanty. Eva hoped that it would be a full pardon but learnt later that there was a condition of future place of residence attached. The Irish community in Melbourne also heard the news in May, and, hoping the exiles would pass through the city after their release from Van Diemen's Land, planned a public banquet in their honour. It was at least two weeks after the decision that official advice left London, and it was not until 26 June 1854 that the *Hobart Town Gazette* carried the official notice that the lieutenant-governor had received a despatch from the secretary of state that Her Majesty had granted a conditional pardon to the three remaining exiles.

There were many farewells, some public in the case of Smith O'Brien. Letters were written to the many friends they could not call on personally and in July the three exiles and Patrick Smyth left Launceston in pairs to cross Bass Strait to Melbourne.

The greatest ordeal for the Irish rebels during their exile in Van Diemen's Land was the separation from their loved ones and their native land, as well as, for some, lack of funds. Any additional punishment was of their own making. The privations Smith O'Brien suffered on Maria Island could have been avoided. O'Doherty, McManus and O'Donohue were well aware that their visit to Smith O'Brien at New Norfolk outside their districts could be followed by some additional penalty if it became known to the authorities, which it did.

But they were treated as heroes by many of the inhabitants and were frequent guests of many of the well-to-do settlers. O'Doherty suffered dejection as a result of his separation from Eva but he was fortunate in the excellent professional experience he gained at St Mary's Hospital. On the whole one must agree with Sir William Denison that the Young Irelanders were treated leniently during their stay in Van Diemen's Land.

CHAPTER 5

Reunion

As the sloop, *Ariel*, passed through the heads of Port Phillip Bay in mid-July 1854, after crossing Bass Strait from Launceston, Van Diemen's Land, O'Doherty and John Martin came on deck and peered northwards through the wintry mist towards Hobson's Bay in the distance. The two Irishmen were headed for Melbourne, the capital of the young colony of Victoria, where their fellow countrymen wanted to fete the exiles on the granting of their conditional pardons. Smith O'Brien, their leader, and Patrick Smyth, who had come to arrange another escape (now no longer necessary) had crossed earlier on the steamer, *Ladybird*.

As the *Ariel* neared Hobson's Bay, the harbour for Melbourne, the two former rebels noticed how crowded it was. Ships of all sizes were moored close to one another with one or two like their own either moving slowly towards the mouth of the Yarra River which emptied into the harbour, or outwards to Port Phillip heads. A ferry was steaming in the direction of Geelong, on the southwest of Port Phillip Bay, and another was coming from that direction. The *Ariel* drew close enough to allow recognition of the ships which lay at anchor. Towards the outside could be seen the two warships, *Electra* and *Fantome*, which the former governor, Charles Joseph La Trobe, had requested the British government to send to protect the young colony. On the portside of the shipping lane a red swallow-tailed pennant adorned by a white star fluttered from a high-masted ship. She was the *Red Jacket*, of the White Star line from Liverpool. Closer in, passengers were transferring into ferries from another White Star line clipper, the *Mermaid*, only just arrived from her home port in England. But by no means were all the ships in the harbour clipper ships from England. The numerous flags flying from masts indicated home ports in numerous countries in Europe and on some the Stars and Stripes of America fluttered proudly.

The *Ariel* hove to opposite the river mouth for port officials to board and for a ferry to tow her up the river. The two Irishmen marvelled at the density of shipping in the young colony's harbour — a result of the magical lure of gold. Commencing as the pastoral settlement of Port Phillip Bay in 1835, the area had been granted separation as a colony in 1851. Almost simultaneously with the declaration of the new status came reports of two discoveries of rich goldfields — Clunes and Buninyong. Several new and equally rich fields followed.

The change in the young colony was electrifying. On the first reports most of the able-bodied men left Melbourne to try their luck on the fields and sailors on ships in Hobson's Bay deserted for a similar purpose. The streets were full of shops selling spades, picks, ropes, buckets and tents for use on the goldfields. As the news of the discoveries spread to the other colonies ships from their ports brought hundreds of optimistic men expecting to make their fortunes. By September 1852 a great rush from overseas began. Ships from Europe brought thousands of would-be diggers frantic to share in the new-found wealth. From California came multitudes of "forty-niners". By July 1854, when O'Doherty and Martin came in the *Ariel*, the rate had slackened a little but it was still such that the inhabitants exclaimed, "And still they come".

As the *Ariel* was being towed up the meandering river the two exiles were still discussing the goldfields. Although there had as yet been almost no communication with the shore, O'Doherty was beginning to feel the excitement that so many men in Victoria had experienced during these heady times. There was emerging an aspect of his character which would never leave him. Although most of his life he would adhere to one profession there would be times when he sensed an urge to speculate, and gold would always have an attraction for him. Disregarding the reports that he had read in the Van Diemen's Land papers that thousands had returned from the goldfields empty-handed with their hopes dashed, he raised with Martin a desire to try his luck on the fields. Here was an opportunity to strike it rich and take a fortune home to Eva. Martin could not be enticed into such a risky venture and endeavoured to persuade his companion not to be so foolish.

A large group had assembled on Queen's Wharf to greet them. Foremost was "Long John" O'Shanassy, the acknowledged leader of the Melbourne Irish community. Born at Thurles in County Tipperary, Ireland, where Smith O'Brien had been arrested while on the run after the 1848 rising, John O'Shanassy had migrated to Australia in 1839. He was now a successful businessman and had been elected as second member for Melbourne in the colony's Legislative Council. He had emerged as the leading opponent of the government which was dominated by nominated members and squatting representatives. He supported the miners in a dispute with the government over harsh licence fees. Later he would become premier of Victoria and be honoured with a subsequent knighthood.

With O'Shanassy were Patrick O'Brien, another member of the Legislative Chamber, Rory Ireland, Thomas Cosgrove, Michael Gallagher, Patrick McGrath and several other members of the committee which had been meeting at the Farmers' Arms in Little Collins Street to plan the reception for the exiles. Also in the group were their comrade in exile, Smith O'Brien, and Patrick Smyth. After warm greetings and congratulations the gathering transferred to the Criterion Hotel in Collins Street to continue this preliminary reception in more congenial surroundings. After further expressions of camaraderie and affable conversation, O'Doherty left with Patrick McGrath with whom he would stay until the main reception, also planned to be held at the Criterion on the next Saturday.

In the next few days O'Doherty had an opportunity to look at Melbourne, which showed all the signs of a city unable to cope with a fourfold increase in its population in three years. There had been some attempts to provide a firm surface in the centre of most streets but woe betide a bullock or horse team which had to leave the centre on a wet day. The animals would slither and slip about and in many cases become hopelessly bogged to the accompaniment of colourful language from their drivers. From those streets came an offensive odour of animal excretions which nobody had bothered to remove. Shops selling provisions, mining tools, clothes and gaudy gifts were prominent, but the establishments which attracted most attention were the numerous hotels, some open twenty-four hours a day. They were crowded with noisy miners (the more fortunate ones) in colourful shirts who had come to the city to spend their new-found wealth. The laughter and loud talk of the diggers were often punctuated by squeals of women who were helping them to dispose of their fortunes as quickly as possible.

During the week O'Doherty arranged to meet Patrick Smyth at the Criterion Hotel. In the main bar of this stronghold of the American community, many of whom had begun a search for gold in California five years earlier, the two Irishmen declined the offer of one of the white-shirted, bearded bartenders to mix them a mint julep and settled for whisky. Their discussion began with remarks about the city of Melbourne but soon centred on a possible venture at one of the goldfields. O'Doherty quickly found that his fellow Irishman was fired with an enthusiasm similar to his own. After the function to be held the next day in their honour they would make plans to join the thousands digging for the yellow metal.

Shortly before 4 p.m. the following afternoon, Smith O'Brien, Martin and O'Doherty entered the Criterion Hotel and were ushered into the concert hall amid vociferous applause from the crowded audience who filled it to overflowing. The three exiles were conducted to the stage by deputations from the Melbourne and Geelong subscribers to the testimonial fund. John O'Shanassy led the Melbourne representatives and John Myles, another member of the Legislative Council, headed the Geelong deputation, closely followed by John Harvey from Bendigo.

Smith O'Brien, as leader of the rebels, was the first to be honoured and O'Shanassy read and presented an address in which congratulations and gratification for his liberation were expressed and reference made to the leader's sacrifice for his country. The address had been signed by 500 inhabitants of Melbourne and 300 from Geelong, including several members of the Melbourne corporation and the whole of the Geelong corporation. After Smith O'Brien's reply, O'Shanassy rose again to refer to the gift of a gold cup from subscribers from Melbourne and Geelong, who had contributed £1,000($2,000) and £400($800) respectively. The cup was not on view at the gathering as Messrs Hackett of Elizabeth Street, the artisans entrusted with the task of suitably embellishing it, had not completed their work. When the ten-inch (twenty-five centimetre), twenty-two carat gold cup was delivered later the testimonial committee was entirely satisfied with the adornments which included a statue of liberty, the Smith O'Brien family coat of arms, an Irish wolfhound, an inscription of the donors' esteem for the leader of the Irish rebels and many other Irish emblems.

O'Doherty and Martin were next honoured by Patrick O'Brien, MLC, presenting each with a purse of 200 sovereigns and reading an address which included the following passage:

> Fellow-labourers in the cause of Ireland with our distinguished countryman, Smith O'Brien, and companion of his six years' captivity, you are equally entitled to any honour which admiration for true patriotism can suggest. Your short political careers were marked by a sincerity, a disinterestedness and devotion of the noblest cause; while the fortitude with which you sustained your trials and sufferings must command the respect even of political adversaries. We congratulate you upon your release from captivity, and trust it is but the precursor of your speedy restoration to your

homes and families. As a small token of our respect and esteem for your characters, and as a mark of our appreciation of your sacrifices, we beg you to accept these purses of two hundred sovereigns each.

Martin replied briefly but O'Doherty responded by reading a long reply which he had prepared beforehand. After expressing gratitude for the welcome and the handsome gift, he endeavoured to justify the offence for which he had been transported in these words:

> Cast, in the pursuit of my medical studies, into the very midst of the horrors which then afflicted my country, I encountered the demon of famine in all its horrible shapes, — in the withered forms of what were once stalwart peasants shrivelled into less compass than that of an Egyptian mummy, — in the pestilent carcasses of those afflicted with the famine scurvy, — and in the forms of the wretched creatures who used literally to be piled together in the fever sheds, happily unconscious, in their wild delirium, of the horrors of their condition. All these I witnessed for months together, and believing in my soul as I did, that these horrors were aggravated to an intense degree by the heartless policy of a Government with whom I conceived the interests and lives of these people was the least item of consideration; is it wonderful that, fired by the revoluntary excitement of the time, I should have raised my voice in favour of deposing this Government, that thereby the people might save themselves?

With the formal part of the function completed, the gathering transferred to the Criterion's dining room, where mine host Samuel Moss, "set forth a collation in his usual admirable style". The bill of fare, in keeping with the occasion, included roast turkey a la liberated; roast goose, a la patriot; gallantine a la Brian Boru; boar's head a l'O'Connell and many more delectable dishes similarly named. Due justice was done to these and other good things, and excellent wines, liqueurs and punch added to the festivity. Then began, in the custom of the day, numerous toasts, not only to the guests of honour, but to their country, their hosts, families and the "Gentlemen, unconnected with Ireland, who contributed to the testimonial fund".

Smith O'Brien and Martin left Melbourne in the 613 tons Peninsular and Oriental steamer, *Norna*, on 25 July for Ceylon.

There Smith O'Brien left the ship to visit a brother at Madras, India, and finally went to Brussels where he was joined by his family. Martin went to Paris where he lived for a few years before returning to Ireland.

No contemporary records of O'Doherty's movements between 22 July 1854, the date of the testimonial dinner, and 12 March 1855 when he left Melbourne, could be traced. Later evidence shows that he carried out his decision made with Patrick Smyth to look for gold. On 28 February 1856 Smyth wrote from Dublin to O'Doherty in Paris. Much of the letter deals with problems which Smyth was having with the Irish organisation in America relating to the disposition of funds with which he was supplied to take to Australia to help him engineer an escape for Smith O'Brien. However, there is a brief reference to the gold digging. An extract reads: "To have remitted to New York the money remaining on hand would have left me destitute in a strange country. What happened you can tell. I joined in the diggin [sic] speculation. You got pretty well out of it." Years later in a political speech in the Queensland parliament O'Doherty referred to his mining experience in Victoria but only in a general way.

So, there is no doubt that while Smith O'Brien and Martin were boarding their ship to return to Europe, O'Doherty and Smyth were purchasing their equipment for their mining venture. From Smyth's letter of 1856 it appears that while the two compatriots may have tried the same field it is unlikely they shared the same claim. The newspapers regularly reported the amount of gold being brought from the various diggings and included in the several fields producing well at this time were Bendigo, Ballarat, Castlemaine, Avoca and Maryborough. On all of these, thousands of O'Doherty's countrymen were digging for their fortunes alongside Englishmen, Scots, Germans, Americans and men from many other countries including China.

O'Doherty, either alone or in company with Smyth, probably boarded a Cobb and Co. coach outside the Criterion Hotel or one of the other coaches leaving hotels in Bourke Street, and after an all-day journey and several stops for changes of horses, he would have arrived on his chosen goldfield. The roads to the fields were dirt tracks which horse and bullock drays and human feet turned into powdery dust in dry weather and into quagmires after rain. Those who could not afford the coach or drays walked, and O'Doherty would have seen many men and women and children, too, heavily laden, trudging along towards their first field or changing fields. Reports of new fields were still being made, and those who had not struck it rich at one field, often transferred to the new strikes full of excitement and hope — hope that would very often be dashed.

O'Doherty's first glimpse of his chosen field would have been a sea of tents where the diggers lived. Many of the stores providing the necessities — including sly grog — were under canvas also. More substantial wooden buildings housed licensed premises, drinking taverns and dancing saloons where diggers with gold to dispense quenched their thirst, entertained female "gold-diggers" or listened to and watched the visiting artists, singers and dancers who thronged the fields. In the surrounding country, the Australian bushland, with its native eucalypts and acacias, hid the huts of those shepherds who had stayed with their masters, the squatters, many of whom were providing the meat which the hungry miners ate ravenously.

Although there is no firm evidence which reveals which field O'Doherty chose, it seems likely that at some stage he was at Ballarat. Events at that field in the last half of 1854 — part of the period O'Doherty was in Victoria — culminated with the episode in Australian history known as the Eureka Stockade. The events began with the imposition on the diggers of a harsh licence fee of £1.10s. ($3) per month and a still harsher method of collecting the fee. In some licence hunts, officers on horseback conducted the search like an English fox-hunt. Diggers not having a licence on their person were chained to logs until the fee was paid. This was often done by other miners. In the final event in the campaign between the government and the diggers at Ballarat the miners in a hastily built stockade were attacked in the early hours of Sunday, 2 December 1854 by troops sent to the scene by the governor, Sir Charles

Hotham. Fourteen miners were killed and another eight died later from wounds received. Of the seventeen miners whose origins were known, ten came from Ireland while another twelve, who recovered from wounds, also hailed from the Emerald Isle. Captain Wise, who led the assault, died of wounds and another four of his troops met a similar fate.

The known presence of two men at Ballarat during these events provides the evidence that O'Doherty may have been there also. The first of these was Peter Lalor, the miners' leader. He was a younger brother of James Fintan Lalor, the prominent Young Irelander, who in 1848 had endeavoured to convince others in the movement that for the Irish peasants land was the burning question, not the repeal of the union of England and Ireland. When the papers reported the emergence of Peter Lalor as the leader at Ballarat, it is quite probable that O'Doherty would have at least paid him a visit. However, it is most unlikely that O'Doherty took any part in the Eureka Stockade episode. Subsequently events showed that the former rebel was prepared to take the risk of jeopardising his conditional pardon under special circumstances, but the dispute of the miners with the Victorian government did not fall into that category.

The second man, whom O'Doherty may have met at Ballarat, was Dr Alfred Carr, who later was to take action which could have had serious consequences for the former rebel. Dr Carr apparently did not keep the best of company and was friendly with James Bentley and his wife, Catherine, who were proprietors of the Eureka Hotel — an establishment of dubious reputation. (Bentley was a former prisoner from Van Diemen's Land.) On the night of 6 October 1854 the Bentleys were entertaining a few friends, of whom Dr Carr was one, after the hotel had closed. Two miners, James Scobie and Peter Martin, wishing to obtain liquor, knocked on the door and accompanied their quest with remarks not complimentary to the hotelier. When their request was refused the miners staggered away, but shortly afterwards they were attacked by a small group of assailants and Scobie was kicked to death. Strong evidence pointed to Bentley and his staff as the culprits but a subsequent coroner's inquiry returned an open verdict.

This finding was received with dismay by the miners who felt certain of Bentley's guilt. A letter in the *Ballarat Times* criticised the conduct of the inquest, claiming that "so far from the inquest being conducted in an impartial manner, the proceedings of the coroner savoured strongly of the desire to smother the case, in the eyes of the jury". The leading name in a list of nine of the jurors and six miners who signed the letter was Peter Lalor. In the next issue of the paper Dr Carr defended the coroner and demonstrated a dislike for miners. When another inquiry also exonerated Bentley, the miners held a mass meeting on the spot where Scobie was murdered. At the conclusion of the meeting, the miners, instead of dispersing peacefully as their leaders had hoped, ransacked Bentley's hotel and then burnt it to the ground.

Eventually the Bentleys and two of their staff were tried for Scobie's murder in the Melbourne Supreme Court. Catherine Bentley was acquitted but her husband and two accomplices were sentenced to three years' hard labour for manslaughter. The evidence of Dr Carr, who had not only been present in the hotel on the night Scobie had been murdered but had also examined the body later, was criticised in the *Melbourne Argus* which said that, "According to his [Carr's] statement no wound had been inflicted by the spade; nor were any of the wounds of a serious nature. Indeed he seemed to treat the cause of death as a very light affair . . . . It does not lie within our province to criticise the professional accuracy of this gentleman's evidence; but we feel it our duty to animadvert upon the singular manner in which it was given . . .." Later Carr was the only witness who testified favourably for Bentley when a number were called to comment on the character of the prisoners.

Early in 1855 Kevin's longing for Eva, which had always been with him during his search for gold, apparently became uppermost. The desire to be reunited with her reached such heights that he realised that he was not content to return to

Europe like Smith O'Brien and Martin and wait for her to join him there. This was a time when he would risk the consequences of being apprehended while breaking the condition of his pardon by going back to Ireland for their reunion. Such a decision meant a voyage in secret. It would be courting disaster to travel openly as Kevin O'Doherty on a ship bound for England or Ireland. He must seek a ship's master who would agree to his travelling incognito. These thoughts were no doubt in his mind as he left the goldfields and returned to Melbourne.

In the middle of February 1855 the *Melbourne Argus* announced the arrival in Port Phillip Bay of a new ship, the *James Baines*, which, on her maiden voyage, had broken the record from Liverpool to Melbourne. The *James Baines* was one of four wooden ships, built by Donald Mackay of Boston in America, to be added to the Black Ball line of gold clippers at a time when men were scrambling for fast voyages to Victoria's goldfields. The Black Ball captains were celebrated for their navigation. The voyage to Australia followed the usual route, sailing southwards off the west coast of Africa, rounding the Cape of Good Hope and then crossing the Indian Ocean to their destination. However, to shorten the time of their voyages they took their ships further south than any ships had sailed before. At 50° south the winds were much stronger than those encountered further north and although the risks were higher their boldness was generally rewarded by record runs.

By leaving Liverpool on 9 December 1854 and arriving at Port Phillip on 12 February 1855, Captain Charles McDonald had made the voyage in less than 64 days. Like his colleagues he drove his ship hard and took risks, but he had broken the record. As was the custom in this age, many of the 700 passengers who had travelled on the 2,215 ton ship paid their respects to her captain in the newspapers. In the *Melbourne Argus* of 14 February, sixty-four first-class passengers praised the strict discipline which had been maintained, and the order and cleanliness, whereby the health and comfort of the passengers had been greatly promoted. They begged the captain to accept the accompanying piece of plate. A similar number of second-cabin passengers thanked the ship's master for his attention to their wants and for his personal courtesy and trusted their testimony might not prove unacceptable among the brilliant honours with which his career as a seaman had already been crowned. The third-cabin passengers claimed they had joined the ship because, before leaving their numerous and respective homes, Captain McDonald's character and reputation were known to them and it was thus they were induced to travel on his ship.

After reading these reports and making private inquiries, O'Doherty decided correctly that McDonald would be sympathetic to his plan. There is, of course, no record of the negotiations but it was agreed that O'Doherty would be one of the first-class passengers when the *James Baines* left Melbourne on her return voyage to Liverpool. It is not known when O'Doherty went aboard. Perhaps he accompanied the visitors on 9 March when "a large party of ladies and gentlemen" travelled by special train from Melbourne city to Sandridge and were transferred by steamer aboard "this splendid vessel", and was present when included in the numerous toasts during the revelry which followed, was "the health of the dashing commander of this prince of clippers". What is known is that O'Doherty was safely aboard when the vessel was towed from Hobson's Bay by the lighter, *Lowestoft*. Discarding the lighter's help, the *James Baines* passed through Port Phillip heads. She would return to England by sailing the second leg of the Great Circle route via Cape Horn.

The vessel's passenger list for this voyage, still preserved, contains no "Kevin O'Doherty" for, of course, he was travelling under an assumed name. However, among the second class passengers there is an entry of "Dr Carr, surgeon". This was the same Alfred Carr who was present in the Eureka Hotel on the night the miner, Scobie, was murdered; the same Alfred Carr whose evidence was criticised in the *Ballarat Times* by Peter Lalor and his friends and by the *Melbourne Argus*; the man who had proved no friend of the miners; no friend of the Irish. O'Doherty must have been well aware of the Ballarat doctor's identity and his hostility. Even if the Irishman had not been at Ballarat he would most probably have been acquainted with Carr's attitude through the press. His presence on the ship would have caused O'Doherty no little concern and no doubt made him wonder whether this potential enemy would take action to inform the authorities on the arrival of the ship in England. Would Carr report him for breaking the condition of his pardon?

The log of the *James Baines* for the voyage on which O'Doherty travelled is not available, but that for a similar voyage which the vessel made in 1856 with Charles McDonald still in command, reveals the route which the gold clippers sailed and the conditions encountered. After leaving Port Phillip the ships sailed due south off the west coast of Van Diemen's Land (Tasmania) until they reached 50°S and then turned eastward. Sailing between latitudes of 50° to 60°S, they continued well south of Van Diemen's Land and New Zealand until they were to the east of Cape Horn. Then turning northwards they sailed in the mid-Atlantic Ocean to Liverpool. No call at any port was made throughout the voyage. Reports in the log of the 1856 voyage of the *James Baines* reveal many days of "dark gloomy weather, thick fog, heavy rain, snow falls and at times the thunder and lightning of storms". Ice islands were met between longitudes of 160° and 100° east and latitudes of 56° and 60°S, with temperatures well below freezing point. An occasional iceberg was sighted. Even when the ship turned northward into the Atlantic Ocean it was several days before the weather improved.

Testimony of McDonald's heroic sailing and the speed of his voyages is seen in this passage relating to the voyage O'Doherty made in the ship taken from Basil Lubbock's book, *Colonial Clippers*:

> Leaving Melbourne on the 12th March 1855, the *James Baines* made the run home in 69½ days, having completed the voyage to Melbourne and back in 133 days under sail. Black Ball captains were celebrated for their daring navigation and McDonald was no exception in this respect. His passengers declared that the *James Baines* was nearly ashore three times whilst tacking off the coast of Ireland under a heavy press of sail, and that when McDonald put her round off Mizenhead the rocks were so close that a stone could

have been thrown ashore from her decks. It was a lee shore, and if she had missed stays she must have been lost. But as McDonald said, when remonstrated with for taking such risks, it was a case of "we have to make a good passage".

The *James Baines* reached Liverpool on 20 May 1855 and one can imagine what thoughts were going through O'Doherty's mind as the time came for him to go ashore. After ten long weeks at sea — made so much longer when one is separated from one's loved one — Kevin could now begin to believe that it was no longer a dream — the dream was becoming a reality. He would soon be reunited with Eva in the flesh, he could hold her in his arms and all would be well. However, enough of these fantasies, he thought, as he raced around the dock to inquire about a passage on a steamer to Dublin. He had deliberately travelled light so as to be unencumbered in making as quick a departure as possible. He gave a generous tip of half a sovereign to his cabin boy whose support he had won during the voyage by several acts of kindness and generosity in keeping with his character. The lad looked after Kevin's luggage first and directed him towards the terminal where the Dublin ferries were docked. Kevin was experiencing all kinds of feelings, mostly excitement at the thought of seeing Eva and his beloved Ireland again, relief that all seemed to be going to plan. Perhaps his fears about Alfred Carr were unfounded since he was as yet unchallenged. He had never been afraid to take a risk as his previous actions had shown and a risk he was prepared to take to join Eva. Perhaps his philosophy was like that of Monro, Earl of Montrose when he said:

> He either fears too much,
> Or his deserts are small
> Who will not put it to the touch,
> To gain or lose it all.

Kevin arranged his transport to Dublin, being able to embark within a few hours. He relaxed and breathed more freely as he saw the shores of England fade away in the distance. Now it was a case of "Dublin, here I come". Although of a sanguine nature there had been times during the past six years when Kevin wondered whether he would ever set foot in his native country again. It was hard to believe it was actually happening. How could he wait to see Eva again? At last, the ferry docked at Kingstown. Kevin was on Irish soil once more and felt that he could walk to Galway to see Eva. But there was no coach till early next day. He would spend a night at the Shelbourne Hotel, St Stephen's Green. He wasted no time reserving a seat on the first available coach to the west, and returned to the hotel.

Since secrecy as well as speed was the essence of the exercise, Kevin decided to keep as low a profile as possible while in Dublin. There were too many "Castle people" — Anglo-Irish and English sympathisers — about to take any unnecessary risks. After an early meal he returned to his room to spend a quiet night reading. However he was too excited to concentrate on his book. When he finally fell asleep he had a horrible dream that he had missed the coach. As he awoke, day was dawning. He quickly packed his few belongings to go and catch the coach.

He sat in the coach looking at the landscape for which he had yearned so long, savouring each moment and congratulating himself that fortune was still favouring him. He visualised his meeting with Eva. Would her feelings still be the same towards him? After all it was six years and she had been only in her teens when he left Ireland. Perhaps she was a romantic young girl who had fallen in love with him because he was the image of a republican hero to her. He began to feel a little nervous. However the die was cast and from now on he must accept whatever fate had to offer. He need not have had any fears. Totally unexpected as his arrival was, the Kelly family soon recovered from the shock. The welcome was overwhelming. The usually shy and reticent Eva, encouraged by her fond parents, threw herself into his arms and wept for sheer joy. What a wonderful moment. The fairytale and the dream had finally come true. Her Kevin had returned and like the gallant hero he was he had come to get her. It was a miracle. He had survived two long voyages across the world, six years of living in strange lands, exposed to all kinds of dangers at times in Van Diemen's Land, on the goldfields and on the ships in which he had travelled. He had survived the risk of violence, epidemic disease and shipwreck and brought with him a few grains of the small amount of gold he had won in Victoria. Best of all, he had been preserved. But no time was to be lost, for he could not tarry long.

They sat up till the small hours discussing their plans. Kevin would return to England and arrange a marriage time and place in London. All his movements would have to be undertaken in secret. From London he would travel to Paris where his Uncle George and John Martin were living. There he would secure accommodation for them both and arrange to continue his medical studies in preparation for his final examination which he hoped he would be able to take sometime in the future. Paris would be their home until a full pardon was granted. Accompanied by his Uncle George he would meet Eva and her father for the clandestine marriage in London. After spending two days and three nights at the Kelly home Kevin reluctantly made his departure. He could not afford to take too many risks. The couple were careful to stay within the confines of the Kelly property. The moments sped by like magic for the young lovers but they felt far happier at this parting than they had done six years earlier when the prospects of a reunion had looked very bleak indeed.

Kevin sent word from Paris to the Kelly family that Cardinal Wiseman had agreed to conduct the wedding at Moorfields Church, London on 23 August 1855. Uncle George, with whom he was staying for the time being, was willing to come to London for the wedding. Kevin had arranged to attend the Paris Anatomy School and also to obtain clinical experience at the Pitié Hospital. Although Kevin had made all these movements unchallenged and had had no indication that Dr Alfred Carr had taken any action to report his illegal presence in England, the English doctor had not been inactive in that regard. However, the latter had taken some weeks to move, apparently thinking it necessary to make inquiries from the shipping agents before making a report. Finally on 2 July, by which time O'Doherty had moved around without any problem, Carr decided to write to Home Secretary Sir George Grey. His letter read:

> Dr Alfred Carr feels it's his duty to communicate to Sir George Grey that Mr Kevin Izod Dogherty, a State prisoner, who received a pardon conditionally that he should not return to England, was a first class passenger by the "James Baines" Royal Mail ship which left Melbourne on the 11th March ult. and arrived at Liverpool on Sunday, May 20th ult. Dr Carr has just ascertained that the name of this person is not to be found in the official list of passengers given by the Master of the ship to the Government officials — a copy of which has been forwarded to Dr C. by the ship's agents at Liverpool — Evidence also exists that the Master of the ship was cognisant of Dogherty's being on board — either entered on the passenger list under a false name or not entered on it. The recent agitation in Hyde Park induces Dr Carr to think that Sir G. Grey should be immediately acquainted with this fact.

An official, in drawing Sir George Grey's attention to the letter, asked the question: "Shall the Irish Government be informed of this?." The minuted reply read: "Yes, but without any reference to the Hyde Park meeting." A further instruction of 4 July 1855 directed that a letter be written to Ireland.

In addition to Dr Alfred Carr, O'Doherty had at least one other enemy in Galway, who informed the police of his presence at Killeen, the Kelly home. This unfriendly action is revealed in the following letter of 9 July 1855 from Thomas Arthur, sub-inspector of police at Portumna, County Galway to his inspector-general at Dublin Castle:

> I have to inform the Inspector-General that it is whispered about the County that a Mr Kevin Izod O'Dogherty, one of the Young Ireland party who was convicted and transported during the year 1848 and subsequently escaped from one of the Penal Settlements of Australia is shortly to be married to a young lady (a Miss Kelly) who resides with her family within a few miles of Portumna. It appears that the parties became acquainted in Dublin during 1848, and would have married at the time but for Mr O'Dogherty's conviction. Since his escape he has been residing somewhere in France where he has been studying at the medical profession and it is thought that he will now come over here in disguise for the purpose of marrying the young lady and bringing her out of the County. I have ascertained that a strange gentleman was staying with the Kelly family about a month ago and I am strongly of the opinion that Mr O'Dogherty was the person. In case he should return to the

County again I should wish to be informed how I am to act and whether under the circumstances the arrest of the party would be desirable on the part of the Government.

Dublin Castle forwarded a copy of the sub-inspector's report to Sir George Grey. Reference was made in the covering letter to the information supplied by Dr Carr but there was also an admission of doubt as to what action should be taken if O'Doherty were seen again. The Home Secretary's office had not advised Dublin Castle of the conditions of O'Doherty's pardon nor given any instructions for his apprehension. The bureaucratic omission of not informing Dublin fully about O'Doherty was of course in his favour and the bungling explained why no apparent attempt was made to follow Eva and her father when they later left Ireland for the wedding in London.

Before his marriage O'Doherty wrote to Gavan Duffy with whom he had been closely associated during their incarceration in Newgate jail after their arrest in 1848, and who was now a member of the House of Commons. He beseeched Duffy to approach Lord Palmerston, prime minister of England, with a view to granting a full pardon. Duffy in London replied that an approach had been made to the prime minister but he declined to give an answer one way or the other. Smith O'Brien's friends, who had made a similar request, believed that Palmerston would probably refuse the requests if he were pressed unduly. Duffy suggested that an approach be made to other influential friends, who he believed would be more likely to succeed, as "English Governments have no affection" for him.

In a second letter O'Doherty told of the arrangements for his marriage to Eva and again pressed the matter of a full pardon. Relevant portions of Duffy's reply are quoted:

> I congratulate you. A man going to marry his first love and to live in Paris has nothing to desire in the world. Bye and bye the idea of home will arise and please heaven be gratified. I have returned home to Blackrock, without getting an answer from Palmerston. Yes, I am going to the South of Europe. When I am clean gone I have reason to hope he will give one in the affirmative — but heaven only knows.

Since Kevin had departed Eva had been floating in a dream world, thinking almost continually of her imminent reunion with her beloved, the man for whom she had patiently and faithfully waited during six long and difficult years. She was an attractive, vivacious and intelligent young woman of good family and some means. There was no lack of young suitors who would have counted her hand a rare prize. However, she had never wavered since making her promise to Kevin; she had no doubts of the "rightness" of her decision and always felt intuitively that they would finally be united. She had not considered, however, as she had longed for that reunion that they would be living anywhere else but Ireland. Now she had to adjust herself to the idea of leaving her family and her familiar environment for a foreign one. Apart from those heady months during 1848 and 1849 she had always lived with some members of her family. She could write French but had had no opportunity to converse with French people, and would have no family nor close friends in Paris, at least no friends of her own sex. She knew John Martin through his letters but had had little face to face contact with him. Most young women like to be near their mothers during their early years of marriage and motherhood and during the nineteenth century this was certainly more usual than it is today. Eva had a few misgivings and uneasy moments when she contemplated these prospects and she felt some disappointment at not being able to have a wedding at home in the midst of family and friends. However, like Kevin, she was made of stern stuff and she did not allow these considerations to daunt her resolve. They were not of major importance. So in this frame of mind she set off for London with her father. After travelling to Dublin by coach they spent two nights and one full day there to enable Eva to do some essential shopping. They deliberately avoided making contact with anyone whom they thought might disclose their plans, for it was imperative they travel without the authorities knowing their movements.

It was when they had boarded the steamer for Liverpool and settled into their cabins that Eva came on deck. It was a lovely

August day with the sun shining on the calm waters of the Irish Sea. As she saw the coast of Ireland recede slowly, the reality dawned upon her. She was leaving her own native country, the soil from whence she and thousands of her ancestors had sprung: for how long was she leaving it? Would she ever see her family and home again? There were so many uncertainties hanging like a dark cloud over her head. Would Kevin get his full pardon? If so, when? What if they became ill in France — perhaps either one could perish there. The Celtic blood that filled her veins had made her not a little fey and she had a strong feeling that this man to whom she would soon be wed was destined to achieve more remarkable things in his life. She knew that they were destined to share many adventures together, that there would be great joys and great tragedies; but of one fact more than any other she was certain — their love and faith in each other would sustain them through all the trials and tribulations that might beset their future paths. She knew that the coming months and years would require great strength and courage and she felt a spiritual strength within her breast as if an inner voice spoke and said, "You can do it." This realisation came upon her as she sat gazing across the great expanse of water which seemed to go on into infinity. She felt part of that infinity and knew no more fears. This vision, this experience would sustain her in time to come when her strength and courage would be sorely tested. She relaxed, and turning to her father, who sat quietly beside her, she said, "I'm sure everything will go well." He nodded, he understood. No more words were needed.

Kevin and his uncle were waiting at the church when Eva and her father arrived. Despite the empty church the couple felt extremely happy as Cardinal Wiseman solemnised the ceremony.

The next day Kevin and Eva travelled to Brighton where Eva applied to the French vice-consul for a travel certificate for France. On the document, dated 24 August 1855, a copy of which still exists, Eva saw her married name written for the first time. The pass gave Mrs Mary Eva O'Doherty, rentière (a person of independent means), permission to travel in France for one month. If she wished to stay longer it would be necessary to obtain *un passeport regular*. There is no record of Kevin's travel documents for this period.

On a certificate issued by the British consul in Paris after he conducted a second marriage on 30 November 1855, Eva is described as a spinster. The couple apparently attempted to hoodwink the authorities into thinking that the Paris ceremony was their first marriage. Had the London marriage become known it would have been evidence that Kevin had been in England, thus breaking the condition of his pardon.

In Paris the newly married couple first resided in Rue du Faubourg Saint Honoré on the right bank of the Seine, where Uncle George Doherty and John Martin had accommodation. Not long after, they transferred to the Latin Quarter and had rooms in a rambling rooming house at 26 Rue de Lacepède. This was within walking distance of La Pitié Hospital where Kevin had arranged to attend surgical clinics. The hospital was founded by a royal edict in 1612 by Louis XIII. It was built to put beggars to work. A few years later children were admitted and in a separate building prostitutes were housed. In 1656 it became a general hospital and was still functioning in this capacity when O'Doherty attended for his clinical studies. La Pitié was demolished in 1904 and a Moslem mosque (La Mosque de Paris) was built on the site. Adherents of that faith were still worshipping there when the authors visited the area in 1978. La Pitié was established as a separate hospital in the grounds of the nearby Saltpetrière Hospital in Boulevard de L'Hôpital and functioned from 1904 to 1911, but the two hospitals were placed under one control in 1964.

The delirium of happiness which Eva experienced during the weeks following her marriage faded fairly rapidly. Kevin was absent for long hours during the week and the rooming house was a far cry from the family home at Killeen in Galway. She was quickly pregnant and suffered from morning sickness. Most women pregnant for the first time appreciate the presence of their mothers. Eva's mother was far away and, further, she had no female friend in Paris in whom to confide. Coming over in the ferry from Ireland to England she had realised that there would be periods of trials and tribulations. She was surprised that such an experience had come so soon. Later, when she had returned to Dublin, she wrote to John Martin about her feelings at this time. She said, "I really look back with a sense of horror to my life in Paris. From the state of my health during that period my mind suffered considerably and I felt as if I were the most wretched of human creatures."

Martin had also shifted to 26 Rue de Lacepède and had given Eva comfort and support during her ordeal in Paris. In her letter she thanked him in these words, "Of all the friends I have known none has been more genuinely and delicately kind than yourself — it occurs to me I have not at all deserved it, and that it required all the patience and goodness of your nature to be all that you were to me in many hours of loneliness in a strange land."

Besides Gavan Duffy, who, on Kevin's behalf, had continually lobbied Palmerston for a full pardon for the exiles, Lord Inchinquin, (formerly Sir Lucius O'Brien, Smith O'Brien's brother) had been working towards the same goal. Their hopes rose at the end of April 1856 when there were suggestions in the press that, with the cessation of the hostilities in the Crimean War, full pardons would be granted for political prisoners. Success came on 8 May 1856 when a deputation on behalf of the Young Irelanders waited on the prime minister. That night Duffy wrote to O'Doherty, who again had risked going to Ireland, taking Eva with him so that she would be in Dublin for the birth of their child expected towards the end of May. Duffy's letter read:

> You are free to remain in your country. The deputation who presented the memorial have just seen Lord Palmerston and got his answer, which is a full and unconditional assent that O'Brien, Martin and yourself should return to Ireland. I have lost three years in the British Parliament but I count some compensation that I have been able to effect this for my old friends and confederates. I hope to see you in Dublin within a fortnight.
> P.S. By the way I would advise you to keep quiet for a week or so, and then let it be supposed you have just come from France. Pray make my congratulations to a certain fair poetess on this event.

The decision was published in the papers the next morning. Later in the day, Palmerston, on being asked in the Commons to confirm the newspaper reports, said:

> Her Majesty, following the impulses and dictates of those generous feelings by which She is so eminently distinguished, has determined to take advantage of the return to peace, and of the unexempted loyalty, which has prevailed from one end of her dominions to the other, to do an act of grace and clemency towards all persons under sentence for political offences, with the exception of those unhappy men who have broken all the ties of honour and have fled from the place of banishment. The amnesty will be general and will include Mr O'Brien, Mr Martin and those others who have been referred to by my Honourable Friend.

The amnesty, proclaimed by Sir George Grey, on 19 May 1856, was granted to eighteen political prisoners. Insofar as it applied to O'Doherty it referred to the offence of which he had been convicted and announced:

> Whereas upon consideration of some circumstance humbly represented to us on behalf of the said Kevin Izod O'Dogherty we are Graciously pleased to extend Our Grace and Mercy unto him and grant him Our Free Pardon for the said offence whereof he was convicted as aforesaid.

Kevin was free at last and his destiny now lay in his own hands once again.

CHAPTER 6

Graduation and Migration

Eva would have preferred to have gone home to Killeen to have her first baby but Dublin was chosen for the confinement as Kevin's conditional pardon was still in force when the arrangements were made. He wished to be with Eva and there was less likelihood of his illegal presence being detected in the large city. News of his full pardon had come before the birth but because Gavan Duffy had suggested Kevin keep quiet for a week or so, the couple decided not to alter their plans for the confinement to take place at Bloomwood, Monkstown, not far from Blackrock where Kevin's mother had gone to live after the death of her husband. On 26 May 1856, Eva gave birth to a son, to whom the names William Joseph Kelly were given.

As Kevin was now free to remain in Ireland, he could prepare himself for his final examination in medicine. He decided to stay in Dublin. As soon as Eva and the baby were strong enough to travel, they left for Killeen. Kevin took rooms at 51 York Street in the city not far from the Royal College of Surgeons and made inquiries regarding his preparation for the examination.

At this time the College of Surgeons recognised two standards for admission to the college — a minimal one for admission as a licentiate and a higher standard as a fellow. Candidates for the fellowship were required to study for six years and were not admitted before the age of twenty-five years. In addition to the certificates of training for the licentiate award, the applicant for the fellowship was required to produce evidence of attendance at courses of comparative anatomy, botany and natural philosophy. He was obliged to show that he had served as a house surgeon or a dresser in a hospital and to present a medical thesis or observations on six or more medical cases. Kevin was advised to undertake the higher examination since admission as a fellow would give him greater status in the profession and in the community. He took this advice and planned to present himself for the fellowship examination in the winter of 1857. In his application of 27 October 1856 he referred to his service as a house surgeon at St Mary's Hospital, Hobart, pointing out that attendance there was recognised by the London College of Surgeons, and also to his attendance at the surgical clinics at the Hôpital Pitié, Paris, as well as his dissection at the Paris Anatomical School. His certificates and experience were acceptable and when he presented for the examination he performed creditably. His graduation certificate dated 11 June 1857 was signed by Hans Irvine, president, and several other members of the college. And, so, nine years later than he once anticipated, Kevin had finally graduated in medicine. Writing of his success to John Martin he said:

> I have been these six or seven months past entirely devoted to the work of obtaining my long coveted diploma. Thank God, I have got it and can hold my head some inches higher than I could these few years past . . . . I had to go thro' a court of seven disciplines having determined to pass the seven examinations for the degree of "Fellow" of the College. By dint of hard work I was enabled to present myself last week before the Court with confidence and won my crown easily. I am off tomorrow to the country to take counsel with Eva as to our ultimate proceedings.

Although buoyed up by his success in his "finals", O'Doherty was not a happy man. He felt great concern for his native land and sensed a somewhat hostile attitude in some of its inhabitants towards himself. The Ireland to which he had returned appeared a crushed country. After the Great Famine hundreds of thousands had migrated, mostly to America, and there was very little sign of nationalism in those who remained. Nobody spoke of the repeal of the union with Britain. The Catholic middle and upper classes had given up any thought of independence. Many of them sought minor government posts and titles from Dublin Castle, being dubbed, "Castle Catholics".

Gavan Duffy had begun publishing the *Nation* again in 1849 but the paper seemed to have lost its previous fire. Even Duffy allowed Irish nationalism to lie dormant. He had become deeply involved in the Tenant Rights Association, striving to obtain for tenants the three Fs — fair rent, fixity of tenure and the right of full sale of the tenant's interest. It was to be supported by an Independent Irish Party in the House of Commons, having no relation whatever to any of the British parliamentary parties. But, it was not long before prominent members accepted positions with the British government and both the Tenant League and the Independent Irish Party were lost causes.

Part of the failure of the two bodies was due to the attitude of Archbishop (later Cardinal) Cullen towards Duffy. Cullen, an Irishman, had been in Rome from 1820 to 1849 where he had experienced the nationalism of the Mazzini-led Young Italy movement, which had a very definite anti-papal content. Unfairly, Cullen considered Duffy, a fervent Catholic all his life, to be an Irish Mazzini. Duffy, dispirited by these events, decided to emigrate to Australia. Before he left, he wrote that, "The ultimate for which I had alone laboured — to give back to Ireland her national existence — is forgotten or disdained. Till all this be changed, there seems to be no more hope for the Irish cause than for the corpse on the dissecting table."

O'Doherty, too, of course, was a Young Irelander. He shared Duffy's despair for his country and also sensed the attitude of the church towards Young Irelanders, including himself. In the same letter in which he told Martin of his success in his examination, he wrote:

> I must confess to you, what I dare say you will not be surprised at — that I have taken an intense dislike to this place and I am going down to Eva, determined, if I can, to infuse the same feeling into her — poor thing, she has had so little opportunity of judging for herself that I almost fear she will be inclined to urge me to remain and try my chance in this good city which I verily believe dislikes me as much as I dislike it, and wishes me, moreover, with the same amount of fervour I am beginning to wish myself, safe in the Antipodes — I have had a very encouraging letter from an old friend, Father McEncroe, the factotum of the Irish in Sidney [sic] recommending me to be off there as quickly as possible, promising plenty of nuggets. Would it not be queer if within the next six months I should be sailing up that noble harbour? What do you think of the matter? If I remain in this city I can only hope to prosper by bowing down in humble submissiveness to the wiles and behests of the most Reverend Doctor Cullen, which in truth, Catholic though I be, I should find very difficult to do.

There was a further reason for Kevin's unhappiness — the attitude of his brothers, William and John. They had not approved of his involvement with the Young Ireland movement and displayed no enthusiasm for any Irish nationalism. While Kevin had adopted the prefix "O" to his name his brothers had remained "Dohertys". They had not changed.

While Kevin was reticent about this problem Eva unburdened her heart in letters to Martin. When she wrote in June 1857 she referred to the pleasant news of Kevin's examination success and then said this:

> This is very good but there is a great deal which is not good with regard to us — first, I think from what K says his health is by no means good and next, Wm (his brother) is still persisting in the course he first adopted — the irritation this man is causing him is, I know, one cause of his being ill . . ..
>
> Believe me, I am not talking with passion or prejudice now for I do assure you Wm Doherty is a man of a bad and dishonest nature — crooked, crafty and jealous to an inordinate degree. John I scarcely blame for he is passive — a mere tool in his brother's hands — the women are small and spiteful.

In view of Eva's feelings toward her in-laws she, no doubt, would have accepted Kevin's plans to leave Dublin but the couple deferred the idea of migrating and returned to the city where Kevin set up practice at 18 Hume Street, off St Stephen's Green East. He was appointed a surgeon to the nearby St Vincent's Hospital and lecturer in anatomy and physiology at Ledwich Medical School. The practice was quite successful but Kevin found time to study for two more qualifications. He was admitted, after examination, as a licentiate of the Kings and Queens College of Physicians and after studying for six months at the Coombes Maternity Hospital he gained an equivalent diploma in obstetrics. O'Doherty was now a very well qualified medical practitioner.

Despite the despair of Duffy and O'Doherty for their country and their belief that the spirit of nationalism was completely lost, steps were, in fact, being taken to revive it. In 1856, the year that O'Doherty returned to Ireland, Jeremiah O'Donovan, called O'Donovan Rossa, after his birthplace, Rosscarbery, and other young men in Skibbereen, County Cork, formed the Phoenix National and Literary Society. They, no doubt, hoped that, like the mystical bird after which the society was called, nationalism would rise again from the ashes of the 1848 rebellion, for their organisation was a cover for a secret society which demanded from its members the taking of an oath which renounced allegiance to the Queen of England and the promise to make Ireland an independent republic.

At the time there were also stirrings towards Irish nationalism in America and France to which many Young Irelanders had fled after 1848. James Stephens and John O'Malley were becoming active in Paris and Stephens, aide-de-camp to Smith O'Brien at Ballingarry, went to Ireland to form a secret society. He found O'Donovan Rossa in Cork and the two joined forces. O'Malley went to America to further the cause among thousands of his countrymen who had migrated there.

Others who were prominent in these fresh movements towards an insurrection in Ireland were Michael Doheny, Thomas Clarke Luby, John O'Leary and Charles Kickham as well as Irishmen who had fought in the American Civil War. The movement, first called the Irish Republican Brotherhood, was best known as the Fenians. After several years of intense activity, Stephens was deposed as head of the organisation because he deferred the date for an insurrection. The rising, when it did take place in 1867, was led by Colonel Thomas Kelly, an American Civil War veteran and a Frenchman, General Cluseret. Like the 1848 rebellion, the Fenian insurrection was a dismal failure. There were widespread arrests and heavy sentences. In an attempt to rescue Colonel Kelly who had been arrested in Manchester, England, a policeman was shot dead and three Fenians involved, Allen, Larkin and O'Brien were executed — the Manchester martyrs. Several of the Fenians, including John Boyle O'Reilly and John Flood, were transported to West Australia, the only Australian colony still accepting convicts.

O'Doherty, as a Young Irelander, was most likely approached by Stephens to join the movement. There is no evidence of his activity in the cause and his participation was most unlikely. He had already made remarkable progress in his profession, had begun to raise a family, and, disenchanted with Ireland, he and Eva were seriously contemplating migrating to Australia. As events transpired, the family had left Ireland well before the year of the insurrection — 1867.

In August 1858, after several months' silence, Eva wrote again to John Martin in Paris. Her letter revealed glimpses of a woman sometimes living in fantasy, having to deal with mundane problems; an awareness of her own unworldliness and endeavours to correct it; an ambition of pursuing a literary career. Her opinion of the Dohertys remained unchanged:

> I will not try your patience with a long yarn — only just to tell you that I have had many tormenting troubles of the mean and earthy sort which, by the way, more acutely try a body strongly inclined to live in the moon apart from such influences, than even the sable woes of tragedy . . . . My first downright assimilation with the actual took place only of late years, and since my marriage and I did not fancy it at all — how many annoyances came upon me — some like serpent bites — others like stings of hornets — the consequence was a sort of bewilderment and sourness which I am only just now laying in the red sea . . .
>
> Now about my literary pursuits. I have not been able to write as much as I should wish for the last few months on account of my

health but I am now again able to resume business. Lietch Ritchie, Messrs Chambers' literary hack, wrote to me and seems to have rather a good opinion of my powers . . . Mr Ritchie says after a little time I may expect to be paid £1 per page . . .. To confess a truth, I am downright afraid of you for I fear that my efforts partake of the misty moonbeamy kind — I shall improve, and learn to paint creatures with real life blood in their veins instead of airy nothings . . . .

The Dohertys — I mean William and the females — I like them less today than I did — for I read them now more clearly than ever. William, I would not trust where his own interests would be involved although he is very polite and plausible — the feminines are freezing and spiteful to a degree below zero.

Eva gave no details of any basis for her allegations against William Doherty. She apparently suspected something more than his disapproval of Kevin's involvement in the Young Ireland movement. His standing as a dentist was quite high in the community and he was apparently satisfied with the control of Ireland from Dublin Castle. Maybe she had reason to believe he was a Castle Catholic.

John Martin's reply to Eva revealed how well he knew this intelligent but relatively naive young woman. He appreciated her weaknesses and her strengths. As a true friend he pointed out in rather blunt language those weaknesses and gave sound advice to help her achieve her ambitions to be a successful novelist:

But in all sincerity and seriousness I say that I have remarked in you a tendency to a diseased state of mind which shows itself by giving gloomy and unreal views of the people and circumstances among which you live and also of the creatures of your imagination . . . . If your taste for literary work is so strongly fixed, you must continue to write. But I would advise you not to write for the purpose of earning good money . . . . I believe not only that your writing is good at present when your perverse ignorance of real life and real men and women renders your compositions objectionable but that you have — aye, have eminently — the task, genius and power to *know* life and to paint it like a true artist. But to know it you must employ the means of knowledge. You must not shut your eyes and ears, and lock yourself up in a little dark corner of your own, and keep gazing through firm-shut eyelids at the fantastic forms and colours that appear in the darkness.

During the next two years Eva had little time to write as she produced two more sons — Edward Hyacinth on 3 April 1858 and Vincent Kevin on 23 August 1859, both of whom were born at Hume Street.

During his visits as a surgeon to St Vincent's Hospital O'Doherty frequently met Reverend James Quinn, president of St Laurence O'Toole's seminary in Harcourt Street, Dublin, a most successful boys' secondary school. A firm friendship developed between the two men — a friendship which was to last until Quinn's death twenty-five years later. In view of Archbishop Cullen's attitude to the Young Ireland movement, Quinn's friendship with O'Doherty surprised many in the Catholic hierarchy, particularly as the seminary head was regarded as Cullen's man. Cullen and Quinn were distant relatives and the archbishop had been Quinn's lifelong mentor. No other superior had had as much influence on the younger man's development of religious attitudes and policies. Cullen frequently visited the seminary for dinners and for musical and academic functions. But Quinn had too much independence to follow his mentor blindly on all subjects and the Young Ireland movement was one in which he differed from Cullen. In fact, he went further than just having his own opinion on the matter. He endeavoured, unfortunately without success, to bring Cullen and Duffy, the former Young Ireland leader, together in an amicable relationship, but neither was sufficiently flexible to change his attitudes in the slightest degree.

O'Doherty often discussed his thoughts of migrating to Australia with Quinn, and, when in April 1859 the latter was appointed Bishop of Brisbane at the Moreton Bay settlement, which was expected to soon become a separate Australian colony (Queensland), the doctor took the necessary steps to relinquish his practice and arrange travel for himself, Eva and their young family to the continent.

O'Doherty approached the Black Ball shipping line, which owned the *James Baines*, the vessel on which he had travelled to England in 1855. He suggested that he and his family travel on one of its ships while he acted as ship's surgeon in lieu of payment for himself. The company accepted his proposal and arrangements were made for the O'Dohertys to travel on the *Ocean Chief*. The *Ocean Chief*, a smaller ship than the *James Baines*, being 1,026 tons as against 2,215, was nevertheless considered a worthy vessel. Her agents described her as a "splendid specimen of naval architecture" and claimed that she was "acknowledged by all judges to be one of the fastest and handsomest ships in the world".

When the *Ocean Chief* left Liverpool on 5 July 1860, under the command of William Brown, the passenger list recorded the O'Doherty party among the saloon passengers as Dr and Mrs O'Doherty, children William, Edward and Vincent and servant, Edith Mills. It did not, of course, record that Eva was five months pregnant.

The ship followed the usual route taken at this time — southwards down the Atlantic Ocean off the African coast, around the Cape of Good Hope and then eastward across the Indian Ocean towards Australia with Melbourne as the destination port. The voyage was uneventful during the first stage with the weather becoming hotter as the ship neared the equator which was crossed on 30 July, twenty-five days out from Liverpool. When off the Cape of Good Hope, however, a terrific south-east gale of five days' duration was experienced. From then on there was "a series of easterly and baffling winds" which slowed the vessel's progress. The *Ocean Chief* did not reach Port Phillip until 2 October, taking 89 days to complete the voyage which did not enhance her reputation of being one of the fastest vessels in the world. There is no record as to how Eva fared during the voyage but the family register lists the birth of another boy at Geelong on 8 November 1860 — Kevin Izod Louis. It is assumed that arrangements were made for the confinement to take place at the home of one of the many Irish families with whom Kevin had made contact in 1854.

Kevin, anxious to reach Sydney, where, on the advice of his friend, now Archdeacon McEncroe, he had decided to commence medical practice, sailed for that city two weeks after their arrival in Melbourne and before the birth of the baby. The *Sydney Freeman's Journal* announced his arrival with the comment that, "If high accomplishments in his profession unanimously acknowledged and a passionate, intelligent devotion to the cause of freedom, be merits and titles to success, we can hope for it for friend and fellow-countryman — Doctor O'Dogherty." The same paper and the *Sydney Morning Herald* advised the public that the newly-arrived doctor could be consulted at his residence at 27 Botany Street. Eva recovered from her confinement very quickly and with her four young sons sailed for Sydney on the *Wonga Wonga* in December in time to spend her first Christmas in Australia at their Botany Street home.

O'Doherty very quickly fitted into the Sydney Irish community and at the St Patrick's Day banquet, 1861 was invited to take a major role. The *Freeman's Journal* predicted that the 1861 celebration "will long be pointed at as the platform where men of all creeds and nations united and fraternised in honour of the Irishmen's patron saint". Among those attending were many Englishmen and Scots as well as numerous Irishmen with adherents of both Protestant and Catholic religions mingling freely. The function was chaired by Terence, later Sir Terence Murray, speaker of the New South Wales Legislative Assembly. Born at Balliston, County Limerick, Ireland, Murray had migrated to New South Wales in 1827, but not before Daniel O'Connell had "impressed upon him indelibly that moral suasion was more successful than brute force for obtaining right". Other members of the Legislative Assembly present included Henry Parkes who later in 1867 and 1868 was to become hysterical about Fenianism and see Irish rebels behind every bush.

In accordance with the custom of the times there was a very long toast list. In his capacity as chairman, Terence Murray proposed, "The Queen, God bless Her", and the journal claimed that "the toast was drunk with enthusiasm, the band playing the National Anthem". The paper went on to report: "The chairman in proposing the second toast, said it was one of a cognate character with the last and needed no expression from him to induce them to respond cordially to it. The toast was 'Prince Albert, the Prince of Wales and other members of the

Royal Family'. As British subjects, they should feel an interest in the family of which the Queen was the head, and of which of late years two of the princes had visited two of Her most important colonies." Among the toasts which followed, the function honoured the administrator of government, the New South Wales parliament and the army and navy. O'Doherty's task was to respond to the toast to "Our Fatherland". In an eloquent speech he said:

> In an assemblage such as I see around me, representing as it does various creeds and countries, I am precluded from addressing myself to the subject of my toast in any narrow or sectional spirit; and deeply gratified I am to be so. It was not amongst the least of the inducements which led me to link my destiny to this young country, that in it no such narrow exclusiveness was allowed to find a place. In it the Fatherland of one is as the Fatherland of all; and, as this meeting testifies, the name of Ireland's patron saint can here be honoured by gentlemen who hail from the shores of Old England or from the north of the Tweed as heartily as by the Catholic sons of Ireland . . .. I freely confess, gentlemen, to retaining as strongly as I ever did, my sympathy for the national existence of my country. The people of England and Ireland are today united in too close bonds of a common language and common interest to wish for more than that modified independence which in these colonies is so great a blessing; and for the life of me I cannot conceive why such a national existence should be incompatible with the most cordial good feeling between the two peoples . . .. I trust I may be allowed in this assembly to express the hope that that sentiment of nationality, which is now the watchword of so many of the old nations of Europe, may find a hearty response in Ireland, and that it may be given to us again to see Queen, lords and commons assembled in council, infusing the breath of national life into her . . ..

O'Doherty had modified his goals for Ireland. In his *Irish Tribune* of 1848 the former rebel had named Britain as a jackal foe who was driving Irish sheep and oxen from Irish fields and confiscating her corn. He had then urged his fellow countrymen to "ease their longing thirst, deep, deep in the blood of the English foe". In Melbourne in 1854 at the end of his convict days he had claimed that the ravages of famine and fever in Ireland had been aggravated to an intense degree by the heartless policy of a government with whom the interest and lives of Irishmen was the least item of consideration. Now he was advocating a modified national independence which he believed could be compatible with the most cordial good feeling between the two peoples. Why this change of heart?

In Victoria in 1854 he had seen his countryman John O'Shanassy taking his place as a member of the Victorian Legislative Council. He, no doubt, learnt that most of the grievances of the miners had been solved after the Eureka Stockade. Now his fellow Young Irelander, Gavan Duffy, was minister for Lands in the Victorian government led by the Irish O'Shannassy. He was satisfied with colonial government which he claimed was so great a blessing.

There were other factors at work to alter O'Doherty's attitude. The previous fervid nationalism of many Irishmen who came to Australia was modified in the process of settling in the new land. Like them O'Doherty had migrated to practise his profession and make a home for Eva and their young family and even if he were so inclined any active participation in rebellious activities would have had a low priority. But he was not so inclined. After discussions with Bishop Quinn before he left Ireland and with Archdeacon McEncroe on his arrival in Sydney any sympathies he may have had with the Fenians — and such would have been most unlikely — would have vanished. And so the former Young Irelander now felt quite at ease at the St Patrick's Day banquet at which the chairman initiated the proceedings with a toast to "The Queen, God bless Her". He did, however, feel strongly that the type of government which the colonies enjoyed should be granted to Ireland.

While Kevin was establishing a medical practice Eva was surprisingly busy in the literary field. Although but newly-arrived in the colony, with four boys under five years, the youngest being the baby born in November 1860 at Geelong, she began contributing regularly to Poet's Corner in the *Sydney Freeman's Journal*; between January and November 1861 approximately forty of her poems were published. They included original verse — many written after her arrival and some she brought from Ireland as yet unpublished — and translations into English verse, several poems of the Frenchman, Beranger.

Eva was an Irish patriot, first and foremost, and although she would settle in her adopted country and raise her family there, that invisible chain that bound her to her homeland would never be severed. In her first poem published in the *Freeman's Journal*, she hailed her new country, Australia, with hope for a "Glorious future's rosy dawning" — a future for the "freedman's greatness", but referred to the "sadness of the exile's story". This theme of the exile is echoed and re-echoed in many of the poems she wrote in 1861. "A Flight Across the Sea" summed up her feelings in that heart-rending cry for her native land:

> O Ireland of that spring-time fairest!
> O Ireland of the murmuring streams!
> Fair clime on earth of memories rarest,
> Of early hopes and golden dreams —
> With heart strings round thee fondly twining,
> With eyes thro' space and time that strain
> Across that waste of waters shining,
> The exile flies to thee again!

and in *Shadows*, where she refers to Glenmaloe in the following way:

> For my heart to that spot is clinging,
> Far, far away!

Brought up in a well-to-do family with its attendant privileges, and intelligent and enthusiastic enough to take advantage of competent governesses, Eva still had a great empathy for the poor and underprivileged — she was a socialist at heart. These values are quite apparent in several poems which appeared during this year. In "The Ruined House" an old man returned after years of absence to look at the cottage now in ruins, where he had raised his family. He thought of his loved ones and recalled those days before the rich man's son evicted him and chased him off to the workhouse. The last stanza sums up the old man's feelings very adequately:

> And the old man came to his cottage door
> To see the home he lov'd once more;
> Then I heard him pray: what asked he there?
> A broken heart has but *one* prayer!

It is not surprising that Eva translated the poems of Beranger, for like herself he was a true patriot and champion of the underdog. In "My Mission", "Song of the Cossack" and "The Niggers and the Puppets" those of poor or lowly birth or disadvantaged by their colour are exploited by the rich and powerful. At least six of the poems relate to that universal and greatest of all human emotions — love, — and fervently Eva pours out her declarations of love for her favoured one in "My Star":

> My star of morn, my star of eve,
> My only joy, my only pain.
> Mine evermore or sad or bright,
> While memory holds her reign.
> Thou't ever live before my sight
> Tho' morn be past, and night remain!

And also in "Anacreontic":

> My love — it is a draught divine,
> Pure and bright as purple wine,
> Foaming, sparkling, bubbling up
> From my heart's red ruby cup;
> And I pour it, wild and free,
> Every day and hour for thee.

While a great number of the poems show a personal love, a patriotic love, a sympathy for the oppressed, there is also present in many a thread of sadness, nostalgia, often despair and melancholia to a point of morbidity. All or some of these qualities can be found in poems like the "Dead Leaves" and "Dead Years", where she is looking back into the past with longing and seeing only despair and woe for the future. In the poems "No More" and "Song of Deidre" (which she took from the Irish of Owen Roe O'Sullivan, an eighteenth century Irish poet) and the "Magic Glass" Eva deals with the human tragedies of sorrow and hopelessness, when the lovers fail to be reunited. In the "Magic Glass" the lonely old man, utterly deserted and alone, cries in his despair:

> "Am I, in sooth, to wander all alone
> Upon the earth?" he said, with shuddering moan,
> "Ev'n thy presence, sorrow, fain would I behold
> To fill the pulseless void of being still and cold."
> But sorrow with averted eye
> Swept on her sable pinions by;
> In that wide waste of vacant, torpid death,
> For him might breathe again no quick'ning breath —
> Within the magic circle of that frozen rim,
> Love, Hope, and Sorrow — all alike are dim!

A similar story occurs in "Song to Deirdre" — the passionate cry of desperation:

> Frenzied with love for you;
> Praying above for you;
> Torn with that longing, and sorrow, and pain;
> Ah! tho' I'd sigh for you,
> Ev'n till I'd die for you,
> Never on earth shall we two meet again!

As well as this more serious and sober strain in her character, Eva was not devoid of a sense of humour, as can be seen in the poem, "Ballinalea", wherein she describes a charming little village reputed for its great beauty — "Another Eden calmly blest". Two lovers stood admiring the glorious scenery and as they did, they saw two little pigs dancing for joy, totally oblivious of their impending fate:

> And there behold! two nice little pigs,
> Who danced all manner of reels and jigs;
> Arcadian "grunters" of truest breed,
> Graceful as Dryads and Fauns indeed,
> Who poked each other in frolic and fun,
> Divartin' themselves till the praties were done!
> Little they knew that blessed morning
> Of bacon cured, or pork for corning;
> Little they dreamed of the next fair day,
> Down by the village of Bonalea!
> "Ah! such is the fate", as the minstrels say,
> Even as those little pigs that play!
> Thus did I moralise that day,
> Down by the village of Bonalea.

Eva's poetry is, in many ways, reminiscent of Robert Burns', and although her writing is not to be compared with his, either in content or technique, there is no doubting the sincerity of her sentiments. Many of their themes are similar. They were both great patriots, they both loved their native countryside and sang in praise of their rivers, lakes and mountains; but above all a trait which they shared in large measure, was humanitarianism, having a great love of their fellow man; they both championed the cause of the poor and the oppressed. Although they came from entirely different social backgrounds, they ardently believed liberty and justice to be the right of every man, and not just the prerogative of the rich. While Burns immortalised many Scottish folk songs, Eva was responsible for reviving many of the old Irish folk tales and legends as can be seen from "In the Fairies", "The Ard Righ's Bride", "Song to Deirdre" and others.

The tendency to a melancholy strain exhibited in many of her poems was a characteristic not uncommonly found in nineteenth century literature. It was a time of great social, political and economic upheaval in Europe largely due to the Industrial Revolution, while Ireland was experiencing the terrible potato famines. The majority of the population, both rural and urban, was adversely affected. Eviction and banishment to the workhouse was a common occurrence. Charles Dickens in his *Oliver Twist*, Elizabeth Barrett in "The Cry of the Children" and Thomas Hood in "The Song of the Shirt" all attempt to expose the gross injustices and the dreadful living conditions experienced by so many.

Eva made no extravagant claims for her poetry. She told journalist Spencer Browne that, "The best that we do must have in it some inspiration from outside things — patriotism, affection and events; but of my best I do not think there is much that counts." Henry Kellow, in his *Queensland Poets*, said that, "She was inspired by patriotism, affection and events, and at the time when she wrote she found an audience attuned to all three; but to a new generation patriotism wears a different face, old affections lose their personal appeal, and the crowding events of today diminish the importance of yesterday. Therefore Mrs O'Doherty's verse has lost the interest derived from the circumstances in which it was produced."

In May 1861 Bishop Quinn passed through Sydney on his way to his new diocese of Brisbane. He was welcomed at a "grand tea party and musical soiree" given by St Benedict's Young Men's Society at their hall in Abercrombie Street where 500 people had gathered. Among the special guests named in the press as attending the function were Dr and Mrs O'Dogherty, along with His Grace, the Archbishop of Sydney, John Bede Polding and Archdeacon McEncroe. O'Doherty was also among those mentioned as farewelling Quinn when he left Sydney in the *Yarra Yarra* a few days later.

Quinn returned to Sydney in October 1861 and as Eva, in her reminiscences, states that they came to Queensland "at the insistence of Bishop Quinn", it was probably during this visit that O'Doherty was persuaded to leave Sydney for the northern colony. He relinquished his practice at 457 Pitt Street, at which address he had been practising since May 1861, and with Eva and their four sons boarded the Clyde-built, 700 tons paddle steamer, *Telegraph*, under the command of Captain O'Reilly on 26 February 1862. Two days later the *Telegraph* rounded Cape Moreton and entered and anchored in the bay overnight. The next day the steamer proceeded up the Brisbane River and the family was greeted at the Australasian Steam Navigation Company's wharf by Bishop Quinn.

The colony to which the O'Dohertys had come had commenced as the Moreton Bay penal settlement in 1824. In 1842 the area was declared open for free settlement after the closure of the penal station. Pastoralists, with their flocks, moved in to join others who had already taken up land beyond the fifty miles (eighty kilometres) radius from the convict settlement required by law. At the end of 1859, when the population had reached 23,500 and only a little over two years before O'Doherty's arrival, the area had been granted separation from New South Wales. At the time only one quarter of the colony's area situated in the south-east was occupied by Europeans but in the next twenty years, land-hungry pastoralists, sugar planters and gold miners would push out to the north and the west into the unsettled territory, much of which lay in the tropics.

One of O'Doherty's first tasks was to become a registered medical practitioner in Queensland. This was achieved on 3 March 1862 and the four members of the medical board who signed his certificate, George Fullerton, William Hobbs, Hugh Bell and Frederick Barton, are prominent names, not only in medical history, but also in the annals of the colony itself. O'Doherty was listed as No. 14 in the medical register, being the fourteenth doctor to be registered since separation. Another twenty-three doctors in the colony had been registered by the medical board of New South Wales before separation. O'Doherty, with qualifications in surgery, medicine and obstetrics obtained by examination in Ireland, when the medicine practised there was of a very high standard, was the most highly qualified doctor in the colony.

O'Doherty next took steps to commence practice and set up a home for Eva and their young family. This did not take long. On 7 March 1862, two newspapers, the *Queensland Times* and the *North Australian*, circulating in Ipswich, a town of 3,500 inhabitants, situated 23 miles (thirty-seven kilometres) west of Brisbane, announced that Dr K.I. O'Doherty had commenced practice at his residence at Forbes Terrace, Thorn Street within one door of Mr Panton's.

Ipswich was almost as old as Brisbane, the capital city. Only three years after the penal settlement was established, it had commenced as a convict outstation, called Limestone, providing burnt lime to be used in building in Brisbane. In addition to lime burning, George Thorn, "the father of Ipswich", managed a cattle herd and crops were grown for the settlement on the "ploughed field". It was renamed Ipswich with the declaration of free settlement. At first keen rivalry existed between Ipswich and Brisbane. The squatters, who sent their wool to Ipswich for transfer to Brisbane by boat down the Bremer and Brisbane rivers, had hoped that Ipswich would become the capital of the new colony. People wishing to reach Ipswich from Brisbane in 1862 travelled either by one of the river steamers which plied between the two centres catering mainly for cargo or by coach over very rough roads. The O'Dohertys probably travelled on the *Ipswich*, a paddle-steamer, which was the only vessel making this trip which had adequate accommodation for passengers — a far more comfortable journey than by coach.

By this time, Ipswich was well-established, and had been declared a municipality in 1860. The famous Cribb and Foote store was already functioning and was to continue to serve the inhabitants for several decades. The religious needs of the citizens were satisfied by churches which had been built by the many denominations practising in the colony and cultural activities were provided by a school of arts. Primary education was available at a national school and for those needing medical care not available at home a voluntary committee conducted a public hospital. To slake the thirst of the community Irish innkeepers ran St Patrick's Tavern and the Harp of Erin Hotel in competition with other proprietors whose establishments rejoiced in such names as the Queen's Arms.

It is interesting to conjecture why O'Doherty went to Ipswich and did not set up his plate in the capital city, Brisbane. He was well-qualified and it is certain he would have been confident of his ability to be successful in his profession wherever he went. Population figures and the number of doctors practising suggest that neither town was over-doctored. The Irish doctor had settled in very quickly and it appears that he received help in this regard — help which no doubt came from his friend, Bishop Quinn. It seems plausible to suggest that O'Doherty went to Ipswich to support the bishop in a dispute with Father McGinty, the parish priest there.

Forbes Terrace, where O'Doherty put up his plate, was a row of terraced houses in a style popular in the colony during this period. Built by George Goggs, it changed hands in 1861 and was renamed after its new owner. Mr Panton's house, mentioned in O'Doherty's advertisement, was "Claremont", then a commodious stone house in Milford Street, which Panton sold to George Thorn in 1863. One of Ipswich's landmarks, it is preserved by the National Trust.

Soon after his arrival, O'Doherty offered his services in an honorary capacity to the Ipswich Hospital which had been opened in 1860. O'Doherty's colleagues on the visiting staff were Henry Challinor and Thomas Rowlands — English graduates. Challinor had come to Queensland in 1849 as surgeon-superintendent on the *Fortitude*, one of Reverend Dumore Lang's immigrant ships. Outside his profession Challinor was prominent in the Congregational Church and politics, being a member of the Queensland Legislative Assembly. Dr Challinor was a man who voiced his opinion no matter what the opposition — he had a social conscience. Rowlands had preceded O'Doherty by twelve months and already was an esteemed practitioner. Although both men had graduated in medicine before O'Doherty, they soon came to respect his superior skills. At a time when any special medical event was featured in the newspapers several articles appeared in the Ipswich press, revealing O'Doherty's prowess as a surgeon, and his relationship with his colleagues. They also indicated the treatment and medical beliefs current when anaesthetics had been available less than twenty years and such other aids to medical practice as X-rays, blood transfusion and antibiotics were still several decades away. The *North Australian* carried the following accounts:

19 April 1864
Two very successful operations at the Ipswich Hospital have been performed during the week. The first and most important was that on a female patient, named Banks, suffering from cancer of the breast, the entire removal of which was accomplished in twenty minutes by Dr O'Doherty assisted by Drs Challinor and Rowlands. The difficulties attendant on removal of the entire root of this distressing disease are generally of no ordinary character, and the inhabitants of Ipswich must congratulate themselves on the fact that the hospital has on its staff such successful operators.

15 November 1864
Another operation has been performed on a girl named Ann Kelly, aged 8 years, who was suffering from a tumour of the ankle-joint. In many hospitals amputation would have been resorted to, but not so here — for Dr O'Doherty, assisted by Drs Challinor and Rowlands and Mr Heeney, performed the operation of excision, or resection, of the diseased portion, leaving the foot perfect . . . . It is justice to our hospital surgeons to notice such cases as the above, and that the public know they are skilfully and successfully treated.

28 December 1864
A case of snake-bite has occurred in North Ipswich to a man named Cornelius Clifford, of which I think it only just to the public to send you the full particulars, as I consider, under God's providence, the treatment the man received, and the attention paid to him, have saved his life. The man in question was bitten by what he described to me as a diamond snake. After a lapse of two hours he was taken to Dr Challinor, who slightly scarified the wound, and ordered the man to hospital; the patient was gradually getting worse, and so much so that the Rev. Father Goulding, who had been watching him from the commencement, considered it his duty to administer the last rites of the Church, and to send for Dr K.I. O'Doherty, who promptly attended, and immediately scarified the hand so deeply that the man lost a pint of blood. Brandy and ammonia were then administered, and the man, supported by others, was compelled to walk up and down the verandah. Stupor again, however, came on, and it was found necessary for a period of an hour to strike him with a heavy whip across the back to prevent his going to sleep. The man was then left in charge of Mr Heeney, the house surgeon, who remained with him for the night. I have seen the man three times, and I believe him quite recovered. There are so many quack remedies suggested for snake-bite, that when a really serious case occurs, it is only fair to the public to inform them how it has been treated and the results.

One of the first people whom O'Doherty met when he arrived in Ipswich was Father William McGinty, the Catholic priest. McGinty had come to Ipswich in 1852, nine years before the arrival of Bishop Quinn in Brisbane. During this time the priest had almost become a law to himself. His superior, Archbishop Polding in Sydney — Ipswich was then part of New South Wales — had paid one visit to see McGinty but for all practical purposes was a long distance away and the priest had much scope to develop his own independence. He not only attended to the religious needs of his flock but also directed their electoral activities, often spending the day at the polling booth on election day. However, in his own way, he was a vigorous pastor and had raised over £7,000 ($14,000) from which John Petrie was paid to build St Mary's Church in 1859. The erection of the church did not absorb all the funds and there was a balance of over £1,000 ($2,000). McGinty and his two fellow trustees, Patrick O'Sullivan, a member of the

CHURCH OF ST. ANDREW,

WESTLAND-ROW, DUBLIN,

this 31st day of Augt 1881,

I Certify that Kevin Izod Dougherty Son of William and Anne Dougherty was Baptised according to the rite of the Catholic Church, on the 21st day of Sept A.D. 1823, *Twenty three* Sponsors being John Dougherty and Annabella Gale as appears from the Baptismal Register of the United Parishes of St. Andrew, St. Mark, St. Peter, and St. Anne, kept in the Church of St. Andrew, Westland-row, Dublin.

Patrick J Brennan
Curate of said Parishes.

O'Doherty's baptismal certificate (St Andrew's R.C. Church, Dublin)

Eva O'Doherty, c.25 years *(Poems "Eva of the Nation",* 1909)

O'Doherty, c.25 years
(Monica Carroll, Dublin)

"Lisdonagh", Headford, Ireland, home of John O'Flaherty, Eva's maternal grandfather. (Photograph by David Burke)

Ivy House, Headford, Ireland, Eva's birthplace (Photograph by David Burke)

Royal College of Surgeons, Dublin (Courtesy of Patrick Logan, Dublin)

John Martin, Young Irelander, close friend of Kevin and Eva O'Doherty (National Library of Ireland)

William Smith O'Brien, leader of the Young Irelanders (National Library of Ireland)

Daniel O'Connell, the Great Liberator
(National Library of Ireland)

Elm Cottage, Oatlands, Tasmania, O'Doherty's first residence as ticket-of-leave holder (National Trust of Tasmania)

No. 50

Downing Street
1 April 1834

Sir

At the instance of the Secretary of State for the Home Department I transmit to you herewith a conditional Pardon which Her Majesty has been graciously pleased to grant to William Smith O'Brien, John Martin, and Kevin Izod O'Doherty

Pardon

Lieut. Gov'r Sir W'm Denison

Prisoners

British Government's advice to lieutenant-governor of Van Diemen's Land of the conditional pardon granted to O'Doherty and other exiles (Public Records Office, Kew, Surrey, UK)

Prisoners of the Crown in Van Diemen's Land, and I have to instruct you to give these persons the immediate benefit thereof. —

  I have the honor to be
   Sir
  Your Most Obedt. Servant
   Newcastle

Queen Street, Brisbane, c.1867 when the O'Dohertys arrived (Oxley Library)

Eva O'Doherty, c.40 years (Courtesy of Caroline Nesbitt)

O'Doherty aged 59 (Australian Medical Association, Qld)

Brisbane Hospital in the 1870s (Oxley Library)

William O'Doherty, graduate in dentistry, aged 23 years (Courtesy of Caroline Nesbitt)

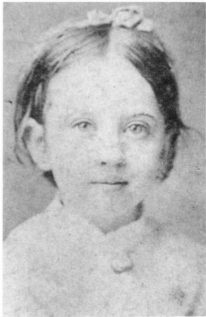

Gertrude O'Doherty, aged 8, only child to survive her parents (Courtesy of Caroline Nesbitt)

Dr William Hobbs, with whom O'Doherty was involved in a bitter dispute over the treatment of psychiatric patients (Australian Department of Health)

Dr John Thomson, who, as a young house surgeon, accused O'Doherty of being too drunk to operate (Royal Brisbane Hospital Archives)

An artist's impression of the former St Stephen's Church and St Stephen's Cathedral, Brisbane (Brisbane Catholic Archives)

Dr Kearsey Cannan, defended by O'Doherty when charged with lax administration at Woogaroo Asylum (Australian Medical Association, Qld)

Bishop James Quinn, whom O'Doherty loyally supported in many controversies (Brisbane Catholic Archives)

Invitation card issued to Kevin O'Doherty jun. on the conferring of the freedom of the city of Dublin on his father (Courtesy of the late Mrs A.G. Melhuish)

Eva O'Doherty c.75 years (*Freeman's Journal*, Sydney)

"Frascati", elegant O'Doherty home and professional rooms in Ann Street, Brisbane (Oxley Library)

O'Doherty c.75 years (*Freeman's Journal*, Sydney)

Rented cottage at Rosalie, Brisbane, where Kevin and Eva O'Doherty spent their last years (Photograph by Ross Patrick)

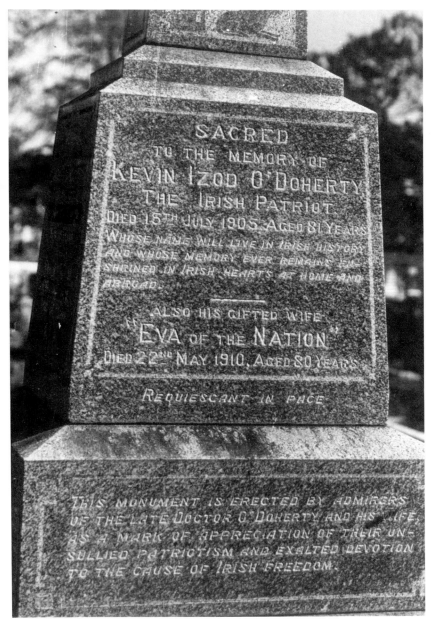

Inscription on the O'Doherty memorial in the Toowong Cemetery (Courtesy of the late Dr Garth May)

Caroline Nesbitt, great-great-granddaughter of Kevin and Eva O'Doherty (Family collection)

Queensland Legislative Assembly and Christopher Gorry, a member of the Ipswich Municipal Council, agreed that the remainder of the funds should be used to build a convent for a religious order which they hoped to attract to their city, and to purchase an organ for the church.

Bishop Quinn, believing that he should be involved in all that was going on in his diocese, claimed that he should have access to the funds. The trustees, suspecting that the bishop would endeavour to transfer the money for use elsewhere, refused his request.

The dispute was at this stage when O'Doherty arrived in Ipswich. In the events which followed, O'Doherty demonstrated the strong support that he would give the bishop over the next twenty years. Central to the current dispute and many more which were to follow was Quinn's absolutism. He believed that his policies should be accepted without question and his dictates obeyed to the letter. Threats to refuse sacraments to any who disagreed were frequently made and often carried out. In all public disputes, particularly when the laity was involved, O'Doherty was the bishop's staunch ally.

Bishop Quinn's reaction to the refusal of the trustees to hand over any monies was to make arrangements to remove McGinty from Ipswich. When this intention became known, the Ipswich Catholics petitioned his lordship not to continue with the proposal. The bishop went to Ipswich to reply to the petition. After he had celebrated mass at St Mary's Church one Sunday in May 1862, he detained the congregation to announce his strong denial of any intention of misusing the building fund. He also made it very plain that "interference between a bishop and his clergy was neither Catholic nor seemly". Smarting under the refusal of the government to grant him financial assistance under the Grammar Schools Act to build a Catholic Grammar School, the bishop then accused Christopher Gorry of having "been guilty of a scandal on his co-religionists" by accepting an appointment as trustee of the proposed Ipswich Grammar School. Under the threat of excommunication Gorry had already resigned the position.

Then followed a series of meetings at which O'Doherty

played the role of peacemaker and strong advocate for the acceptance of the bishop's wishes. In July 1862 Reverend Scully, Quinn's vicar-general, who had been sent by the bishop to take McGinty's place after the Ipswich priest had been relieved of his duties, clashed violently with "Paddy" O'Sullivan at a meeting after mass. When it appeared that the dispute between the two men might progress to physical action, O'Doherty "stood up to speak, which diverted attention of the excited people" and proposed that a deputation wait on Father McGinty who was still opposed to the bishop's requests. The proposal was accepted and the meeting concluded peaceably.

With McGinty still holding firm, another meeting was held a month later, at which O'Doherty, one of the main speakers, said that, "Unless Catholics are prepared to support the Bishop in preference to Father McGinty, they may as well turn Protestants, for they will no longer be Catholics. The Bishop has been charged with acting in too severe a manner with Father McGinty, but having known him for several years, I believe that if he has one fault more than another it is that of being too mild . . .." He then proposed the following resolution which was carried unanimously — "That, realising to its full extent the pain indicted upon the Bishop by such an act of disobedience, we hereby tender to His Lordship the expression of our respectful sympathy, and at the same time beg to assure him of our determination to assist, so far as is in our power, in carrying out any measures he may deem necessary to vindicate his authority as the chief pastor and administrator of the church in this district."

Through the vigorous efforts of O'Doherty and other members of the congregation the dispute was finally settled in Bishop Quinn's favour. Gorry had provided no trouble. O'Sullivan, who had denounced "new-chum priests who attempted to interfere with the liberties of their flocks" was antagonistic for some months but was eventually reconciled with the bishop. It was McGinty who suffered most. Up till this time, his stipend, in accordance with legislation, was paid by the government. Bishop Quinn advised the authorities that McGinty was no longer an officiating clergyman and his stipend was stopped. However, moves were made to have the matter debated in parliament and Dr Challinor, not a Catholic, but a champion of civil liberties, moved that the salary be restored. The motion was carried unanimously. Towards the end of 1863, McGinty officiated again at St Mary's, but, soon after, he was transferred to Rockhampton and later to Bowen.

O'Doherty's next public support for his bishop came in 1864 during the bitter debate relating to state aid for denominational schools. The Queensland Board of General Education, created under the Primary Education Act, ceased to give financial aid to non-vested schools (schools whose property was not vested in the government and included denominational schools) which had been paid by the New South Wales government before separation.

The Anglican bishop, Edward Tufnell and the Catholic Quinn joined forces — some called it an unholy alliance — and held mass meetings in the populated areas of the colony. After meetings at Dalby, Drayton and Toowoomba the bishops came to Ipswich to speak at the School of Arts on a Tuesday evening in October. Not long before the meeting was due to commence, the secretary, fearing that violence might erupt among the excited hundreds who had gathered, advised the mayor, who had convened the meeting, that the premises were not available.

When the deferred meeting took place the next evening in the open, O'Doherty took his place among the speakers on the temporary platform and moved the first resolution — "That, as all indiscriminately contribute to the public revenue, out of which the education grant is voted by Parliament, the grant should, in the opinion of this meeting, be so administered as to allow all to partake of its advantages; and that such grant is at present not so administered." At times there were heated verbal exchanges and loud interjections and the meeting ended in disorder.

The bishops' crusade was criticised by most of the newspapers — the *Northern Australian*, a pro-Quinn journal, being an exception. The *Brisbane Courier* predicted that, "The agitation is likely to share the fate of others of a similar character, and to die a natural death, unregretted, except by a few prelatial devotees." This, however, was not the outcome. Later the Board of Education amended its regulations so that those non-vested schools, who conformed to the new measures, received a subsidy towards salaries and books.

As to be expected O'Doherty soon assumed a significant role in Ipswich Irish community affairs. At the 1863 St Patrick's Day banquet in proposing a toast to fellow colonists who hailed from "Old England and north of the Tweed" he said:

> I assert but a truism when I say that the best and dearest interests of Ireland have long been sacrificed at the shrine of religious strife — no blight more emasculating ever fell upon any country. Fruitful in resources — rich in all that contributes to the greatness of other countries, it yet presented the sad spectacle of a land from which people were obliged to fly in despair from famine and disease. That this state of things has resulted from the working of the fell spirit of sectarian rancour, no Irishman present will, I think deny. Our Scotch and English friends, who at home so readily dispose of the fact of Irish distress by attributing it to defects in the character of the people, have but to follow those people to any of the English colonies to be convinced of the injustice they have done them. There is no impartial man who will not admit that the high qualities displayed by the working portion of the Irish colonists speak trumpet-tongued in their favour, as showing them to be well fitted, if allowed fair play, to prosper in their own land . . ..

An Ipswich "occasional correspondent" to the *Brisbane Courier* claimed that O'Doherty had "proved by his own argument that the best use to put an Irishman to was to expatriate him for his country's good".

In September 1863 O'Doherty strongly supported a move in Ipswich to raise funds to send to Dublin for the erection of a monument to honour the memory of Daniel O'Connell, the Great Liberator. Speaking at the initial meeting, O'Doherty said that, "No son of Ireland is there who will not be anxious to say something in favour of O'Connell, and especially no one who, like myself, had been one of the recruits of the great man, and fought with him in his last battle for freedom." The former member of the Young Ireland movement made no mention of that movement's disagreement with O'Connell. The Ipswich modest total of £67 ($134) was added to the £8,000 already in hand from which the monument, which stands in O'Connell Street, Dublin, was erected.

O'Doherty's name was often mentioned in the press in connection with events outside his profession, his church and the Irish community. His voluntary services in fighting a fire in the town — there was no fire brigade — were praised by the *Queensland Times* in these words: "Dr O'Doherty and his assistant, Mr Fitzgibbon, greatly distinguished themselves in passing buckets of water to the fire."

The most important public event to take place in Ipswich during this period was the opening of the first railway line in Queensland. The government, after much debate, decided that the settled areas of the south-west section of the colony should be connected by rail and that as river steamers were providing adequate public transport between Brisbane and Ipswich, the line should extend westward from Ipswich and not towards the capital city. Lady Bowen, the wife of the colony's governor, was invited to turn the first sod for the new railway on 25 February 1864. O'Doherty was one of a number of the town's leading citizens who each contributed a guinea to a fund to provide extra facilities for the function, above those provided by the government and the Ipswich corporation. At a ball held in the School of Arts to celebrate the occasion O'Doherty was a steward. Seventeen months later when the first section of the line, from Ipswich to Bigge's Camp (Grandchester) was officially opened on 31 July 1865, O'Doherty was an official guest and again a steward at a second ball attended by the governor and Lady Bowen.

During their sojourn in Ipswich, Eva seldom put pen to paper. In the relatively small town there was little intellectual stimulation. Like most other wives of professional men at this period she occupied her spare time by attending meetings of the Ipswich Ladies' Benevolent Society and similar activities. While in Ipswich she gave birth to two more babies. John Paul was born at Forbes Terrace on 30 June 1862 and Jeanette Marie Annunciata also came into this world at Forbes Terrace on 22 February 1864. Kevin and Eva were saddened by the deaths of both babies in the first year of life — the little girl at

Little Ipswich, to which western suburb the family had shifted in 1864. During the 1860s the infant mortality in Queensland was 140 per 1,000 live births — one baby in seven died before reaching its first birthday — with infectious diseases being the main killer. The death of two babies in one family — even a doctor's family — was not surprising.

By the middle of 1865 O'Doherty had decided to move to Brisbane. There were probably two reasons for the shift. The dispute between Bishop Quinn and Father McGinty had been settled and the doctor's strong support would be invaluable to the bishop closer to the headquarters of the church, and secondly, O'Doherty, having professionally conquered Ipswich, wished to try his hand in the capital city.

CHAPTER 7

Member of Parliament

People wishing to travel from Ipswich to Brisbane in 1865 still had two means of transport from which to choose — river steamer or road coach. The paddle-steamer, *Settler*, commissioned for this service in 1863, was vying with the *Ipswich* for popularity with passengers wishing to make the journey by water, while other river steamers, plying for cargo, such as the *Brisbane*, the *Amy*, and the *Emu* also had provision for a few passengers. For those desiring to travel by road, John Nolan's coach left the North Star Hotel, Ipswich, at 6 a.m. and 2 p.m. daily for Brisbane. (Later in 1865 Cobb & Co. took over Nolan's run.) With the road improved, the O'Dohertys may have travelled by coach and sent their furniture and heavy baggage by steamer. If they did Kevin and Eva would each have paid 8s. (80 cents) for the journey and alighted at the Prince Albert Hotel, South Brisbane. As their destination was a house at the corner of George and Turbot Streets, North Brisbane, from which Kevin would practise, a horse-drawn cab would then have taken them over the temporary iron-bark wooden bridge spanning the Brisbane River which had been opened, only a few months before, on 24 June 1865 by Governor Sir

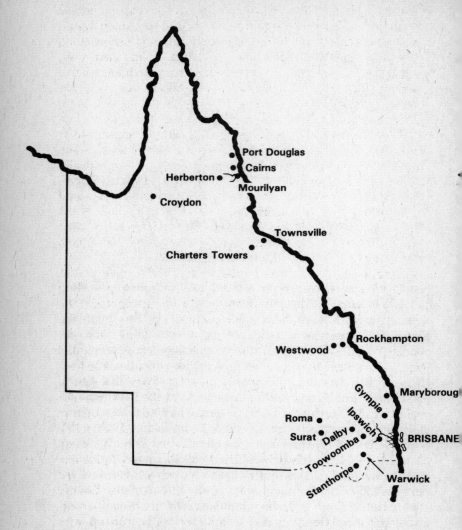

QUEENSLAND. Showing places mentioned in the text.

George Bowen. In addition to carrying traffic, the temporary bridge would serve as staging from which workmen would erect a permanent iron bridge. However, the first bridge stood only until November 1867 when one of its spans gave way, followed by the collapse of other sections a few months later. A permanent bridge, named the Victoria Bridge, was not opened until 1874.

The buildings which comprised the city of Brisbane were a mixture of stone, brick and wood roofed with shingles, slate or galvanised iron. Some were substantial structures, some roughly built and most were of one storey but occasionally two- or three-storey edifices were to be seen. In Queen Street, the main thoroughfare, new brick shops with plate glass windows were replacing old buildings as well as being built in the empty spaces left by the disastrous fire of December 1864 which destroyed fifty premises between George and Albert Streets including two banks and three hotels.

There were reminders of the convict era. The former convict barracks were being put to good use including providing accommodation for the young Queensland parliament. On the rise where later the General Post Office would be built, the former female factory, having served first as a jail, was now housing a police office. In other city streets commercial and public buildings were being erected among private residences. The city boasted a few gracious homes. Dr Hobbs had returned to his elegant home in Ann Street where the first governor had lived until an appropriate Government House was built in George Street near the botanical gardens. Other fine residences were beginning to dot the landscape on Wickham Terrace and in the nearby suburbs of Kangaroo Point and Milton. However, many of Brisbane's 13,000 inhabitants lived in substandard accommodation which the *Brisbane Courier* described in 1864 as "paltry humpies, which are neither airtight nor water-tight in floors, walls or roofs, run up with frailest materials, and partitioned off into what are called rooms that will hardly afford space for a cat to jump . . .".

The Anglican church, consecrated in 1854, stood on a site which would later become part of Queen's Park in George

Street. The Roman Catholics worshipped in their church in Elizabeth Street, which, when it was being built in 1850, the *Brisbane Courier* said would be an ornament to the city. Ann Street was the site of a Presbyterian church but in William Street Dr Lang's Evangelical Chapel had long since become a telegraph office.

The Board of Education was continuing its programme of building national schools, having completed the Normal School (from the French, *école normale* — a school for training teachers) at the corner of Adelaide and Edward Streets in 1862. Meanwhile the two bishops, Quinn and Tufnell, were still conducting their denominational schools. There were no public secondary schools but several private establishments were willing to provide appropriate education for young ladies and gentlemen. New additions of a library and reading room for the School of Arts established at the corner of Queen and Creek Streets had been completed. Thirty-five hotels provided for the thirst of the inhabitants and often served as meeting places for various organisations.

The Brisbane Municipal Council, created in 1859, was converting former bush tracks into reasonable carriageways by cutting down trees, filling holes and reducing hills, thus making it possible for the heavy-laden horse and bullock drays to pass. When the O'Dohertys arrived in 1865, Turbot Street was being extended up to Wickham Terrace to create a thoroughfare, which would link up with Edward Street later. Shopkeepers in Queen Street were joining forces for the watering of the road surface in dry weather and bridges in Queen and Elizabeth Streets made progress possible over the waterway in Creek Street.

So far the council had made no attempt to tackle the serious problems of drainage and sanitation. During downpours of rain the water followed the natural channels, often causing severe flooding to shops and houses in the city's main streets. Some of Brisbane's citizens were availing themselves of the services of private nightmen to empty their cesspools; others buried the nightsoil on their premises while some, living near the river, still emptied excreta down its banks.

Soon the ponds in Roma Street, on which Brisbane had depended for its water since the beginning of the convict era, would be replaced by the Enoggera reservoir. If O'Doherty wished, he could, along with other inhabitants, advise the Brisbane Gas Company to connect his house to the gas supply soon to be available.

Both the Queensland government and the Brisbane Municipal Council were erecting important buildings. The foundation stone for Parliament House had been laid on 14 July 1865; the Government Printing Office in William Street had just been completed and a three-storey Immigration Depot was nearly finished not far away. Up near the jail on Petrie Terrace new military barracks were being built and Brisbane's first Town Hall in Queen Street was almost ready for occupation.

It was into this Brisbane that O'Doherty transferred to practise his profession. At first there were not many patients and newspaper reports suggest that the doctor was deliberately making public appearances to make himself known. His name was included among those specially mentioned as attending the half-yearly meeting of the Queensland Steam Navigation Company whose ships sailed to Sydney, Queensland ports and up the river to Ipswich. He was listed in January 1866 as one of a number who had contributed to the Lying-In Hospital in Leichhardt Street, Spring Hill. In the next month he and his friend Bishop Quinn were among those mentioned as having accepted the invitation of the Board of the Water Commission to inspect the progress of the building of the Enoggera Reservoir. Arrangements had been made for an employee to "fire off a salute of petards" during the inspection. Unfortunately, one of the petards exploded prematurely, inflicting severe eye injuries and shattering one hand of the employee. Dr O'Doherty was reported as rendering immediate attention and supervising the transfer of the patient to the Brisbane Hospital. O'Doherty was always willing to travel into the country to attend patients and not long after arrival in Brisbane he gave evidence at an inquiry into the death of an infant at Cleveland whom he had visited after riding from the city. He testified that in his opinion "death had occurred through the child having been overlaid".

At the annual meeting of subscribers to the Brisbane Hospital in January 1866, a decision to increase the visiting staff of two doctors to four was made and O'Doherty applied. During this period such appointments were made through votes of the subscribers — a rather unusual procedure as most of the subscribers had no competence in judging a doctor's professional ability. The *Brisbane Courier* published the names of three applicants for the positions beforehand — Robert Hancock, an English graduate who had come to Brisbane in 1861, Thomas Temple, also an English graduate who had arrived in 1863, and O'Doherty. The subscribers had time to make inquiries, and the doctors, if they felt inclined, to lobby the subscribers. Dr Temple gained nineteen votes, O'Doherty seventeen votes and Dr Hancock only two votes. Apparently the reputation O'Doherty had gained in Ipswich had reached Brisbane and during the five years Dr Hancock had been in the city he had not made many friends. Dr Temple died a few months later and his place was taken by Dr Bancroft who, in ten years' time, would gain world renown by being the first to discover the adult worm which causes the disease, filiariasis.

O'Doherty had only a short distance to walk from his home at the corner of George and Turbot Streets to the hospital to attend his duties as visiting surgeon every fourth week. The hospital was being conducted in the buildings erected by Patrick Logan, commandant of the penal settlement, in 1827 for a convict hospital on the site where later the Supreme Court was established. A civilian committee had taken over the buildings in 1848 and commenced accepting patients the next year. A full-time house surgeon, assisted by an untrained staff, provided medical attention for the indigent sick under the direction of the visiting staff.

In the early 1860s the committee considered that the George Street hospital had outgrown its usefulness and with this the government agreed. The committee suggested two possible sites for a new hospital — Green Hills (Petrie Terrace) and York Hollow (Gilchrest Avenue). The government, however, had already instructed the colonial architect, Charles Tiffin, to prepare plans for a hospital at The Quarries, Bowen Bridge Road and when the committee protested, advised that body that the government would "be happy to relieve the committee from all connection with the hospital". In reply, the committee said it did not have "any power to remove itself of the responsibility" and accepted the position. At the time of O'Doherty's appointment as visiting surgeon, John Petrie was making good progress with a two-storey, four ward, stone hospital on the Bowen Bridge site. When the new hospital, which most inhabitants claimed was too far from their homes, was opened in January 1867, O'Doherty and the other visiting surgeons either rode out on horseback or drove in their sulkies for which a carriage shed and stables had been provided.

Soon O'Doherty shared with Dr Hugh Bell the honour of being Brisbane's leading surgeon. However, they were still performing external surgery only — removing stones from the bladder, performing amputations, removing cancerous breasts and treating diseased bones. They were using inhalation anaesthesia but many of their patients were dying from sepsis. There were no pathology tests, no X-rays, no blood tranfusions and no antibiotics. While the pharmacopoeia contained numerous drugs, most were ineffective — exceptions being morphia, tincture of digitalis, quinine and silver nitrate. In the 1860s the hospital committee rented a house on Petrie Terrace to accommodate convalescent colonial fever patients, causing much consternation among nearby residents. The colonial fever — probably typhoid — was the forerunner of disastrous epidemics of intestinal diseases which ravaged the colony over the next few decades.

Meanwhile O'Doherty was building up a large private practice. At the end of 1866, while still living at the corner of George and Turbot Streets, he took rooms in Edward Street next to the Normal School. By August 1867 his practice had increased sufficiently for him to take in a partner — Dr Stephen Burke, another Irish graduate. However, the partnership did not last long. In April 1868, Burke moved to Gympie where gold had been discovered a few months before. In view of O'Doherty's attraction to the mineral, it was a move that the senior partner probably fostered and envied. He, no doubt, wished he could have gone with Burke to try his luck on the field. O'Doherty did not restrict his professional interests to the Brisbane Hospital and his private practice. In view of his special training in obstetrics at the Coombe Maternity Hospital, Dublin, he offered his services to the Queensland Lying-In Hospital (later the Lady Bowen Hospital) founded in 1864 in Leichhardt Street, Spring Hill. He served for several months but pressure in other fields restricted his attendance on a routine basis. However, his services were often used in difficult cases — an indication of his expertise in this branch of medicine also.

Very shortly after Sir George Bowen took up his duty as Queensland's first governor, he endeavoured to give the colony protection by forming a defence force. In view of the absence of legislative power, the force had to be a voluntary one. Due to the apathy of the community and the volunteers themselves, adverse criticism of the press and the lack of government financial support, the venture was not a success in the early years. In 1867, however, there was renewed interest and at a meeting of eighty aspiring volunteers it was decided to form a Brisbane Volunteer Rifle Corps. The volunteers elected their own officers and three doctors, proposed as surgeon to the corps, indicated their willingness to serve in that capacity. They were O'Doherty, his fellow Brisbane Hospital visiting surgeon, Joseph Bancroft, and a relative newcomer to Brisbane, Theo Byrne. When a ballot was taken, O'Doherty received fifty-six votes, Bancroft twelve and Byrne eleven votes. So the former Irish rebel, who had been found guilty under the Treason Felony Act of "compassing to levy war against Her Majesty the Queen," was now an officer in the defence force of one of her colonies — albeit a volunteer force to which he was elected by the members themselves. O'Doherty's duties with the "Frog Hollow Rangers", as the rifle corps was sometimes derisively called, were not onerous.

It was not long before O'Doherty was playing an important role in the activities of the Roman Catholic Church. In a few years he became a prominent layman and then for almost two decades he was the leading Catholic outside the clerical hierarchy. His advice on medical matters generally, as well as his personal medical attention, were accepted gladly. Bishop Quinn and the Sisters of Mercy who came to Queensland with the bishop were the main recipients of O'Doherty's services.

But O'Doherty served in other ways as well. The autocratic Quinn trod on many toes among his priests and the laity. Whenever he could, O'Doherty gave the bishop strong support. Only once, when the doctor was nominated a trustee of the Brisbane Grammar School, was there a difference of opinion between the two men. Often when opprobium was heaped on the bishop, some spilt over to O'Doherty, but his public demonstration of his loyalty continued unabated. Mother Whitty, superior of the Brisbane Sisters of Mercy, wrote back to the order in Dublin advising that their doctor was Dr O'Doherty, brother of the dentist in Dublin. She went on to extol his virtues and outline the many ways in which he was helping her with the problems she faced.

In 1858 John Petrie had built for Dr George Fullerton a solid, two-storey, brick house on two and a half acres (one hectare) of land on Duncan's Hill between Ann Street and the Brisbane River. When Dr Fullerton decided to move to a sheep property in the Maranoa district, 300 miles (480 kilometres) west of Brisbane in 1863, Bishop Quinn acquired the house for the Sisters of Mercy, four of whom became trustees, for a convent and school, to which the name, All Hallows, was given. The purchase price was £6,000 ($12,000) and Fullerton demanded ten per cent interest on any unpaid principal. The Order had difficulty in meeting the interest and by 1866 none of the £6,000 had been paid.

O'Doherty was one of a number of Catholics who met the Sisters of Mercy to discuss informally the means by which the debt could be paid. This was followed by a formal meeting on 22 April 1866 over which the bishop presided. At this meeting O'Doherty moved that, "This meeting sees with regret that the debt which the Sisters of Mercy were obliged to incur in purchasing the house and land known as All Hallows Convent and, at present occupied as such, remains still unpaid; and is of the opinion that the community to whose services the lives of the Sisters are devoted, would, if appealed to, promptly relieve them of that liability." His resolution was carried unanimously.

A system of collection was planned and O'Doherty, William Murphy, Alderman Donovan and several priests formed an organising committee of which O'Doherty subsequently became secretary. Mother Bridget Conlan, in her memoirs held at All Hallows' archives, gives the credit for this campaign to "Mr Randall McDonnell, one of Dr Quinn's missionary party, and Dr Kevin Izod O'Doherty".

O'Doherty took every opportunity to publicise the collection campaign. When Archdeacon McEncroe, who had come from Sydney, was invited to lecture on the Benevolent Institutions of Australia, O'Doherty chaired the function. "Before the meeting dispersed, the chairman drew attention to the fact that the debt of All Hallows was still unpaid. He hoped an effort would be made to provide the ladies who occupied it — he meant the Sisters of Mercy — with all they required, which was a house to live in, as they were quite willing to maintain themselves in other respects." A correspondent to the *Brisbane Courier*, "Catholic", was not enamoured of O'Doherty's support for the proposal. He wrote:

> Dr O'Doherty was not slow in taking advantage of a Brisbane audience . . . in appealing to the generous sympathies of the Irish heart . . . to subscribe five or six thousand pounds for the purpose of buying Dr Fullerton's house for the Sisters of Mercy . . . to purchase a shapeless structure with low ceilings, small rooms, and, the principal accommodation in the attic . . . . Let the doctor who seems to be the oracle of this new subscription advise them to abandon that expensive establishment, take a cottage for the present, and ask the public to subscribe a sum of £3,000 for a brick convent on some cheap eligible site . . . .

In his opposition "Catholic" was a voice crying in the wilderness. He was also astray in his description of "Adderton", the name Dr Fullerton had given his home. When the house was built, the *Courier* said, "The rooms are large, well-lighted and lofty, and every modern appliance has been adopted."

In Brisbane, twenty teams of collectors were given districts into which the city was divided and from whose residents they were expected to solicit subscriptions. It was not a propitious time for such a financial drive as the colony was facing a grave economic crisis. The Agra and Masterman's Bank had failed and the Queensland government proposed to issue unsecured notes, a scheme which Governor Bowen would not approve. When the subscriptions to the liquidation fund were published in the press, O'Doherty's team had surpassed all others. O'Doherty himself was accredited with £17.10s. ($35). It was a personal donation — not a sum collected from others. With individual subscriptions ranging from one shilling from the poorer classes to £5 ($10) from the governor, O'Doherty's donation was a truly generous gift. In addition, his wife, Eva, collected £3 ($6) from her friends.

The money raised by the collection campaign did little to reduce the principal of £6,000, for it totalled only £391. Mother Vincent then persuaded the bishop to allow her to conduct a bazaar and art union. The *Brisbane Courier* had this to say about the prizes donated:

> The buggy has been ordered from the establishment of Bennett and Edds who have promised it will reflect credit on its builders and those concerned in the grand drawing. The engraved cross is on view at Messrs Flavelle Brothers and is most creditable to that firm. The suite of drawing-room furniture, when seen will prove that Brisbane is not behind even London in such works. The Irish poplin dress, as worn by the Princess of Wales and the Limerick shawl have arrived.

When Governor and Lady Bowen arrived at the School of Arts to open the bazaar on 24 September 1867, they were met by "Bishop Quinn, several of his clergy, Honorable George Harris and Dr O'Doherty". This time Eva played a more active role than her husband by conducting one of the many stalls at the bazaar.

The total receipts from the bazaar and the art union were over £3,000 ($6,000) and when heavy expenses were deducted, the All Hallows debt had been reduced to approximately £4,000 ($8,000). An anonymous benefactor arranged to take over the remaining debt, charging the order a more reasonable interest of 3 per cent. Further functions in the following years finally freed the Sisters of Mercy of all debt and the campaign of which O'Doherty was one of the main initiators concluded successfully.

The Irish doctor was associated with the Sisters of Mercy in another public service — St Vincent's Orphanage. The orphanage first functioned in Terrace Street, New Farm but was soon transferred to Nudgee Beach. The following extract from Mother Bridget's memoirs tells of these early beginnings:

> The children in Terrace Street arrived there in December 1866 in a bad condition with ecsema [sic] and had to undergo Dr O'Doherty's sulphur treatment. The result was a new skin from top to toe. [The condition was probably scabies for which sulphur was often used with satisfactory results.] Unhappily every newcomer introduced an epidemic and when doctor found measles had arrived he required the sisters and the children should be quarantined .... Sr M. Columba Griffin was sent in charge with Sr M. Catherine Cotham catching measles, whooping cough and pneumonia. Sr M. Catherine departed this life at All Hallows Convent on 18 July 1868.

The first time after their arrival from Ipswich that Kevin and Eva went to worship at the Roman Catholic church in Elizabeth Street, they noticed that the little building was overcrowded and many worshippers were obliged to stand outside in the cold westerly winds blowing at the time. They also noticed completed foundations for a much larger edifice on adjoining ground — the proposed St Stephen's Cathedral.

Steps towards the erection of the cathedral had been initiated by Bishop Quinn and his parishioners in October 1863., when a meeting of the church hierarchy and influential Catholics had agreed to raise money for the project by an organised system of collection. The foundation stone was laid by the bishop on 26 December, St Stephen's Day. In a description of the plans the *Brisbane Courier* said that the cathedral, in which the architectural style to be used would be a combination of early English and French Gothic, would, on completion, be a credit to the denomination who would worship there and would embellish the city. In July 1864 a further report stated that the foundations had been completed but building progress was punctuated by quiescent periods when work was at a standstill due to lack of funds. Then came the financial crisis which crippled the economy throughout the colony, and the efforts to liquidate the debt owing on All Hallows placed a further burden on the Catholic community.

A revival of activity came in 1867 and O'Doherty headed a subcommittee of five supporters to examine the current position. Later in that year the press published a list of recent subscribers and, as in the case of the All Hallows fund, the doctor had contributed liberally. He continued his generous support and the records of collections in the Brisbane archdiocesan archives show the O'Dohertys contributed 10s. ($1) per week — 2s.6d. (25c) each for Kevin and Eva and 1s. (10c) for each of their five children (fundraising continued until St Stephen's was opened in 1874 — the O'Dohertys had by then had another child).

For many years in early Brisbane the days of the patron saints were declared public holidays and most inhabitants, who were free to do so, took part in some recreational activity — a trip down the Brisbane River to Moreton Bay, a picnic in some favourite spot on the outskirts of the city or taking part in or watching organised sport. Newspaper reports of the period indicate that St Patrick's Day was popular with most of the inhabitants, and not only those of Irish origin joined in the activities. In the evening the Irish community held their banquet. For many of O'Doherty's early years in his new city the Brisbane organisers followed the Ipswich Irishmen's example by inviting him to respond to the toast of "Our Fatherland". In all such speeches he spoke eloquently, made a tilt at the English, plucked at the hearts of his fellow-countrymen and displayed his wide knowledge of history. At one of the first banquets he attended in Brisbane he said:

> Although by a very practical order of mind, patriotism, in its loftiest sense, might be looked upon rather as weakness than an ennobling sentiment — like an obsolete article of *vetera*, to be classed with other interesting relics of antiquity — yet I am still of the opinion that even in this nineteenth century, despite political economists and grasping capitalists, men of "prudence and common sense", the spirit is yet alive, which animated the men of Marathon and Thermophylae, which gave England a Hampden, Scotland a Bruce and Ireland a Grattan and an O'Connell . . ..

> Ireland, indeed exercises an imperial power over the hearts of her children, and can they wonder at their devotion when they call to mind her ancient story, full of interest and genius and contrast it with her modern history of misery and humiliation . . . . Ireland possesses treasures that, in the eyes of thoughtful and learned men, entitle her to respect and admiration.

O'Doherty by no means restricted his activities to those connected with his profession, his church and his native land. Almost from the time he arrived in Brisbane his name appeared in the press, attending public meetings and being elected to various organisations, often as a member of the controlling committee. In August 1866 he was accepted as a member of the Philosophical Society — the forerunner of the Royal Society of Queensland — and in the following month, when the annual meeting of the Queensland Turf Club was held in Tattersall's rooms, he became a member of the club's committee. At the New Year's Day meeting at Eagle Farm the doctor was one of the stewards. In reporting the winter races of 1867 the *Brisbane Courier* said that it was fortunate that Dr O'Doherty was on the course to give immediate attention to a jockey who was injured when his mount, The Prince of Wales, known for bolting propensities, fell in the Champagne Handicap.

The medical profession in the developing colony was held in high esteem — a status which had begun with the fine standard of care given by the surgeon-superintendents of the migrant ships coming to Queensland from the British Isles. A number of these doctors settled in the colony along with the migrants whom they attended during the voyage and the respect for them continued. Members of the medical profession were also among the few in the colony who had received a university education and this was another reason for the community's high regard of its doctors. It was an esteem in which O'Doherty, of course, shared. The Irish doctor was also regarded by many as a loyal British subject, for on 24 May 1866 and 1867, the day being Queen Victoria's birthday, he had donned morning dress and top hat and paid homage to the British Crown by attending the levees given by His Excellency, Governor

Bowen. It was a practice that O'Doherty continued during the rest of his active career in Brisbane.

But Kevin Izod O'Doherty was an Irishman who had taken part in the 1848 rebellion, had been convicted of treason felony and transported to Van Diemen's Land. Were there any in the community, ardent loyalists, who kept these facts in mind and therefore harboured ill-feelings towards him? O'Doherty in his St Patrick's Day speeches said he believed that the English and Irish could live in harmony. But he also alluded to past wrongs which he believed England had committed against the Irish. Although he had modified his attitude towards the repeal of the Union of England and Ireland, he advocated that his native land be given the type of government which the colonies enjoyed. There were probably some Brisbane inhabitants who harboured ill-feeling towards him on account of his earlier rebellious activities and his Irish nationalism as well as for his religious beliefs.

The press kept the England-Ireland question alive by repeating the news of Fenian activities which the editors read in the English papers which arrived regularly in the colony. The *Brisbane Courier's* own opinion was given at intervals in editorials. On 9 December 1865 that paper said:

> Of all the delusions that have dazed the sanguine and impulsive sons of the Emerald Isle, none, surely has been so preposterous or so contemptible in its inception, progress and results as that of the "Fenian Brotherhood" . . .. What is it that the Irishmen want and are likely to gain by rebellion at this date? What are the wrongs that have been inflicted upon them and that they are called upon to redress?

The editor then went on to say that many Irishmen were strongly opposed to the Fenians and mentioned that, "Recently, an eminent Irishman, Charles Gavan Duffy, who has learned in Australia, the error of his ways during his early career in Ireland, has returned home for a brief sojourn; and he will doubtless improve the occasion by enlightening his fellow-countrymen upon the futility and wickedness of rebellion."

In January 1866 the same paper pointed out that the Fenian movement was more serious than at first believed and in doing so referred to the uprising in which O'Doherty had taken part:

> It was stated that the Fenian uprising was more contemptible and called for less notice than the Chartist affair of 1848, when a handful of unarmed "patriots" defied the hosts of England in Widow Cormack's famous cabbage garden at Ballingarry, but ended by succumbing to a few policemen. We now hear, however, that the movement is exciting grave apprehensions in Great Britain and elsewhere.

In 1866, collections were made in Australia to assist families of Fenian leaders arrested in Ireland. In Ipswich, Patrick O'Sullivan, who had been a member of Queensland's Legislative Assembly until 1863 and a key figure in the Quinn-McGinty dispute during O'Doherty's time in that city, acted as treasurer for the collections made there. The *Brisbane Courier* commented on his actions and then alleged that there was Fenian plotting in the colony:

> Whilst Mr O'Sullivan may be looked upon as one very much interested in any agitation raised by his countrymen at home, we can hardly reconcile the fact of his having once been a member of Her Majesty's Parliament in Queensland with the position he now holds — only a few years afterwards — that of a collector for a Fenian fund . . ..
>
> He should recollect, however, that no matter the number of his professed adherents, he will find to his cost that any attempt he may make in respect to the encouragement of a popular demonstration of Fenianism will be crushed in this colony. Movements have lately come under the cognizance of the police, which however much they be disbelieved by the general community, are based upon facts. There is at the present time a force being organised, in connection with rebels at home, the object of which — though not as yet openly ventilated — is sufficiently well known to warrant the attention of the Government being directed to it. Night drills are held and various quarters have been appointed for the gathering of Queensland Fenians . . ..

In the months that followed the colonial press kept the subject alive by continuing to report the clashes between the Fenians and the authorities in Ireland.

It was in this social and political climate that approaches were made to O'Doherty to allow himself to be nominated as a candidate for one of three seats for North Brisbane in the forthcoming election for the Queensland Legislative Assembly in 1867. When it was announced that the former Irish rebel had accepted, there was no question by the press as to the possibility of his being an unsuitable candidate on account of his participation in the 1848 rebellion or for his later expressions of Irish nationalism (as O'Doherty had been granted a full pardon he was eligible to stand for parliament). Apparently the *Brisbane Courier* thought that the doctor, like Gavan Duffy, had seen the errors of his ways. There was no suggestion that, like O'Sullivan of Ipswich, he had a tendency towards Fenianism; no suggestion that he was taking part in night drills or gathering with the Queensland Fenians. However, one correspondent raised the possibility that due to his religion he might press hard for more state aid for non-vested schools.

At this period in Queensland's history there were no political parties, as were formed later, to select and support a candidate. The first step towards securing a seat in the Assembly was the written invitation signed by a number of electors to the proposed candidate requesting him to allow himself to be nominated to represent their interests in the House. The candidate replied stating his attitude to what he thought were the important issues. This correspondence was published in the press and the candidate then mounted an individual campaign with the help of a few friends. Nomination was made on the hustings a day or two before polling day. The elections for the various electorates were not held simultaneously and it was possible for a candidate defeated in one electorate to stand for another electorate in which voting had not yet taken place. The franchise was based on property, but, as many of the working class met the prescribed conditions, it was in practice close to adult male suffrage. As yet women had no voting powers.

In his answer to a "numerously signed requisition", O'Doherty addressed himself to government spending, the land question and immigration. He claimed the previous government had "outrun the stable" and involved the colony in a load of debt which should not have been incurred. He would "give his warm support to any measure calculated to confine spending strictly within legitimate income". At a time when many were claiming that at least pastoralists' lands should be made available for agriculture the doctor advocated that the land between the coast and the Main Range and along the new railway on the Darling Downs should be available for agriculture and defined the remainder as "the true inheritance of the flock-masters". This latter suggestion was not one that would endear the aspiring candidate to the squatters, some of whom were a strong force in the young colony's parliament. The doctor believed that a restoration of a land order system to migrants instead of assisted passages would secure a better class of settler and would place less strain on the treasury. Again, this was not a provision to which the squatters would take to kindly as they would most likely be unwilling to sacrifice land for such a purpose.

The press took up the question of the subject of state aid to religion, on which O'Doherty had been silent. There would be a need for the doctor to state his position on this before polling day particularly as he was a Catholic and a close ally of Bishop Quinn who had fought a hard campaign for restoration of state aid to denominational schools. From correspondence in the *Brisbane Courier* it appeared that it was a subject on which other electors wished to hear O'Doherty's intentions.

O'Doherty delivered four campaign speeches — at the Logan Hotel, Kangaroo Point, at the Sir John Young Hotel, Spring Hill, the Royal George Hotel, Fortitude Valley and at the School of Arts in Queen Street. His views on state aid were given at his first meeting in these words:

> It has been assumed that there is danger that if elected I will go into the House as a tremendous bugbear in favour of state aid to religion. A generation ago when I was a young man with hot blood in me, I was mistaken enough as some supposed, to risk my life and lose my liberty in an attempt to secure civil and religious liberty for my native country. After some time, when an amnesty was granted me, I returned to my native country, and I can candidly tell you I could not remain there. I had seen the effect of civil and religious liberty in Australia, and I determined to come out and settle among you. It is not likely that I came out with a desire to impose fetters, the existence of which compelled me to leave my own country. I

am totally opposed to state aid to religion and will be as long as I remain in the colony. I believe, in the church to which I belong, we do not require state aid and we are well enough able to support our own church without assistance . . . . With regard to education under the present system, I hold that the question was settled some years ago. There was then a great agitation which has totally died away, and the main cause of it has disappeared. That is, that the non-vested schools, which are prepared to conform to certain regulations receive the same support as those under the Board, and therefore to my mind it does away with the principal objection which was then raised. [In 1864, the Board of Education, after first having given no aid to non-vested schools, commenced to give some financial support towards salaries and books to schools which conformed to the Board's regulations.]

With no opinion polls like those which appeared in the twentieth century the electors relied on the press for predictions of the outcome of the election. The *Brisbane Courier* surveyed the chances of eight candidates likely to nominate for the North Brisbane electorate. The paper expected two of the sitting members, T.D. Pugh and W. Brookes, to be returned — the third, G. Raff, was retiring from politics. Of the other six candidates the paper said that, "Dr O'Doherty has pretty well worked up the electors, and from the first meeting at Kangaroo Point to the last one at the School of Arts, appears to have carried them by storm." Mr Pritchard was expected to run the doctor close if he did not beat him.

Great interest was taken in the elections and about 1,000 assembled at the hustings to assist in the nominations. The eight candidates addressed the gathering. O'Doherty "good humouredly revised the claims of all the other candidates and concluded by advising the crowd that by way of getting rid of their embarrassment amidst a choice so rich and varied to 'call in the doctor' ". In later years O'Doherty claimed that he was nominated by an Englishman and seconded by a Scot.

When the inhabitants of Brisbane went about their business on polling day they were surprised and shocked to see placards in the streets, spitefully worded against O'Doherty and read in the press two advertisements — one, the official announcement urging the electors to vote for the doctor and the other reading:

VOTE FOR O'DOHERTY
and
CLASS REPRESENTATION!
CLASS LEGISLATION!
STATE AID!!!
and
DENOMINATIONAL EDUCATION
Queenslanders!!!!! Beware of
Wolves in Sheeps' Clothing

The polls closed at 4 p.m. and counting commenced immediately. With a small number of voters the result was known by 6 p.m. when "there could not have been less than two thousand present". The returning officer, Mr Halloran, declared the state of the poll as follows: T.D. Pugh, 635; K.I. O'Doherty, 615; A.B. Pritchard, 603; W. Brookes, 439; J.M. Shaw, 256; W. Coote, 68; C. Campen, 56; T.M. Smythe, 36. With three representatives required, Mr Halloran declared Pugh, O'Doherty and Pritchard duly elected. Around 4 p.m. the doctor had been called to visit a patient at Oxley, travelling by horse and sulky. Returning to the city well after 6 p.m. in the dark he called to the driver of a vehicle going the other way, "How did the election go?" Back came the answer in a North of Ireland brogue, "Bad enough, that bloody papist, O'Doherty got in." It was a tale the doctor often related.

Although three representatives were required it was not compulsory to vote for three candidates. In a review of the election it was officially announced that 210 electors had voted for O'Doherty only — "plumper votes". One source claimed that had such a procedure been illegal and the O'Doherty "plumper" voters forced to vote for three candidates then Brookes would have most likely beaten O'Doherty. Brookes was one of the migrants brought out by Reverend John Dunmore Lang and with his supporters shared the reverend gentlemen's hatred of Catholics. Of course the argument was purely academic and O'Doherty had been fairly elected.

On 6 August 1867 the westerly winds stirred up the dust as O'Doherty walked along George Street to take his place in the thirty-two-member Legislative Assembly still sitting in the old convict barracks in Queen Street. Charles Bernays in this *Sixty Years of Politics in Queensland* referred to the Irish doctor's entry into parliament in these words, "The Third Parliament met on 6 August 1867 and here we find for the first time, the genial medico, Kevin Izod O'Doherty, member for Brisbane. No man was better known in his day." Practice demanded that the "Address in Reply" to the speech with which the governor had opened parliament be used to give at least one or two members an opportunity to make a maiden speech. Accordingly O'Doherty delivered his first speech in the Assembly by seconding the "Address in Reply". The *Brisbane Courier* commenting on his efforts, said, "O'Doherty made a creditable maiden display and those who elected him, need have no fear of his being found on the wrong side when their interests are concerned, and the division bell rings."

While there were no political parties in the modern sense in Queensland in the 1860s, many writers suggest that there was a sharp division between the squatters on the one hand and the town members on the other — town liberals. The position was not as clear-cut as this for there were factions within both groups and members, including some leaders, changed sides at a whim, often to secure a ministerial post. Further, any member supporting the government who did not vote against it often was considered to have no political courage. In these circumstances, O'Doherty decided that, at first, he would be an independent and sit on the cross benches.

In the debate on the "Address in Reply", Pritchard, one of the North Brisbane members, believed to be a supporter of town interests, defected to the opposition, thus bringing about the defeat of the government, led by Arthur Macalister, on the floor of the House and shortly afterwards the ministry resigned.

A public meeting — such meetings were popular in this period — was held to consider the resignation of the ministry and the part that the Brisbane representatives played in the events leading up to it. Pritchard was condemned for his defection, but O'Doherty was praised by none other than the Baptist parson, Reverend B.G. Wilson, who said that "he highly approved of the conduct of Dr O'Doherty in that debate, and he had laid his constituents under a lasting obligation which they would not soon forget. The sentiment which he gave utterance to, to let bye-gones be bye-gones was the best sentiment which was uttered during the debate." The doctor had begun his political career impressively.

CHAPTER 8

A Public Man

One of the measures introduced by the new "pure merino" government led by Robert Mackenzie, who had replaced Arthur Macalister as premier, was the Prevention of Contagious Diseases Bill, which had as its object the reduction of venereal disease. Its provisions included the compulsory medical examination of prostitutes and the detention in hospital for a period of up to six months for those found to be suffering from such a disease. Detention could be extended and penalties for offences against the legislation included imprisonment. There was no provision for action against males who frequented brothels or who suffered from venereal disease.

O'Doherty, who supported the bill, gave his reasons for doing so in typical O'Doherty language, reported in Hansard as follows:

> He [O'Doherty] must confess that for more than a year past, from professional experience in Brisbane, he had been well convinced of the necessity that there was for passing a measure of this kind — the absolute necessity there existed for it, and that, on highest moral grounds. There seemed to him to be no doubt whatever, that

with the last section of immigrants that came from the old world into this colony, there came also a species of contagious disease of this kind that was rapidly infecting every young man in the colony. He had no hesitation in stating that at this moment, there was stalking about in this town as frightful a form of venereal disease as there was in the world. It was stalking abroad amongst those unfortunate females unseen and unknown to those who had dealings with them, or to anyone. It was a dreadful form of disease, though it was quite possible to be cured; and those unfortunate women were walking centres of the most frightful disease to which the human body could be subject.

The bill became law in 1868 and for over forty years opinion on the measure was polarised. While O'Doherty and his fellow legislators saw nothing wrong with the double standards demonstrated in the legislation, there were many in the community who thought differently. Several womens' groups, holding that the statute degraded their sex, petitioned parliament for its repeal. They found allies in the churches who formed a "Social Purity Society". One correspondent to the press used language as colourful as O'Doherty to express his opposition — "Let the above Bill become law so that the accommodation shall be kept clean for the patrons of the brothels. Then, they can violate every moral and social law with safety while they wallow like swine in animal indulgence and gratify their craving for the seduction of the more innocent creatures of the weaker sex."

The debate waged for half a century but finally the abolitionists won their battle when, in 1911, John Elkington, Queensland's second commissioner of Public Health, convinced his minister that the Act was not having the desired medical effect and the proclamation of the Act in Brisbane was rescinded.

In 1867, four years after the Ipswich Grammar School was opened, definite steps were taken to establish a similar school in Brisbane. The *Brisbane Courier* considered the absence of a grammar school was a disgrace to the capital city and said that "after this lapse of time the discredit is all the greater, and must continue to increase until we set heartily to work to redeem our character, and late though it be, follow the example set us long ago by a town inferior to Brisbane in wealth and population." The paper went on to express gratitude to His Excellency, the governor, Sir George Bowen for his donation of £25 ($50) towards the proposal. The Grammar Schools Act demanded seven trustees be appointed — four government representatives and three elected by the subscribers. When O'Doherty's name was mooted as a likely government appointee, Bishop Quinn was very upset and the doctor received the following letter from Robert Dunne, vicar-general.

> I mentioned to the Bishop this morning that you told me you had been spoken of as a trustee of the Brisbane Grammar School, and that you had an idea of allowing yourself to be so nominated, with a view to be serving the R.C. community whatever advantage that position might confer. His Lordship observed that the decision of the Holy See had rendered it incompatible with the duty of a Catholic to allow oneself to be placed in such a position, that he had no power, even were he so disposed, to dispense with or modify those decisions — that hence Mr Gorry was appointed a trustee of the Ipswich Grammar School, he was obliged to insist on his resignation, and in place of such an appointment benefiting the Catholics in any way it would be injurious to their interests. His Lordship was under the impression that he had communicated to you the substance of the foregoing in a conversation in the Ministers' room but to avoid any mistake he wished me to convey it to you.

There is no record of what next transpired between the doctor and his bishop in what appears to have been the only major difference of opinion during their long association. But O'Doherty persisted in his intention and accepted the appointment in a letter of 5 February 1868 to W. Manning, the under colonial secretary, in which he also stressed the continuing resolve of the Catholics to obtain funds under the Grammar School Act to found their own grammar school despite the previous rejection of many applications.

O'Doherty's appointment as a government representative on the Board of Trustees along with those of T.B. Stephens, C. Lilley and A.B. Pritchard was duly gazetted with the subscribers electing W. Brookes, L. Bernays and R. McDonnell. O'Doherty not only served the first term of three years but was reappointed for a further three years in 1871. The doctor also matched the governor's subscription by generously donating the sum of £25 ($50) himself.

A site in Roma Street, on which later the railway station was built, was chosen for the erection of the grammar school. The foundation stone for the school was laid on 29 February 1868 by His Royal Highness, Prince Alfred, Duke of Edinburgh, son of Queen Victoria, who was paying an official visit to Australia. O'Doherty was chosen from the trustees to read an address to the prince prior to the laying of the stone and later read a scroll on which was inscribed an account of the function taking place. The scroll, signed by the prince and the trustees, together with various coins of the realm and copies of the *Brisbane Courier* and the *Daily Guardian*, was placed in a receptacle and sealed beneath the foundation stone.

Although known for his genial nature, O'Doherty, if he felt strongly about a subject, was not afraid to voice sentiments at a time which some of his listeners considered was inappropriate. One such occasion was the official opening of the Brisbane Grammar School by Governor Blackall on 1 February 1869, approximately twelve months after the foundation stone ceremony. Deputed to say a few words by way of friendly counsel and advice to the boys enrolled at the school, his speech included the following:

> I do not consider myself the right man in the right place. I deeply regret the absence from among us of the men whose province I consider should be to address those words of counsel and advice on this most important and solemn occasion to our young lads. I refer to the dignitaries of the Churches — The Bishops of the Episcopal and Roman Catholic Churches. I am persuaded that I echo the feelings of everyone present when I deeply regret their absence from among us today. I indulge in the hope that the cause of their absence is not of a permanent character. For my part I must candidly confess that I would not have been here if I had thought it would be so . . ..

O'Doherty then went on to say that he hoped that the edifice being opened would be the first of three or four colleges, which, affiliated together, would fulfil not only the educational requirements of the colony but also the religious requirements of every section of the community. He was quite willing to avail himself in the interests of his own boys of the advantages of the school they were inaugurating solely because the time had not yet come when the Roman Catholic portion of the community could avail itself of a similar institution of its own.

Not unexpectedly his remarks stirred up a hornets' nest. The next speaker, Randall McDonnell, felt it incumbent on him to refute the shameful attack made on them by the last speaker and the next day, the *Brisbane Courier* in a scathing outburst questioned the judgment and good taste displayed by O'Doherty. The paper then claimed that Drs Tufnell and Quinn would take all they could get for their own schools, and, until O'Doherty had reminded his listeners of their existence, nobody else thought of them.

Despite the fracas O'Doherty did not change his decisions to continue as a trustee of the school and enrol his boys there. Twelve months before, the boys had been among the first pupils enrolled at the Cleveland national school which was opened at the beginning of 1868. The doctor owned a house in the seaside village at which he often spent the weekends. In the early 1870s the doctor and one of his boys were driving to Cleveland one weekend when his horse bolted. O'Doherty and his son were thrown out but escaped with severe bruising. The vehicle was smashed beyond repair.

After his visit to Queensland in 1868, Prince Alfred had gone back to Sydney. There, on 12 March, an Irishman, Henry O'Farrell, attempted to assassinate the young prince by shooting him with a revolver. The bullet entered the prince's body but struck no vital organ and he recovered. O'Farrell was seized immediately and later executed.

The first news of the attempted assassination suggested that O'Farrell was a Fenian and the *Brisbane Courier* immediately published a tirade against that movement:

> It seems O'Farrell is a Fenian agent and that the curse of the desperate conspirators leagued together under that name, has at length been fairly brought to Australia . . . . There can be no hesitation as to the course which ought to be taken by all peaceable and well-disposed citizens in the face of such facts as we have before us and that is to lose no opportunity of discountenancing in every

possible manner any and every attempt to transplant Fenianism in this land.

The Irish community in Brisbane held a meeting on 14 March which O'Doherty chaired and which passed a resolution which read: "In the opinion of this meeting, it is desirable that the Irishmen in Brisbane and its vicinity should attend the meeting to be held on Monday with a view to giving expression to their sympathy with the Prince on the attempted assassination of His Royal Highness and their detestation of the act then sought to be committed."

The Monday meeting to which the Irish community referred was held on an open space in Queen Street and about 5,000 citizens attended to agree to four resolutions expressing sorrow and regret at the attempted assassination, deep abhorrence of the perpetrator, and that a message of loyalty be sent to the Queen and of sympathy to the prince. O'Doherty was one of the four prominent citizens who proposed the resolutions. In Brisbane thanksgiving services for the prince's recovery were held in all the churches and the inhabitants then put their minds to other business.

In Sydney, however, where Henry Parkes was colonial secretary and feared for his life from the Fenian Brotherhood, a Treason Felony Act, similar to the legislation under which O'Doherty and his fellow Young Irelanders had been tried in 1848, was passed in the New South Wales parliament. Subsequent evidence revealed that Parkes and the *Brisbane Courier* had been mistaken — O'Farrell was not a Fenian.

When the excitement of the attempted assassination of the prince had died down, O'Doherty, along with many citizens, gave his attention to other subjects in which public interest was being shown. Ever since Edward Hargraves had discovered gold near Bathurst, New South Wales, followed by the gold rushes of Victoria, the inhabitants of Moreton Bay settlement, later the colony of Queensland, had been envious of the rich fields in the neighbouring colonies and offered rewards for a similar discovery in their own areas. A small field was discovered at Canoona near Rockhampton in 1858 but soon petered out. Further west, Peak Downs was a small producer for a few years from 1862. Then in September 1867, James Nash discovered a rich field on the Mary River about 100 miles (160 kilometres) north of Brisbane, to which the name of Gympie was given after the Aboriginal name for the stinging tree growing in the area. Access to the new field by road, especially from Brisbane, was difficult. There were two routes — one, traversing Durundur station near Kilcoy and then on through Imbil; the other, nearer the coast, through Maroochy and Caboolture. Both were impassable to drays.

Early in 1868, a committee was formed with the object of having a road between Brisbane and the new field opened to allow horse and bullock drays reasonable passage. O'Doherty, a member of parliament, and no doubt spurred on by the businessmen of the capital city and his own burning interest in the mineral, became its chairman. The committee, which at times met weekly, had no executive power but acted as a pressure group through deputations to ministers, lobbying at every opportunity. In May 1868 came reports of two gangs working on the eastern route — one at the Gympie end cutting through the scrub and another doing likewise at Caboolture where a punt would be required to cross the Caboolture River. In September, work on the road had advanced sufficiently to permit Cobb & Co. to commence a coach run. Soon after it began running, the coach was held up with the passengers being robbed and the mail systematically opened and the notes therein stolen. By November 1868, the coaches were running regularly along the route, leaving Gympie at 6 a.m. one morning, arriving at Maroochy by 3 p.m. and after spending the night there, leaving at 5 a.m. the next morning to arrive at Brisbane at 7.45 p.m. O'Doherty and his committee believed that their efforts had played a major part in this achievement.

In accordance with the practice of the times, O'Doherty, after some twelve months in parliament, met approximately 250 of his electors in the Town Hall to give an account of his stewardship. The main feature of his address was his emergence as a strong opponent of the squatter faction after having sat on the cross benches as an independent. He had now become a true town liberal. He claimed that he had no hostility to the squatters as a class but their advent to power was an unmitigated evil. They did not conceal their contempt for the agricultural interest; the Brisbane Bridge and the railway were laughed at and consigned to the wastepaper basket, and their efforts to provide a passable road between Brisbane and the Gympie goldfield were almost negligible. He dwelt for some time on Pritchard's defection causing the government to fall and gave an account of events in the Legislative Assembly since his entry to parliament. A motion that "This meeting has heard with satisfaction the address of Dr O'Doherty and hereby expresses its renewed confidence in him as one of the representatives of the city" was carried unanimously. However a press critic, who was not present at the meeting, believed that O'Doherty's supporters were carried away by the doctor's eloquence. He said:

> Had I heard the doctor's speech instead of reading it I might have been carried away by the grace of his style and enthusiasm of the moment. The doctor has the faculty, which few of his countrymen who attempt oratory are wanting in, — to talk to a crowd . . . but I confess at being disappointed. The honourable gentleman did not take up public questions — the necessity for increased representation, immigration, railway extension, the bridge to be built . . . .

Shortly after parliament met for the first time in the new Houses of Parliament on 4 August 1868, the Mackenzie government was forced to resign and another election was held. After some indecision as to whether or not his medical practice prevented his giving sufficent time to political duties, O'Doherty decided to stand again. In his campaign addressed to the electors, written in typical prose and published in the press, the doctor again expressed opposition to the policies of the squatters, and this time tackled those subjects which he had been accused of avoiding in his report to the electors a few weeks previously. He advocated the raising of loans to extend the railways and urged increased European immigration. The *Brisbane Courier* saw fit to devote an editorial to O'Doherty's address, agreeing with his policy but criticising his style:

> The tendency of the Milesian mind to the poetical and imaginative is generally acknowledged, and the doctor is the Milesian of the Milesians. When he delivers a set speech or issues a lengthy address it is evident that he commences with two objects in view: the first, a desire to express himself very decisively about men and things, but at the same time to keep on good terms with all parties; the second, to be as brief and as matter as fact as the occasion will permit. In compassing these two objects he seldom succeeds. Before he gets very far his vivid imagination begins to take sportive liberties with his good resolutions and his common sense and gradually bears him away into the realm of fancy; his sketches become more lively in colouring — warmer in tone; his imagery more striking, and his whole style of expression rather ornate and considerably inflated.... A slight dash of it would greatly embellish the Gradgrind phraseology of some of our public men or the colloquial vulgarisms in which others indulge when trying to be particularly forceful. Neither can we quarrel with the doctor's address as a whole. For the most part they are the sentiments of the entire Liberal party and accord with our own.

O'Doherty again polled well and easily retained his seat. "Plumper" votes were much fewer than at the previous poll and there was no suggestion of any of the candidates being returned unfairly. The returning officer declared the poll as follows: S. Fraser, 586; K.I. O'Doherty, 558; T.D. Pugh, 558; W. Coote, 174; E. Lewis, 40.

After a few days of uncertainty, Charles Lilley formed a government and the town liberals expected a better deal. This was not to be. Following changes to his original ministry, Lilley included two Darling Downs squatters, Arthur Hodgson and James Taylor in his team, thus causing resentment among his supporters. It was the beginning of an unhappy term.

One incident which did not brighten the public scene involved the management of psychiatric patients. During Queensland's first decade as a colony, patients suffering from psychiatric illness fared badly. Prior to separation, such patients were sent to Tarban Creek Lunatic Asylum in New South Wales, but when Queensland's first governor, Sir George Bowen, approached his counterpart in the southern colony, Sir William Denison, for a continuation of this arrangement, his proposal was rejected. With no alternative accommodation available, the colony's lunatics, as such patients were called at the time, were admitted to the jail on Petrie Terrace. In unsatisfactory, crowded conditions, the mental patients mixed freely with the criminals. In 1865 they were transferred to Woogaroo Asylum, built reluctantly by the government. At Woogaroo, the forerunner of Wolston Park Hospital, the patients were under the care of Dr Kearsey Cannan who had been appointed surgeon-superintendent. Cannan was a lax administrator and during his term the custodial care of the patients was often harsh. After a number of inquiries which exonerated Cannan, a civil service commission in 1869 reported reprehensible treatment at Woogaroo, but suggested that there were mitigating circumstances.

When the commission's report was debated in parliament, O'Doherty, who had been appointed an official visitor to the institution at the beginning of 1869, defended his medical colleague by blaming the colonial secretary's department for depriving the asylum of medical comforts. Hansard reported part of his speech as follows:

> Again he [O'Doherty] came across an unfortunate patient suffering in the last stages of dysentery — scarcely any life in him. This was a case in which medicine and medical aid were urgently required to save life. The only medicine that would have benefited him was good port wine. He asked the surgeon-superintendent how much wine was given to the patient daily. "My dear sir", said the superintendent, "I have not been allowed to have wine in the place for patients. Medical comforts are not allowed; they were stopped long since; and the only medical comforts I am allowed are vinegar and some other few things [he named] . . .."

O'Doherty's pleading did not save Dr Cannan who was dismissed, with Dr Henry Challinor giving up his well-established practice in Ipswich to take his place. A parliamentary select committee, with the Honourable Arthur Palmer as chairman and O'Doherty as its only medical member, was appointed to inquire into the asylum. The committee recommended extensive amendments to the Lunacy Act but when the legislation was altered the only change was a provision for the establishment of reception houses to which patients in the early stages of mental illness were admitted. These, too, would be the centre of another controversy in which O'Doherty was involved.

As was the case with many members of parliament, O'Doherty was approached by individuals and groups to present petitions to the Legislative Assembly. In May 1870 he presented a petition on behalf of the oystermen of Moreton Bay who requested that legislation be introduced to control their industry. It was a subject which O'Doherty approached with great enthusiasm. In conjunction with the portmaster, Captain Heath, he framed a bill during a parliamentary recess, which provided for the division of Moreton Bay into twenty-six areas for each of which a five-year lease was granted to the highest bidder, giving him the sole right to farm the oysters growing there. The preparation and the delivery of his introductory speech gave the doctor great pleasure. The following is an extract:

> To many honourable members the idea of legislating for that little mollusc, the oyster, was a source of great pleasantry but he thought . . . if they would recollect how intimately it was connected with those joyous periods of their youth when "the feast of reason and the flow of soul" were so kindly if not rapturously associated with feasts of oysters and the flow of brown stout, they would be inclined to regard more generously than they did, the efforts he proposed to make to protect that delicate and delicious mollusc.
>
> Medical men never fail to find in the oyster a grateful and agreeable remedy for the wasting of the sick and the weakness of the convalescent and perhaps the capriciousness of both . . . . He held in his hand, *Pliny's Natural History*, and that distinguished author wrote this of the properties of the oyster — "Oysters are slightly laxative to the bowels, and boiled in honeyed wine, they relieve tenesmus — Calcined oyster shells, mixed with honey, allay affections of the uvula and of the tonsillary glands . . . . Beaten up in a raw state, they are curative of scrofula and of chilblains of the feet".

In later years, particularly when the legislation was being amended, O'Doherty's oyster bill and its introduction were referred to with affection.

On a more sombre note, O'Doherty, now the senior of the three North Brisbane members, led his colleagues in a move against Lilley, premier, and more importantly their leader in the Legislative Assembly. Lilley, so full of promise, well-educated, vigorous, eloquent and a would-be reformer had continued his disastrous course. He was in almost continuous dispute with his ministers, and while acting in his professional capacity as a barrister, imprudently accepted a brief as counsel for a squatter, named McDonald, who had sued the under-secretary for Lands over a disputed land lease. In another unwise step he arranged, while he was in Sydney, an order for three ships for a proposed government shipping line despite the objections of his treasurer, T.B. Stephens.

In February 1870, O'Doherty and his parliamentary colleagues, Fraser and Edmonstone, called a public meeting ostensibly to render an account of their stewardship during the previous session of parliament. Their speeches, however, were devoted to enumerating the shortcomings of the government, attacking the ministry and Lilley in particular. They were acting as a party within a party — a "ginger group" as it were. In later years, had they belonged to a political party, they would have faced expulsion. They were "town liberals" and O'Doherty was treasurer of the Liberal Association which Lilley had revived just prior to separation. But, in the political scene of the times, they felt no allegiance to the man they had at first supported and the steps which they took did not attract any censure.

The meeting, held in the Town Hall on a hot February night in 1870, "in the absence of anything like sufficient ventilation", attracted an audience of 700. O'Doherty, who spoke first, said that when the "pure merino" ministry was replaced by Lilley's government there were high hopes but these were soon dashed. The government's record was a history of violated promises; of conduct weak and vacillating, when an honourable discharge of their duties called for bold and decisive action; winding up with a chapter of unconstitutional acts, which if tolerated, would practically bring responsible government to an end in the colony. While blaming the ministry as a whole for this state of affairs he was particularly critical of Lilley:

The gravest offender he thought was their old friend, Charles Lilley. By his personal folly he allowed his name, and with it the honour of the premiership of the colony, to be dragged in the mire . . . whilst by his political inconsistency, his lawyer-like duplicity, and gross betrayal of his pledges, he had proved himself utterly unworthy to lead the popular cause. The truth was, as many gravely foretold, he was yet too young to have been elevated to so high a position. Like many others he had not yet sown his wild oats . . .

The *Brisbane Courier* agreed with O'Doherty's assessment saying:

> There can be no doubt that Mr Lilley has proved himself unfit for the position of Premier . . . the meeting last night, we venture to state, ought to have the effect of removing from the mind of His Excellency any doubts he may have felt as to the propriety of calling to his counsel, as representative of the Queen, a new, or reconstructed body of advisers at a time when Parliament is not sitting.

Governor Blackall took no action but when parliament met on 26 April, Lilley was humiliated by having to move the Address-in-Reply himself — a task generally undertaken by newly-elected members. Soon afterwards, Joshua Peter Bell, member for Northern Downs, moved a vote of no confidence in the government. Lilley later resigned and Arthur Palmer replaced him. But Palmer's control was shaky and a dissolution and another election followed. O'Doherty's criticism at the public meeting had acted as a catalyst for these events.

In the campaign that led up to the election, the three North Brisbane sitting members joined forces and met the electors as a single group. In O'Doherty's speeches at their meetings he advocated the raising of a loan for the construction of a railway from Ipswich to Brisbane; claimed he favoured free national education; supported a redistribution of electorates and stated that he would vote for the repeal of legislation dealing with the importation of black labour. Professional duties prevented O'Doherty from attending all campaign meetings and one absence was explained by his riding to the Tweed River to attend a man seriously injured by a falling tree.

The ploy of campaigning as a group was not completely successful, for when the poll was declared one of its members, Fraser, was not returned. However, when the returning officer, Arthur Halloran, announced the results, O'Doherty had received by far the highest number of votes of all six candidates — gaining 746 votes with a new member, Ratcliffe Pring, coming second with 615 and George Edmonstone polling 543.

Despite his heavy political commitments, O'Doherty was by no means neglecting his medical practice and there were several press references to his professional prowess during the early months of 1870. An account in January referred to his amputation of the forearm of a sugar-mill worker from Logan River, whose limb had been drawn into the rollers during cleaning operations. A few days later, the press reported an accident to Frank Glynn Connolly, a prominent Gayndah pioneer, while he was travelling between Sandgate and Brisbane. Drs O'Doherty and Mullen "properly set Connolly's fractured thigh but symptoms of cerebral congestion developed themselves and the unfortunate gentleman expired". In its 9 April issue the *Brisbane Courier* announced that "a very important operation was performed at the hospital by Dr O'Doherty assisted by other members of the medical staff. Several pieces of bone were excised from the principal bone of the arm of a girl named Agatha Sullivan, aged fourteen years. The operation was most successful and the patient is now doing well."

O'Doherty was the medical attendant of many prominent citizens and was often called in consultation by other members of the profession. During 1870, Governor Blackall developed a serious illness from which he died on 2 January 1871. He was first attended by William Hobbs, the government medical officer, but O'Doherty and Hugh Bell were called in as consultants. From the outset the medical men realised the hopelessness of the governor's prognosis — a fact that he knew himself. When the funeral procession left Government house in the domain for St John's church in William Street, the three medical attendants walked behind the clergy and ahead of the hearse. The governor was buried in the new Toowong cemetery on the top of a hill — a site which he had chosen himself.

O'Doherty's interest in medicine went beyond the clinical aspects of his private and hospital practice. It spread over the whole range of activities in which the profession could be involved. Mindful of the time spent during his convict days at St Mary's Hospital, Hobart, where Dr Bedford conducted his embryo medical school, later recognised by the College of Surgeons, O'Doherty strove for similar arrangements to be extended to the Brisbane Hospital when consideration was given to a candidate's application for membership of the college.

In 1870 Charles Lilley introduced a university bill into parliament which provided for a system of examinations in Queensland, the passing of which would entitle the successful candidates to degrees awarded by London and other universities in Britain. In the ensuing debate, O'Doherty claimed that he had proposed bringing in a short bill himself with a view to enabling students to avail themselves of the opportunity to studying the profession of medicine in the colony, and if Lilley's bill was meant to apply to the medical profession he would support it. He believed that young men (applications from women to study medicine were still frowned upon) had greater facilities in Brisbane for studying for the medical profession than for studying any of the other learned professions. They had in the Brisbane Hospital one of the finest institutions of its kind in the colonies, and there were gentlemen here capable of giving as good a course of instruction as they could get at home in England or Ireland. Despite O'Doherty's enthusiasm nothing emerged from the legislation, but he did not lose heart and would pursue the proposal vigorously in the years to come.

During her first years in Brisbane Eva appeared to be a happy and dutiful mother and housewife. In July 1867, she was a member of a ball committee endeavouring to raise money for the Brisbane Hospital, and in December of the same year she was among the married ladies of Brisbane who presented a valedictory address to Lady Bowen on the eve of her departure from Queensland with her husband, the colony's first governor. Eva also helped husband Kevin in the drive to liquidate the All Hallows debt by collecting from her friends and conducting her stall at the convent bazaar.

In her home Eva was a busy mother with four boys aged from five to nine years when they first arrived in Brisbane. On 9 March 1866 she gave birth to a baby girl, Eva Mary, but once again the O'Dohertys were to be saddened by the loss of an infant when the new baby died a few months later. The family moved to a larger house on the Mary Street corner of George Street in August 1868 and no doubt Eva was fully occupied with the move — even though the distance had not been great — and in setting up a new home.

But Eva was never really content in Queensland. She often longed for Ireland and particularly for Killeen and her family. She was writing little now. The stimulus of the days of rebellion were, of course, gone and further poems revealing nostalgia for her native land would be dull repetition. She still corresponded with her close friend of the days in Paris, John Martin. In one letter, written at their seaside house at Cleveland, she sent him a photograph of the four boys, but the correspondence contained no discussion of serious subjects. Two letters from Martin, in 1866 and 1867 respectively, dealt with news of his family and their mutual friends. In one, he mentioned the state of the Catholic church in Ireland and the Fenian question, but there was no attempt at character analysis nor any reference to Eva's ambition as a writer — the subjects so much canvassed in their letters a decade previously.

Unlike Eva, Kevin fitted into life in his adopted city quite comfortably. One paragraph in Martin's correspondence confirmed for him that his decision to leave Ireland was the correct one. Martin had written that, "The clergy seem about to destroy the Catholic religion in Ireland in their zeal for the English. Among the educated there are no Irishmen who actively sympathise with the mass of the people of their own country. God help the poor Fenians, who are now breaking stones in the jails of England or pining in the jails in Ireland."

After five years in Brisbane, at the age of forty-seven,

O'Doherty was one of the colony's eminent citizens. In the medical field he was a leading surgeon, and in addition to holding a post on the visiting staff of the Brisbane Hospital, had been appointed to the Medical Board of Queensland. In an uncharacteristic decision he declined this last appointment apparently because members of the medical board received no remuneration for their services. However, some years later, he accepted such an appointment.

He was the leader of the Irish community and the Catholic laity. The results of three polls he had contested demonstrated his popularity among the electors, and in parliament he was held in high esteem by all members. Despite the fracas he had caused at the opening of the Brisbane Grammar School, O'Doherty had remained a trustee and was proud of his boys' achievements in the examinations at the end of 1869. O'Doherty 2 (Edward) had been awarded a special Lilley medal for distinction in Latin and English. A certificate of merit was awarded to O'Doherty 1 (William) for Latin while O'Doherty 4 (Kevin) received honourable mention for his efforts in the rudiments of English, Arithmetic and Latin in Form 1. By this time O'Doherty had become very much a public man.

CHAPTER 9

Many Irons in the Fire

In the early 1870s O'Doherty's keen interest in a wide range of endeavour continued, with politics and the medical profession absorbing much of his time. In one of his first significant actions when parliament met after the 1870 election, he initiated steps towards the establishment of a museum in Brisbane. He proposed that £300 ($600) be placed on the supplementary estimates for 1871 for the formation of a free library and museum. Referring to a large number of mineral specimens collected by government geologists, he suggested these be displayed in a room over the parliamentary library. His original motion was amended by reducing the amount to £100 and deleting the idea of a library. O'Doherty accepted the amendment "on the grounds that half a loaf was better than no bread". In the middle of 1871, C. D'Oyley Aplin, a former geological surveyor, began the task of classification of fossil and mineral specimens in Queensland's first museum — two rooms in Parliament House.

After the Southern and Western Railway was opened with its initial line from Ipswich to Grandchester, it was first extended westwards to Toowoomba and points to the west and south of that town, but not eastward towards Brisbane. Transport between the capital city and Ipswich still depended on river steamers and road coach and bullock drays — a situation with which Brisbane citizens were not satisfied. In 1869 a Railway Extension League was formed and a deputation waited on Premier Lilley to press claims for extension of the line to Brisbane. The League also advocated that, in the 1870 election, support be given only to those candidates who favoured the proposal. O'Doherty, of course, gave the extension his full support. Support also came from businessmen and settlers on the Darling Downs. Inhabitants of Ipswich, at first, strongly opposed the extension. Later, however, they changed their minds in favour of an extension with a terminus at Victoria Point or some other site on Moreton Bay, thus bypassing Brisbane.

At the end of the 1870 parliamentary session, O'Doherty was instrumental in the appointment of a royal commission to inquire into the extension after lobbying had prompted both Houses to agree to a select committee examining the subject. The *Brisbane Courier*, in acknowledging O'Doherty's role in this move said, "Dr O'Doherty did not believe in the question being shelved by being referred to a select committee and it is to him we are indebted for the appointment of the Commission."

When the composition of the commission was announced O'Doherty was one of eight members appointed and Captain H.G. Simpson, MLC, its chairman. Despite his heavy commitments to his medical practice, the doctor attended most of the twenty-eight sessions of the commission, some of them being held in Ipswich and Toowoomba. The commission's majority report was tabled on 2 May 1871 with five members, including Simpson and O'Doherty, agreeing to the opinion that the proposed line would absorb two-thirds of the river traffic, attract traffic from other areas, and, if carried out in an economical and judicial manner, would not entail any additional financial burden to the colony. Dissenting members of the commission were John Scott (Leichhardt) and William Walsh (Maryborough) — both representing electorates well away from Brisbane — and Thomas Prior from the Legislative Council.

O'Doherty, in presenting the report to the Legislative Assembly, moved "That in the opinion of the House, the time has arrived when such extension be carried out". When O'Doherty spoke to his motion on 11 May there was a full attendance of members and the gallery was crowded. After a long and surprisingly tedious speech by the doctor, John Scott, a dissenting member of the commission, moved an amendment that a committee be formed to consider the feasibility of extension of the Northern Railway, which connected Rockhampton to Westwood, further west to Expedition Range. Then followed a vigorous debate lasting late into the night when it was adjourned to the next sitting day.

Meanwhile on the afternoon of 15 May, 2,500 Brisbane citizens met at a public meeting, held on vacant ground in Queen Street next to the School of Arts, over seventy of the city's major business houses being closed during the meeting. A resolution was passed to petition parliament asking for the extension to be undertaken. It was presented to the Legislative Assembly by O'Doherty.

Back in parliament the railway extension debate lasted another two sitting days, being concluded with the defeat of O'Doherty's motion by sixteen votes to fifteen. Both O'Doherty and Scott were appointed to the latter's proposed committee but no action ensued. Then, a second royal commission of which Scott was chairman, but which did not include O'Doherty in its membership, was appointed in January 1872 to examine railway construction generally in the colony. This time one of its recommendations was that the extension to Brisbane should be commenced immediately. Later in the year the Railway Department invited tenders for 500 navvy's barrows and for the erection of a post and rail fence in lengths of one mile upwards along the proposed route. It was a signal that the work would begin.

On 30 July 1873 the river steamer, *Kate*, left Brisbane with 300 passengers, and the *Francis Cadell* followed with 400 more, who would witness the Marquis of Normandy, Queensland's third governor, turn the first sod on the new line at a picturesque spot near the junction of the Brisbane and Bremer Rivers. Almost two years later, the first train carrying passengers destined for Ipswich left Brisbane at 6.30 a.m. on 15 June 1875, with the passengers having to cross the Brisbane River at Indooroopilly by punt, as the bridge had not yet been completed. It was not until 6 July 1876 that passengers could cross without leaving their train.

Another general election was held in July 1871 but the three members for North Brisbane, O'Doherty, Pring and Edmonstone, were returned unopposed. However voting was necessary in most electorates, including Maryborough where the sitting member was William Walsh, minister for Works. O'Doherty and his fellow Catholics in Brisbane were amazed when their attention was drawn to a letter, which had appeared in the *Maryborough Chronicle* of 14 July 1871 signed by Paul Tissot, a French Roman Catholic priest who had come to Queensland with Bishop Quinn. In his letter, Tissot solicited support in the forthcoming election "for that candidate who has hitherto served us so faithfully [Walsh]".

At a meeting of Brisbane Catholics in the Town Hall to consider Tissot's action, O'Doherty pointed out that the majority of Catholics in the colony coming from their native land had felt the curse accruing from religious intolerance in Ireland, and had come to Australia because, under free institutions here, no man would dare question their religious opinions. He feared that such indiscretions as Tissot's letter would pit against them the majority of their Protestant fellow colonists. However, he excused Father Tissot as he was almost unacquainted with the English language. The meeting unanimously agreed with a resolution proposed by O'Doherty:

> Resolved that we, Roman Catholic colonists of Queensland, yield to no other class in the community in our desire to uphold in its integrity the free constitution under which we enjoy the blessings of religious liberty; and we hereby declare that we shall at all times deem it our first duty to resist any attempt to restrict that liberty come from what quarter it may.

Whilst O'Doherty was, no doubt, genuinely concerned with the effect that the patent canvassing of votes by a Catholic priest might have, similar charges would be made against the Church for years to come. Further, it must be pointed out that Walsh had opposed the railway extension to Brisbane in the debate following O'Doherty's presentation of the royal commission report, and that O'Doherty had clashed with the minister for Works after he accused Walsh of successfully altering the membership of the commission. It is also pertinent to add that at a banquet held to honour Walsh after re-election, James Horan, another Catholic priest at Maryborough, said that the late member had been again returned against all kinds of political and other influences which had been brought against him.

In 1863, Robert Towns, a southern merchant, who had commenced growing cotton on the Logan River south of Brisbane, had solved an acute shortage of labour by bringing in natives from the Pacific Islands. Soon pioneer sugar planters, Louis Hope at Ormiston near Cleveland and Captain Whish at Caboolture River, also used the Pacific Islanders or Kanakas, as they were called. Thus began a most controversial aspect of Queensland history, which divided political parties and caused acute personal differences among community leaders. The Polynesians, as they were also called — they were in fact Melanesians — were not always recruited peacefully and there were accusations — often with good basis — of murder and kidnapping, and reference to "black slave traffic" and "blackbirding". On some plantations the Pacific Islanders were treated well. On others "they were compelled to quench their thirst as how and best they could, drinking even, on the admission of the manager, from any pool or puddle".

It was not until 1868 that the Queensland government took action by passing the Polynesian Labourers' Act, which prohibited the introduction of the Pacific Islanders without a licence, and demanded a bond that they be returned to their native lands at the end of three years. Later a government agent travelled on each recruiting vessel.

Responding to a "very generally expressed call outside [parliament] that repeal of the Polynesian Labourers' Act was necessary", O'Doherty introduced a bill for that purpose in 1871. His short bill provided that existing arrangements regarding Pacific Islanders already in Queensland be not disturbed and contained a clause repealing the previous legislation. The doctor referred to the disrepute the colony had earned from the trade, and drew attention to evidence of malpractices committed during recruiting. However, the main reason for his advocacy of the repeal of the Act appears to be that the introduction of the Pacific Islanders had restricted immigration from Great Britain, which should have been the main source of migrants.

O'Doherty's bill was not well received, partly due to the polarisation of opinion on the subject already present in the community, and partly because it contained no clause prohibiting the introduction of the Pacific Islanders. It simply dispensed with existing safeguards, and inadequate as they were often found to be, they were of some use. No progress was made after the initiation of the legislation and after it had lain on the table for some months he withdrew it.

The Irish doctor was more successful when, in 1872, he introduced the first public health legislation to be passed by the Queensland parliament. In the young colony priority was given to legislation dealing with land development, the building of railways, mining and education. When health legislation had been introduced in the 1860s it lapsed for lack of interest. However, panic, the handmaiden of pestilence, frightened the parliament into viewing O'Doherty's bill with favour.

In July 1872, ships arrived in Victoria and New South Wales from overseas with smallpox aboard and from these sources the disease was introduced into those colonies. The *Brisbane Courier* of 10 July reported that, "The outbreak of smallpox is creating a panic at Sandhurst [Port Melbourne]. Nine cases have been reported, three have terminated fatally. The school children have been dismissed and the school closed." On the same day, O'Doherty asked the colonial secretary in parliament, "What action the government was taking in regard to press statements that smallpox had broken out in southern colonies?." Colonial Secretary Palmer replied that a government health officer on board the prison hulk, *Proserpine*, anchored off St Helena, would board every vessel coming into Moreton Bay, and there would be no communication with the shore until the health officer had given permission.

The next day, O'Doherty introduced his legislation, hastily copied from a Canadian Act. It provided for the appointment of a Central Board of Health, which it was hoped would take measures to prevent the spread of infectious disease. The Central Board would have no executive power but would promulgate health regulations which local boards of health, appointed by local authorities, would be responsible for implementing. The bill passed without debate — the smallpox scare had demolished any opposition.

In September 1872, a Central Board of Health was appointed, including in its membership O'Doherty and his medical colleagues, William Hobbs, Kearsey Cannan and Hugh Bell. Arthur Palmer, colonial secretary, was ex officio, chairman, and Captain Simpson MLC and Frederick Rawlins were lay members. No smallpox occurred at the time — in fact the only time the disease entered Queensland was in 1913 when five mild cases appeared. The Central Board could not really be given any credit for the absence of cases in 1872.

At the time that O'Doherty's Health Act was being enacted a hot debate was developing in the medical world as to the nature of infection. The "spontaneous generationists" were adhering to their theory that infection occurred after breathing air which contained noxious vapours given off from the putrefaction of organic matter in certain localities — the miasmatic theory of infection. Overseas, the French scientist, Pasteur, was developing the "germ theory" and he would show that the infectious disease only occurred when the specific organisms were transferred from a source to a susceptible individual.

Henry Scott, the registrar-general, in his report for 1872 revealed that Brisbane was an unhealthy place and wrote of overcrowding and the "filth and general neglect of hygienic precautions". He referred to "foetid stagnant gutters in front of houses and equally filthy back premises" from which it was believed that vapours arose causing the "miasmatic deaths" which were twenty per cent of the total deaths occurring in the colony — many of them in children under one year. In speaking of these deaths in young children O'Doherty revealed that at this stage he belonged to the "spontaneous generationists". He said, "Such a rate of mortality . . . is in no way to be wondered at if we take the trouble to walk through the city streets at night, and inhale for a few hours the foul atmosphere such children are doomed to breathe." A decade later he had adopted the germ theory.

The medical men on the Central Board, led by O'Doherty, wanted the powers of the Health Act exercised to clean up the city. Attention to contaminated cesspools, albeit for the wrong reason — to rid the atmosphere of noxious vapours — would have reduced the amount of intestinal disease in the city. But, the Central Board soon learnt that the Brisbane Municipal Council was opposed to the appointment of a local board of health as it believed that its own bylaws were quite adequate and the Health Act did not provide any funds for the proposed board. The government deferred proclamation of the Act in Brisbane until the Central Board advised it in writing in May 1873 that poor sanitation in the city was responsible for the current epidemics of infectious disease, and that the legislation was supported by every medical practitioner in Brisbane. Even then it was only after a successful writ of mandamus that a local board of former mayors was appointed. However, the council called a meeting of ratepayers to "consider whether a Local Board of Health was necessary". After a number of speakers, of whom O'Doherty was the leader, had addressed the gathering, a motion "that thanks of the meeting be accorded to Dr O'Doherty for his disinterested efforts on behalf of the city" was carried unanimously.

The municipal fathers, realising that the local board could incur expenditure without their approval, gave the new body no cooperation, and they made approaches to the government with the view of having proclamation of the Act, as far as it applied to Brisbane, rescinded. In the meantime the epidemics of infectious disease in the city increased in severity, and the efforts of O'Doherty and his colleagues in the campaign to improve the public health of Brisbane were nullified.

In June 1873, there occurred another of the political crises which marked the Queensland Legislative Assembly's early history. In the small chamber of thirty-two members the defection of even one member to the opposition often meant defeat for the government. With the "painful estrangement" between Boyd Morehead and Premier Arthur Palmer, the government was fearful of facing a vote of no confidence and declined to attend parliament. The town liberals were also having difficulties in that a former supporter, John Handy, a North Brisbane representative, said he would abstain from any action which would defeat Palmer. O'Doherty and his other North Brisbane colleague, George Edmonstone, called yet another public meeting at which it was reported that every foot of space in the Town Hall was crowded with fully two thousand persons who attended. Its purpose was to hear the views of the two senior city members on the subject. The *Brisbane Courier*, in commenting on the political situation, referred to O'Doherty's command of the English language in the following:

> It is quite possible that there is a painful estrangement between Mr Morehead and Mr Palmer; yet it would seem to us, in all deference to Dr O'Doherty, as if such an estrangement might afford the brilliant member for North Brisbane a fitting opportunity for extending his conquests at a time when Mr Morehead may be presumed to be more especially susceptible to the persuasive arts of an accomplished rhetorician. [Mr Morehead was about to be married.] Mr Morehead, though a squatter, is yet human, and might not be wholly invulnerable to even less winged words than those with which Dr O'Doherty's quiver is so abundantly furnished.

It is not surprising that the political turmoil was followed by events which led to a general election in November 1873. This time O'Doherty decided to retire from politics, giving "family reasons" for his withdrawal. The *Brisbane Courier* greeted his announcement with an editorial in which it said:

> Dr O'Doherty may well speak with some honest pride of the honourable position he has so well filled for the last six years.

Unrewarded by any higher solace than the confidence and esteem of his constituents, after a career of unblemished political probity, he retires once more into the ranks of private citizenship, carrying with him the good wishes of all men with whom he has been connected in public life. There are few men in the Assembly who have done better service as the representative of a constituency. There are none, who have imparted less acerbity to the discharge of their political duties. He has been a firm friend, without being an implacable foe, and, while not wanting in decision, his conduct has always been characterised by a cheerful suavity of demeanour calculated to conciliate rather than to offend.

It might have been expected that, during his term as a politician, O'Doherty would restrict his medical activities to his clinical duties only. However, at all times he took a leading role in all aspects of the profession. In continuing his campaign to have the Brisbane Hospital serve as a preliminary medical school, he raised the subject again in 1872 through the hospital committee. On 15 March, William Day, the Brisbane clerk of petty sessions and a committee member, at O'Doherty's instigation, moved, "That in the opinion of this committee the time has arrived when students should be admitted to study in the hospital; that a committee be appointed for carrying out the above resolution." The subcommittee, of which Thomas Harlin, headmaster of the Brisbane Grammar School, was secretary and all the medical staff were members, placed the following advertisement in the *Queenslander* and the *Brisbane Courier*:

BRISBANE HOSPITAL

> The sub-committee appointed to consider the question of establishing a PRELIMINARY MEDICAL SCHOOL at the BRISBANE HOSPITAL, are anxious to ascertain how many Pupils the School, if established, can be expected to attract. Parents who are desirous of giving their sons a MEDICAL EDUCATION, will be good enough to communicate with the Honorary Secretary on or before the 27th instant.
> THOS HARLIN, Hon. Sec.

The proposal envisaged that students would take a preliminary examination in Queensland, and then proceed to Britain or Ireland to spend another two years at a medical school there, after which they would have gained sufficient knowledge and experience to take the final graduation examinations — thus shortening the time that they would otherwise have to spend away from Queensland. However, there was only one response from Goondiwindi to the advertisement and no further action was taken at the time.

O'Doherty was still not discouraged, and in 1874 he grasped another opportunity to press his advocacy for a preliminary medical school in Queensland. Charles Lilley, now a puisne judge, chaired a royal commission "into the working of educational institutions in the colony". O'Doherty and his medical colleague, Kearsey Cannan, appeared before the commission to further the proposal for a medical school. O'Doherty told the commission that the first part of a medical course, which included anatomy, physiology, chemistry, botany and the general treatment of diseases, could be given in Queensland and that the necessary examinations at the same standard of those held overseas could be mounted in Brisbane. Satisfactory experience could be gained at the Brisbane Hospital, the Woogaroo Asylum and the Lock Hospital. Lilley and the other members of the commission were so impressed with the submissions from the two doctors, that in their report they said, "It is at present impossible for students desiring to enter the medical profession to pursue the necessary studies within the colony itself." After outlining considerable supportive evidence they stated, "We therefore recommend the immediate foundation of a University with a fixed annual endowment which would include a preliminary medical school." On 2 May 1876, the *Brisbane Courier* praised O'Doherty for his public-spiritedness in volunteering "to devote his honorary fee, allowed as a visiting surgeon" to help provide scholarships "to assist young lads in prosecuting their studies at the hospital". Unfortunately neither of these proposals materialised and once again O'Doherty was disappointed.

During this period in the developing colony there were many areas too small to support a doctor, and to which a doctor's visit by the only means of transport available — on horseback or horse and buggy — was out of the question. Often there were to be found in such places, unregistered practitioners to whom the inhabitants were pleased to turn for medical advice. The practitioner sometimes held quite sound medical qualifications which were not recognised by the Medical Board of Queensland, or in some cases he had only a smattering of medical knowledge. O'Doherty, as a member of the Medical Board, was jealous of the standards demanded by the board before the practitioner was registered. Forgetting that he, himself, had practised in Van Diemen's Land before he had graduated, he frowned on the unregistered practitioner. Specific evidence of O'Doherty's attitude to these practitioners came to the surface in 1871.

A storekeeper, Simon Ziemen, was travelling alone on horseback from Roma to the small town of Surat when he was murdered. The police called in an unregistered practitioner to examine the body. O'Doherty was so horrified at this action and the methods used in the autopsy that he raised the matter in parliament. He read the police sergeant's report to the Legislative Assembly:

> On the morning of the 29th, I assisted Dr Godfrey to make a further examination of the body; we stripped the whole of the clothes off on that occasion; the trousers and braces off the body; in my presence, Dr Godfrey removed the head from the body, and an hour afterwards the neck; I afterwards escorted the head and neck into Surat; the remaining portion of the body was then buried about 200 yards from where it was found.

O'Doherty told the Legislative Assembly that he thought it was monstrous that government officials should call on "any tinker who might be picked up in the bush" to perform an autopsy, that he should have mutilated the body in such a way, and that the head and neck should have been taken in a tin box into Surat. Any qualified medical practitioner could have certified to the cause of death without mutilating a human body in such a way.

Mr Miles, the member for the district, defended the actions to which O'Doherty objected so vigorously. While he admitted that there was no necessity for the mutilation of the body, he believed Dr Godfrey was far superior to most medical gentlemen in the colony, although he was not registered with the Medical Board. He added that there was no telegraph in the district, and it would have been necessary to send a man on horseback to summon the nearest registered medical practitioner, who was a hundred miles (one hundred and sixty kilometres) away. It would have taken several days for this doctor to reach the scene of the murder and by that time, at this hot season of the year, the body would have been in a very advanced state of decomposition.

O'Doherty, like other medical practitioners at the time, was also critical of many of the midwives who, unsupervised, attended women in labour. He was quite aware of the safe nursing practices of the staff of the Lady Bowen Hospital under the supervision of the visiting medical staff, but was often scathing in his comments regarding the individual midwives practising in the community. He gave vent to his feelings at a magisterial inquiry into the death of a woman after childbirth which a midwife, Mrs Hirley, had attended. O'Doherty deposed that he had been called to see the deceased and when he arrived she was on the point of death from loss of blood. Mrs Hirley told him the confinement had been normal, which he claimed was not the case. Despite the doctor's efforts at resuscitation, the mother died an hour later. She appeared to have been a strong, hale, young woman and had given birth to a fine child; after he had conducted a postmortem examination and found no traces of organic disease, he was of the opinion that death would not have occurred had it not been for the stupid blunder of the midwife.

Midwives were not the only health workers who suffered the wrath of the doctors. In 1871 Dr Kearsey Cannan, president of the newly-formed Queensland Medical Society, in his inaugural speech condemned the "nefarious practice of chemists prescribing for serious illnesses and in some cases visiting patients in their homes". At the same time Cannan advocated the establishment of district dispensaries for the sick poor. With as yet no public transport, some patients were finding it difficult to visit the hospital outpatients at Bowen Bridge Road.

The hospital committee followed Cannan's suggestion and appointed a subcommittee to examine the subject. When its report was discussed in 1872, Moses Ward, a city chemist, claimed that "he, in company with others, was of the opinion that the dispensary was not required. There were no funds to spend on it. In his own experience, gained from living in the poorest part of Brisbane, the dispensary was not needed as there were very few indeed unable to pay for medicine. He did not think it was their duty to pauperise the people." But Mr Harlin who had consulted the visiting staff said that "The opinion of Dr O'Doherty was that great hardships were entailed on the poor from the fact of their having to come so far to obtain medical relief. This opinion, coming as it did from one of the medical staff, had much weight with the subcommittee." The hospital committee followed the advice of O'Doherty and a dispensary was established in Elizabeth Street in 1873 with the medical staff manning it on a roster basis.

The Brisbane Hospital was continually plagued with the problem which all hospitals face — insufficient finance. When, in 1872, parliament was debating supply for the ensuing year, Premier Arthur Palmer announced that, among the grants to charitable organisations, Brisbane Hospital would receive £3,000 ($6,000). Two of the North Brisbane members, O'Doherty and Edmonstone, attacked the premier on the inadequacy of the amount allotted. The premier, unmoved by the criticism, claimed the Brisbane Hospital committee should be more economical. He pointed out that the Toowoomba Hospital was managed at less than half the cost of the Brisbane Hospital, and threatened that consideration was being given to have the government take over the hospital. O'Doherty claimed that the premier had no grounds for his allegations of economic mismanagement and that the Brisbane Hospital received from other hospitals patients who needed expensive treatment. For this reason it merited special consideration. The premier brushed aside this argument and the proposed allocation was not amended.

The premier took almost immediate action to carry out his

threat to assume control of the hospital and the chairman of the committee received advice that a new government committee would be gazetted within a week. Great concern at the government's intention was expressed by all members at a regular hospital committee meeting only four days before the proposed date of gazettal, but most of those present were prepared to accept the action as inevitable. However, O'Doherty had no such thoughts and he urged hasty moves to stall the government. When he was told that such moves could only be initiated at a special meeting of hospital subscribers for which two weeks notice was required, he convinced those present that in the present emergency the rules should be brushed aside. He was successful in having a subscribers' meeting convened two days later. At the meeting, the Irish doctor led the debate and persuaded the meeting to consent to a deputation waiting on the government to put a compromise proposal of a joint government and subscribers' committee to manage the hospital.

The deputation waited on John Bramston, the attorney-general, in the absence of the premier in North Queensland, and it was agreed that all action should be postponed until the return of Premier Palmer. The doctor's recommendation was accepted by the government and after the annual meeting of subscribers in 1873 the affairs of the hospital were placed in the hands of a seven-member committee of which the chairman and three members were appointed by the government and three members elected by the subscribers. The change had no effect on the functioning of the hospital, which continued to suffer from inadequate funding.

Although O'Doherty always harboured resentment towards Britain for the wrongs committed against Ireland in the past and cherished the thought that one day his native country would regain self-government, he advocated racial and religious tolerance in his adopted land. He deplored the racial prejudice and sectarian bitterness displayed by many of Brisbane's inhabitants, including a number of his own countrymen.

Although it was not reported as such in the press, O'Doherty and a Protestant Irish friend, Robert Atkin, believed sectarian differences were responsible for a riot at Warwick following an election in 1871. The disturbance commenced after the returning officer declared that candidate Clark with 282 votes had defeated his rival, Morgan, for whom 265 electors had voted. Clark's supporters started a triumphant procession to Bugden's Hotel. "The scene which then occurred baffles description and was a disgrace to a community professing Christianity." Clark's supporters were attacked with fists, boots, stones and palings. Shots were fired from Bugden's Hotel and some of the attackers were slightly wounded. Additional police were despatched from Toowoomba and Warwick but with the voluntary dispersal of the combatants, the riot was long over by the time they arrived.

O'Doherty and Atkin, concerned that their own countrymen had displayed sectarian bitterness in the Warwick riot, resolved to form a society which would "serve as a barrier against bad and evil passions arising out of these sectarian prejudices". Thus came into being the Queensland Hibernian Society of which O'Doherty was the first president, and Protestants, Robert Atkin and Henry King, the first vice-presidents.

O'Doherty delivered his inaugural speech to the fledgling society on 7 September 1871. Admittedly stressing the objectives of the society hammered out in long discussions in which he had played an important part, he not only espoused the aims of the society but also expressed his own sentiments on such issues as sectarianism, the relationship of the Irish with other colonists, colonial government and the British-Irish question.

O'Doherty announced that the first aim of the society was to destroy the most serious of all barriers to a complete solidarity among his countrymen — religious prejudice and party antipathy. The society was open to Irishmen of all religions. He reiterated his satisfaction with the principles of government in Queensland and voiced his hopes that a similar government would be granted to Ireland. "We are here", he said, "thank God, completely independent of that discord among our countrymen at home. Here the British Constitution is not an empty name."

O'Doherty was conscious of the opinion other colonists held concerning the Irish in Australia. He believed that outsiders might view the new society as a Fenian association or "an instrument to be used by the Roman Catholic clergy for some of those dark purposes which are so frequently and stupidly attributed to those reverend gentlemen". He added that, "We are described as a turbulent and discontented people, fractious and quarrelsome", but he claimed that this arose from the Irish being "the most wronged and ill-governed amongst nations". He advocated the fostering of correct views amongst colonists upon the real character and aims of his countrymen, but in such a manner as would evidence respect for the opinions and feelings of those, who differ from the Irish. He referred to a further aim of the society. It was their duty to give cordial sympathy to such of their struggling countrymen as may be in need of it whether they be long resident in the colony or new arrivals. This last statement resulted in the formation of a Hibernian Benefit Society and in 1872 tenders were invited from "medical gentlemen willing to give advice and attendance to its members" and from "chemists for the supply and dispensing of medicines". In the latter case those tendering were requested to state whether or not the necessary bottles, leeches or cod-liver oil were included.

After his first term as president, O'Doherty retired from the position but remained on the directorate of the society. His place was taken by the Protestant, Robert Atkin. It is difficult to gauge to what extent the society realised the lofty aims that its first president enunciated. No doubt the objectives were achieved in part. However, those colonists of other nationalities, particularly the English, probably looked on the society in the manner that O'Doherty had suggested they might — a Fenian organisation or a vehicle of clerical intrigue. Its teachings did not prevent the "Orange Riot" at Ipswich in 1874, despite the fact that a branch of the Hibernian Society had been formed in that city.

It was in Ipswich that many of Reverend Dunmore Lang's migrants, sharing his anti-popery opinions, had settled after they arrived in Brisbane in 1849. By the 1870s the original migrants and their descendants still voiced their feelings against Catholics, many of whom did not hesitate to retaliate. In O'Doherty's time in Ipswich the ill-feelings between the two groups were fanned by the rival newspapers, the *Queensland Times* and the pro-Quinn *North Australian*. The 1874 riot commenced at the Ipswich School of Arts, where, on 5 November, Reverend Porteus, a Methodist minister, endeavoured to deliver the last of a series of lectures entitled "The Monk who shook the World" (Martin Luther). According to the *Queensland Times*, groups of Roman Catholics, who packed the hall, first interrupted the lecturer with hisses and jeers and then a fight broke out in the centre of the hall. "In a few seconds this part of the hall was one surging and swaying mass of heads . . . . Waddies and life-preservers or 'colts' were freely used, and the blood flowed copiously from numerous heads . . . ." The lecturer retired and Captain Townley, the police magistrate, read the "Riot Act" and ordered the police to clear the hall.

An uneasy peace may have ensued but the Orangemen had arranged to hold a picnic on the following Monday to celebrate the birthday of the Prince of Wales, and many believed that further violence would erupt, as it was rumoured that the Orange picnickers intended to march through the streets of Ipswich on the way to the railway station to board a train for their rendezvous at Oxley, and would display banners inscribed with such slogans as "To Hell with the Pope" and would be headed by a band playing, "Croppies, Lie Down".

These alleged rumours were relayed to O'Doherty, who with Dr Mullen and Mr O'Sullivan jun. waited on Arthur Macalister, the colonial secretary, and O'Doherty conferred with Bishop Quinn. Macalister took action under the Party Processions Act to prevent the display of provocative banners and the playing of incendiary music but decided not to cancel the approval given for the use of the special train to the picnic grounds. O'Doherty was accused by the *Telegraph* of endeavouring to have the train cancelled — an action which he strongly denied, saying that he had no intention of interfering with the Orange fraternity enjoying themselves or availing themselves of the train for that purpose at their own cost. He added that he had waited on the colonial secretary solely in the interest of peace and goodwill.

On the Sunday following the riot at the School of Arts, Bishop Quinn presided over a meeting of 600 Catholic men at Ipswich. The action of those who instigated the disturbance was condemned, and an undertaking given that Catholics would not interfere with any procession of Orangemen, whether bearing banners or not. Then Quinn travelled with Reverend Porteus in the train to the picnic and addressed the crowd in a witty and conciliatory speech. There was no trouble at the picnic nor at Ipswich on the return of the picnickers, due no doubt to the Bishop's endeavours, although a strong contingent of police who travelled in a separate train to the picnic may also have had some influence on the behaviour.

When O'Doherty entered parliament in 1867 he had taken pains to emphasise that he was satisfied with the arrangement by which Catholic schools were given some financial help, provided there was an adherence to the Board of Education regulations. However, the threat that the aid might be withdrawn was always present. The realisation that such action appeared to be a distinct possibility came in 1873 when Charles Lilley introduced a new education bill in the Lower House. Arrangements were made for Lilley to explain publicly the proposed legislation at a meeting in the Town Hall on 25 June. Bishop Quinn and O'Doherty were among those who were invited to take a seat on the platform, while 1,000 people made up a crowded audience. Lilley explained that his bill included provision for free, compulsory education for children up to the age of fourteen years at state expense. However, there was one clause over which he said that "bitterness of feeling would very likely rise". Denominational schools could continue to operate but "the revenue from which education was supported, was raised for secular purposes and civil objects, and the application of it to the teaching of the tenets of any particular church — whether Church of England, Roman Catholic or any other — was a misapplication of it".

As Lilley had anticipated, his proposal that support for

denominational schools should cease, provoked opposition and Bishop Quinn spoke strongly against it. He was supported by O'Doherty who spoke at some length, arguing against the abolition of aid for non-vested schools, but supporting the other features of the bill. He declared himself to be strongly in favour of free education. In the Legislative Assembly the bill aroused a lengthy debate and much to the delight of the bishop and O'Doherty, who voted against the measure, the proposed legislation was narrowly defeated by twelve votes to eleven.

In spite of this setback the government, which had been returned after the 1873 election, pressed on with its education legislation campaign. In May 1874 a non-vested schools abolition bill, introduced by Samuel Griffith, was passed by the Lower House but became a dead letter when the Upper House moved it be read in six months' time. However, the government was determined to formulate a definite education policy, and in July appointed a royal commission to "inquire into the working of the Educational Institutions of the Colony and of obtaining a report as to the best means of rendering those institutions as useful as possible". O'Doherty was nominated as one of eight members in addition to chairman Charles Lilley. On the day set down for the first meeting of the commission the doctor wrote to the colonial secretary resigning his membership. In his letter he said:

> The well-known opinions of seven out of nine gentlemen appointed to carry out the work of the Commission on the question of most vital importance to the Colony at present in connection with education, namely, the question as to the continuance or not of non-vested schools left little room to hope that any efforts of mine would be of use in influencing the deliberations of the Commission.
>
> And when, in addition, the Honourable Attorney-General, in recently addressing his constituents, referred to the Commission in the light of a political engine to be used by the Government for the purpose of advancing in the Colony views on the education question in direct opposition to those which, in common with a large and influential section of my fellow-colonists, I conscientiously entertain, I feel that I have no alternative but to decline taking part in a work whose aims and ends have been thus avowedly prearranged.

The *Brisbane Courier* devoted an editorial to the resignation of O'Doherty and of William Walsh, who held similar views to the doctor. Not unexpectedly the paper was critical of their actions:

> Dr O'Doherty, also, as a retired politician of considerable eminence, and as one always hitherto identified with legislation of a shade both popular and enlightened, was very properly selected as the representative of an important section of the community, whose interests are said to be jeopardised by the policy which last session found an exponent in the new Attorney-General, Mr Douglas . . . . Dr O'Doherty, we understand, has resigned. Of the reasons for that resignation Dr O'Doherty must be the best judge, and that they have had some weight with him we do not doubt. It betokens, however, questionable courtesy or respect to the Government, or indeed to that more undefined, but not less exacting master, the public, that he should have so quickly surrendered a trust which he had only such a short time before accepted.

From the Royal Commission's report came the enactment of the State Education Act of 1875 which produced a "free, secular and compulsory system of education". The Act also created a Department of Public Instruction which continued to provide financial aid to non-vested schools until 31 December 1880, after which date the denominations were obliged to provide all funds for their schools. The allies, Bishop Quinn and Dr O'Doherty, had lost their education campaign.

Another activity connected with his church in which O'Doherty was deeply involved had a much happier conclusion — the completion and the consecration of St Stephen's Cathedral. Since the foundations were laid in 1863 building had been slow but, according to a *Brisbane Courier* report in 1871, satisfactory. The paper added that the edifice already presented an attractive appearance, and that "all the walls excepting that at the eastern end, are so far finished that the parapet is being put in place. Only one pillar remains to be erected and the arches are now being cut. The stone for the pillars, arches, windows, parapets and other particular portions is from Murphy's Creek and is very fine and white."

O'Doherty continued to contribute generously to the cathedral building fund, his donations helping to swell "the funds . . . being liberally donated by the Catholic community, the subscriptions averaging £50 ($100) per week ... supplemented by a like amount from Bishop Quinn who collected a large sum of money for the erection of the edifice during his tour of the colony".

By 1874 the cathedral was ready for opening and Dr O'Doherty was among the prominent laymen who played important roles at the various functions associated with this significant milestone in Queensland Catholic history. He chaired the meeting which finalised plans for the reception of southern church dignitaries invited to participate in the opening of the cathedral — Archbishop Vaughan of Sydney and the bishops of Maitland (Dr Murray), Bathurst (Dr Matthew Quinn) and Goulburn (Dr Lannigan), as well as the rector of Sydney University St John's College (Dr Forrest). When the southern prelates arrived in the *City of Brisbane* at the ASN wharf at Petrie Bight on Friday 15 May, O'Doherty with the Honourable E.H. McDevitt, MLC, T.H. Fitzgerald, MLA and R. McDonnell accompanied Bishop Quinn and Dr Cani when they went on board to welcome the visitors. Then followed a triumphant procession along Eagle, Queen, Edward and Elizabeth Streets to the cathedral, O'Doherty taking his place with the leaders and the whole proceedings being witnessed by 3,000 persons.

At a grand oratorio on the Saturday night, O'Doherty was chosen to present an address to Archbishop Vaughan and his fellow visitors, on behalf of the Catholics of Brisbane. On Sunday Kevin and Eva were among the congregation when Pontifical High Mass was celebrated and the archbishop preached "a masterly sermon". The final function took place on the Monday night with a banquet in honour of the visiting prelates at the Town Hall at which the governor, the Marquis of Normandy, presided and to whom O'Doherty was asked to propose a toast.

During the 1870s mining attracted much interest among the colony's inhabitants. After James Nash discovered the rich goldfield at Gympie in 1867, prospecting for the mineral had intensified in many areas of the colony. New fields were first worked by individual miners but this initial stage was closely followed by the formation of companies, generally consisting of miners in collusion with the more well-to-do citizens. O'Doherty attempted to speculate in various ventures, but on occasions he appears to have been too late in investing and there were no significant returns.

Traces of gold were found in the Enoggera ranges close to Brisbane. In March 1872, a modest enterprise, the Hibernian Gold Mining Company, was formed for the purpose of raising, by weekly subscriptions among Brisbane citizens, a fund to enable the Enoggera ranges to be thoroughly prospected and to sink a shaft at a likely spot. When the company was registered in Brisbane on 21 April 1872, its nominal capital was £500 ($1,000) and O'Doherty was listed as holding two shares of £5 each. The prospectus of a more ambitious venture, the Enoggera Gold Mining Company, set its nominal capital at £10,000 ($20,000) to be used for mining at Fisherman's Gully five miles (eight kilometres) from the Enoggera Reservoir. Neither company returned a fortune to its shareholders.

The access to the Enoggera Range fields was difficult. It was almost impossible to get a vehicle of any description to the fields and equipment and provisions had to be carried on packhorses or humped by the miners themselves. O'Doherty, mainly in his capacity as a member of parliament, but no doubt with extra enthusiasm arising from his great interest in gold mining, led a deputation to wait on the minister for Works and Mines, William Walsh, with a view to improving access to the area and having the gold commissioner, Augustus Gregory, visit the field to mark off the various claims.

The year 1872 was also a period in which numerous companies were formed to mine tin in the Stanthorpe district. In October a prospectus of the Pro Bono Publico Tin Mining Company to work an area of half a mile (0.8 kilometres) frontage to Quart Pot Creek was published. O'Doherty's name was included in the list of provisional directors. However, by this time, several other companies had already commenced operations and apparently the promoters of the Pro Bono Publico Company failed to raise the nominal capital of £10,000 as there is no record of its registration.

In the next year O'Doherty was again mentioned as a provisional director in a mining company — the South Monkland Extended Gold Mining Company — which proposed to mine gold at Gympie. There were several extensions of the date by which applications for shares had to be lodged and the company was not registered until 1875. O'Doherty had apparently lost interest as his name is not included as a director in the company's registration file.

As a member of parliament O'Doherty was frequently approached by sporting organisations to accept a position on the body's executive — a vice-presidency was the position generally offered. However, his involvement went far deeper. He had personal interest in most sporting activities although there is no record of his active participation, except when he was named as "a veteran of the green cloth" when he represented Brisbane in a billiards match against Toowoomba. Further interest developed when his older boys, now teenagers, displayed sporting prowess. In August 1870 an Ipswich football team travelled to Brisbane by the river steamer, *Nowra*, to do battle with a metropolitan team at Queen's Park, opposite the botanical gardens and between Government House and the Houses of Parliament. In front of "a large number of spectators including a good many ladies" Brisbane was victorious by two goals to one. In the evening the visitors were entertained at a dinner at the Australian Hotel, at the corner of Queen and Albert Streets, over which O'Doherty presided.

In August 1873 the Irish doctor was a member of the Regatta Club committee appointed to arrange details of a regatta to be held on the Prince of Wales' birthday on 10 November, as well as to receive subscriptions. O'Doherty had a special interest in the regatta as his eldest son, William, was pairing with a friend, John Devoy, in the first event on the programme — the Youth Skiff race — and he was delighted to see the pair come from behind to win by several lengths. The doctor, now no longer a member of parliament, maintained his interest in the Regatta Club, remaining on the committee, and in 1874 raised through his collections more money for the club than any other member.

O'Doherty, a member of the trustees of the Brisbane Grammar School until 1874, attended the school's annual Foundation Day ceremonies whenever his professional duties permitted. On most occasions he watched with pride as his sons were presented with prizes for academic achievement. Although satisfied with their progress at secondary school level, the doctor was concerned about professional training for them. With no university in the colony, they would have to go elsewhere for tertiary education. As a possible way of solving this problem he wrote to Premier Arthur Palmer in 1872, offering his services as an agent for the Queensland government in San Francisco. He suggested that through such appointment he could obtain, at first hand, information on such important subjects as railway construction and national education, and, at the same time, act as an immigration agent. The doctor stated quite frankly that his chief purpose in the proposal was to secure professional training for his sons, which he claimed was not so readily available in Australia. O'Doherty appears to have taken the rejection of his project philosophically, and continued to pursue his life in the colony in the same manner as before.

Eva continued her role as dutiful wife and mother. She added her contribution to the fund raising for the cathedral and her name figured frequently in the press as the convenor of bazaar stalls and as a participator in similar functions. In 1874 the family left the commodious residence at the corner of George and Mary Streets and moved to Leichhardt Street, the former home becoming a Good Templar's hotel. The doctor, who had been practising at his home, took consulting rooms at the corner of Queen and George Streets.

By this time their last child, Gertrude, born 15 November 1869, was nearly five years old, having, unlike the previous three children, survived the epidemic diseases of infancy. Being the only daughter and with nine years separating her from the youngest boy, Kevin, she became the family favourite, especially with her father. One of his letters written whilst he was absent from the family home reads as follows:

Dearest Darling Titsum Kitsum, I send 20000000000 million kisses and I chance also sending you a little dried bouquet which I bought when it was quite fresh and blooming at a bazaar we had lately here — and I bought a delicious pocket for you in which you will find the bouquet. This pretty pocket was made and all the nice lace on it worked by Mrs Hamilton Scott and it was worked for you — It will be such a pretty little pocket to wear when you go to school to put any little stray lolly in that my little ducksum may wheedle out of somebody. I shall soon be sending myself to you and when I do I promise I will send you a number of real kisses.

CHAPTER 10

His Expert Advice

By 1875 O'Doherty had been in Brisbane ten years and his standing in the community and his profession was such that he was consulted on a wide range of subjects. If the subject related to his native land, he and Bishop Quinn often gave a joint opinion. Such a case was the centenary of the birth of Daniel O'Connell, the Great Liberator, who first saw the light of day on 6 August 1775.

To some Irishmen in Australia the approaching event posed a dilemma as they pondered its significance in their adopted country. An anti-Irish attitude was still prevalent in some quarters. The Fenian rising had been given a great airing in the Australian newspapers and the memory was still fresh. In most colonies the Catholic Church was at odds with the government over financial aid to its schools. So in a number of Irish communities the problem was not how the centenary should be celebrated but whether it should be celebrated at all.

To Bishop Quinn and O'Doherty the centenary posed no problem. With great enthusiasm they suggested that the date should be commemorated not only by Irish Catholics but by members of all nationalities and creeds, for they claimed that

O'Connell was far more than a Catholic emancipator — he was the greatest advocate of civil and religious liberty. Accordingly, a reluctant mayor, after being presented with a petition of which O'Doherty was the instigator, called a public meeting in the Town Hall "to consider the best mode of celebrating the approaching centenary of Daniel O'Connell". Among a large attendance at the meeting were a number of Non-conformist ministers of religion. O'Doherty, in leading the discussion, extolled the virtues of O'Connell and outlined grand plans for the proposed celebration. He concluded by moving that a public banquet be held to honour the event. The Protestant clergy strongly opposed O'Doherty's suggestion. Reverend F. Brentall said that, "Protestants could not be expected to combine with the movement while they remembered that much of the hatred, the bigotry and the feeling between the two classes arose from that stateman's [O'Connell's] combination of politics and religion, he having caused the priesthood of Ireland to declare from the altar the way in which their flocks were to vote." The Protestant faction was too strong for O'Doherty and his superiors, and finally a motion was passed that: "This meeting is of the opinion that it is inexpedient, in this dependency of a nation, cherishing the memory of illustrious sons, to single out for honour of a public demonstration, one whose fame principally rests on services to a particular church in Ireland."

Nothing daunted, Bishop Quinn and O'Doherty pressed on with plans of their own to celebrate the centenary on the first weekend in August. The children of the Catholic schools in Brisbane initiated the proceedings by attending a special mass at St Stephen's Cathedral on the Friday morning. The mass was sung by the Very Reverend Dean Tissot, whom the Catholics of Brisbane had castigated four years before for advising his flock how to vote in a Maryborough election — he was celebrating his fiftieth anniversary of his ordination and first mass. In the evening a large audience packed the Cathedral where an oratorio and an oration on the life and work of O'Connell provided the important section of the celebrations. The choir and orchestra performed under the baton of Herr Rosenstengel and O'Doherty delivered the oration. Commenting on the choice of orator the *Brisbane Courier* said:

> There is no one better entitled to speak on such a subject; and of all the men of '48 who acquired fame or notoriety in the cause of what they conceived to be Irish freedom there is not one who has more honorably sustained his consistent patriotism than Dr O'Doherty himself. Nursing no hatred of England as some of his less magnanimous associates have done, he has learned and proved by honest unpretending service, loyally rendered in laying the foundations of freedom in his adopted country, how the old wrongs may be redressed by peaceful means in a country where the rancour of political and religious differences need no longer live.

To those in the audience, who, like O'Doherty, had known O'Connell in Ireland and "felt the magnetic influence of his presence" there were many memorable passages in the oration of which the following was not the least:

> I had been taught from the time I could interpet the meaning of words to regard O'Connell as something higher than a mortal man — to look up to him as a second Moses, who emancipated me from worse than Egyptian bondage — who had enabled me to hold my head in my own land with a proud consciousness that, in following the faith of my fathers, I was no longer to feel I carried a badge of degradation. It is only these who, like myself were made to realise, even in my early childhood, the full consciousness of being the victims of an odious penal code, who can form a conception of boundless love and gratitude towards a man of whom it may in truth be said that by almost his own unaided genius against the power of a bigotted King, and scarcely less hostile Lords and Commons, led on too by the greatest warrior of the age [Wellington], succeeded in carrying the cause of civil and religious liberty to a triumphant issue.

Of those of Irish descent born in Australia who opposed the celebrations he said:

> They are jealous of their Australian dignity, which they consider compromised by celebrations of men and events which have no direct connection with their native land . . . . I have no wish to lessen in the hearts of our youth the ennobling sentiment of attachment to, and reverence for, their native country . . . . Will they not understand through the force of their own patriotic feeling, how impossible it would be to tear from our hearts the sacred memories

of beloved Ireland?

O'Doherty's oration was followed by the singing as a chant of a special ode composed by Eva. One stanza reads:

> Slaves lying low in the pallor of death,
> Did ye not waken to life in his breath?
>   Led by his prophet might
>
> Rose ye to manhood's height,
> Flashing the sword of right,
>   Forth from its sheath!
> Refrain
> Rolling from shore to shore,
> From Erin's inmost core,
> Echoed by thousands more,
>   Hear ye that name!

Bishop Quinn signified his great enthusiasm for the celebrations by announcing at a special lunch after mass on the Sunday that "from that day he would take back his old name of O'Quinn".

While O'Connell's centenary called for a celebration, at least in the minds of many Irish Catholics, there was a feature of life in Queensland at this period that called for concern rather than for rejoicing — the severe mortality, particularly in the young in the population, from infectious disease. There was one lay person in Brisbane who deplored the heavy toll sufficiently to express his thoughts in a letter to the editor of the *Brisbane Courier* in July 1875. Reverend Sutton, an Anglican parson, claimed that he had recently buried the last of six children of healthy and caring parents, all having died from infectious disease; another family living close to the Queensland Club had lost six out of eight children and he had lost three from seven children in his own family. He pleaded for action to reduce this slaughter. Sutton's claims were supported by reports from the registrar-general, who stated a high infant mortality rate in 1875 had been followed by an even higher toll in 1876. In this latter year one baby in four died in its first year of life.

O'Doherty and his colleagues on the Central Board of Health had been striving to initiate measures to reduce this mortality from the time the Health Act was introduced. In this campaign to improve the public health of Brisbane, O'Doherty received strong support from Dr Hugh Bell. While O'Doherty was drafting regulations and making approaches to the government and the municipal council, Bell was preparing scientific papers on appropriate subjects. They were frustrated, however, by the opposition of the municipal fathers, the well-meaning but haphazard efforts of the local board of health and the indifference of parliament. The council still opposed the existence of a local board of health. The unsystematic approach of the local board of health is borne out in a report in 1876, in which it proudly boasted of its assumption of the management of the cleansing of the city itself after the failure of private contractors to perform the work satisfactorily, but then went on to say that, "In three-fourths of the city the old cess-pits continue as an existing nuisance, but, to insist on their entire removal under the present circumstances does not appear expedient." The government continued to give a low priority to health legislation and although amendments to the Health Act were introduced they were allowed to lapse.

Believing that health education would strengthen the campaign for improvements in the health of the city, O'Doherty and Bell persuaded the Central Board of Health to organise a scientific meeting at the Town Hall in August 1876 — the first to be held in the colony — to which medical practitioners and prominent citizens were invited. In addition to papers on public health there were static exhibits. In a paper on state medicine O'Doherty referred to what had been achieved in the colony already, but strongly stressed the far-reaching reforms still necessary. Bell followed with a treatise on drainage and sanitation with Dr de Zouche advocating a system of notification of epidemic diseases.

In May 1877 O'Doherty regained a former forum in which to press for reform. He returned to parliament but this time he was appointed to the Legislative Council. The *Brisbane Courier*, forgetting how loudly it had sung his praises when he resigned from the Legislative Assembly in 1873, was now far from laudatory:

> The doctor is regarded by a large number of his fellow-colonists as a representative man, and his attainments and social position entitle him to respect; but we should be stultifying ourselves were we to pretend that as a legislator he has been a success; or that he is likely to contribute largely to the work of the legislature in future . . . . His geniality of manner and disposition render his partisanship less obnoxious and less striking than many other men but he is too thorough an Irishman to be able to deal with public questions without strong party bias.

The *Telegraph* threw some light on its fellow paper's change of mind:

> And with regard to O'Doherty, we consider it a pity that he has so long held aloof from the legislature. He has often had the opportunity of entering one or other of the Houses since his retirement from the Assembly some years ago, but it is only now that he has allowed the wishes of his political friends to avail. It is quite obvious, however, that in the eyes of the *Courier*, the real sin of the Ministry is not filling up the vacuum in the Council, but in selecting men unlikely to give effect to the principles which that journal advocates.

In May 1878, Premier John Douglas introduced into parliament a bill, drafted by O'Doherty, which proposed that the Central Board of Health be empowered to make regulations on important public health subjects — quarantine, vaccination, drainage and sanitation, and adulteration of food. In criticising the legislation, the *Brisbane Courier* raised a subject which has been hotly debated by politicians, administrators, lawyers and academics for ages:

> It has often been objected that the clause which is usually found in every act of parliament giving the ministry power to make regulations under it, virtually gives them the power to interpret the act as they please — that we are already governed by regulation rather than by law. The proposal in this instance, however, goes far beyond that . . . Parliament is, therefore asked to take this power from a responsible minister and give it to an irresponsible board.

On a proposal to make vaccination against smallpox compulsory, the *Courier* pointed that even the premier, when alluding to this provision, said, "I do not think that public sentiment would justify us coming to such a conclusion." The local board of health agreed entirely with the *Brisbane Courier* and decided that it would wait on the premier to put its views. By the end of 1878 the bill had not been passed and finally lapsed. Children, and adults too, continued to die from infectious diseases and the death rate from intestinal diseases, which some of the proposed measures would have reduced, would reach an all time high in the next decade.

In March 1876 the O'Dohertys left Leichhardt Street to return to George Street. They took up residence at No. 6 Harris Terrace at the corner of George and Margaret Streets, which the agent described as a two-storeyed house consisting of dining and drawing rooms, six bedrooms, servant's room, bathroom and offices, and being very well appointed and elegantly finished, with patent closets draining to the river.

O'Doherty retained his opinion that professional training for his sons should be obtained overseas. As their secondary education at Brisbane Grammar School was nearing completion, it was decided that William, the eldest boy, should study dentistry at Philadelphia in America, and the second son, Edward, should follow in his father's footsteps by studying medicine at the Royal College of Surgeons, Dublin. The third boy, Vincent, had become a bank clerk, while young Kevin had transferred from the Grammar School to the newly established Christian Brothers School, which commenced in the old St Stephen's Church in 1875 before transferring to temporary premises on Gregory Terrace the next year.

Shortly after settling in the new residence at Harris Terrace, Eva and the two eldest sons left Brisbane to join the Pacific Mail Steamship Company's ship, the *Zealandia*, on her voyage from Sydney to San Francisco to enable William to be enrolled in dentistry at Philadelphia. Eva and Edward then continued to Ireland, where the second son commenced the study of medicine. Both boys progressed creditably in their studies.

In February 1877 Edward's friends were delighted to read a press report that he had made an excellent beginning, taking second place in an examination in which there were 130 competitors. William also achieved great distinction by qualifying in dentistry in 1879 with "the second best examination ever passed at the university".

The *San Francisco Monitor* announced the arrival of "Eva of the *Nation*" in an article which referred to "Dr O'Doherty's reputation among the men of '48 as that of a chivalrous and patriotic gentleman" and claimed that "Eva's poetic effusions exerted no small influence over the minds of her fellow countrymen". She had taken a manuscript of her poems with her to arrange publication by a San Francisco firm. When she returned via America in 1877 the published work was waiting for her. Cherishing the memories of the days of 1848, she dedicated the poems to "The Felons, John Mitchel and John Martin". Most of the poems had been written in the heady days of the rebellion, but for a small number she had chosen aspects of her adopted land as the subjects. One such was entitled "Queensland", of which the first stanza reads:

> Thou art, in sooth, a lovely land,
>   As fair as ever fancy painted.
> In virgin freshness calm and bland,
>   By shadows dark untainted.
> But ah! upon the bright expanse,
>   The glory of a clime Elysian,
> 'Tis but a cold and soulless glance
>   That meets the gazer's vision.

It was a harsh picture of her adopted colony. But surely she was describing the reality of many parts of Queensland before her eyes. When compared with the lush green of the Irish landscape, due in part to the softer light found in the higher latitudes, the light of this subtropical clime was indeed harsh and dazzling — frequently bleaching out with its intensity much of the rich colours of flowers, grass and trees.

In 1870, the Queensland government had built a reception house at Petrie Terrace to which lunatics and inebriates were admitted for a short term instead of being sent directly to Woogaroo Asylum. Dr William Hobbs, government health officer, was responsible for the overall management of the reception house and Charles Adams, an experienced but untrained warder, was appointed superintendent. With Hobbs' approval Adams administered to all patients, when they first arrived, a routine treatment of a cold bath and thirty grains of the hypnotic, chloral hydrate.

In October 1876, a magisterial inquiry was held to examine the cause of death of Thomas Hassett, who died at the reception house a few hours after admission — he had been given the routine initial treatment. Evidence revealed that Hassett, who had been on a four weeks' drinking bout, was voluntarily admitted to the watch-house at midnight on a Sunday night. He was examined in his cell by Dr Hobbs about twelve hours later. A diagnosis of delirium tremens had been made, and Hassett was transferred to the reception house.

O'Doherty, who had performed a postmortem examination on the deceased, was called as a witness. He submitted that the treatment Hassett had received from the time he had been placed in the police cell was erroneous. He considered that it was unscientific and inhumane for a man suffering from delirium tremens, a diagnosis with which he agreed, to be kept in the lockup without treatment for the time Hassett had been; it was highly improper for a man suffering from delirium tremens, after being in the cells so long, to be washed with cold water. He believed the reception house superintendent acted to the best of his ability but there should be a resident surgeon at the reception house. He objected to the treatment of patients at the institution without supervision as being altogether wrong in principle.

It is not surprising that the case and O'Doherty's criticism attracted much attention in the press. The *Brisbane Courier* condemned the management of patients at the reception house, saying that, "There is repeated proof that warder Adams' cold bath treatment has hastened out of this world some of the poor creatures who had been committed to his care." The paper expected O'Doherty to have a solution:

> Dr O'Doherty has spoken out very plainly in this case. He thinks the Reception House the more important of the two asylums and if he means as regards to the initiation of treatment of those who may be killed, cured or become confirmed lunatics, he is undoubtedly right. He is of the opinion that the institution should have a resident surgeon and he is probably right there also, but even without going to that length, perhaps Dr O'Doherty can recommend some tentative line of action in regard to the treatment of persons newly ad-

mitted, of a less rigorous and more rational character than the system hitherto in force.

The *Week* claimed O'Doherty had accused Dr Hobbs and warder Adams of being unscientific and inhumane. In drawing what was probably a fine line, the Irish doctor, in a letter published in the *Telegraph* of 23 October 1876, denied this but reiterated what he had said in evidence:

> As regards the stereotyped treatment of cases on admission to the Reception House as described in evidence of Dr Hobbs and Mr Adams, I think, on the very face of it, the charge of unscientific is not misapplied . . . . To leave cases to be treated, at the most critical period of their ailment, by Warder Adams is both unscientific and inhumane.

In 1877 the government appointed a royal commission under the chairmanship of William Graham, MLC, and with Drs John Thomson and Joseph Bancroft among its members, to inquire into the management of the Woogaroo Asylum and the reception houses. In a report condemning the care of patients at the Brisbane reception house, the commission said, "We consider the indiscriminate compulsory bathing wrong and reprehensible" and that, "The administration of baths and chloral by a non-medical man is irregular and dangerous." Some of the wording of the report resembled the language used by O'Doherty in his letter to the *Telegraph* in October 1876. This did not escape Hobbs who was given a copy of the report before it was officially published. In a letter to the colonial secretary, he claimed that, "Throughout the report I recognise the 'fine Roman hand' of the writer of the letter in the *Telegraph* of 25th October 1876." (The letter appeared in the issue of the 23rd, not the 25th of October 1876.) Hobbs also stated that the medical members were activated by professional jealousy in their criticism of his care of the patients.

Speaking to the report under the privilege in the Legislative Council, O'Doherty strongly denied that there had been any collusion between himself and the members of the commission, as implied by Dr Hobbs. In this he was supported by Graham, the chairman of the commission. Hobbs was also a member of the Upper House and the other members enjoyed what turned out to be a slanging match between the two medical members. In reply to O'Doherty, Hobbs claimed that the Irish doctor had told him before the magisterial inquiry that he was "going to pitch into the whole thing". The debate continued with similar remarks and further verbal sallies between Hobbs and O'Doherty and comments from the remainder of the House.

The press welcomed the new turn of events. The *Queensland Evangelical Standard*, published by a directory of Nonconformist parsons, sided with Hobbs, a former Reverend Dunmore Lang's immigrant, in a sectarian swipe at O'Doherty:

> This "atrocity" perpetrated at our door set the Legislative Assembly on fire. Each speaker, more than another, went in for "slating" Dr Hobbs and Superintendent Adams and even the dignity of the Upper House ruffled up in the common cause. Dr O'Doherty's hydrophobia infected the medical members of the Commission, and alarmed the public; insomuch that it seemed as though Dr O'Doherty were to be asked to take over Woogaroo and the reception-house, and manage the whole concern himself, with nuns for nurses, those highly accomplished and self-denying ladies — so secret withal.

Further debate in the press included an editorial in the *Brisbane Courier* which stated that Dr Hobbs had no grounds which could justify the insulting accusations brought against members of the commission. Eventually, new legislation provided for the appointment of an inspector of asylums and reception houses but it was not until 1918 that O'Doherty's recommendation, that a doctor should examine mental patients in the initial stages, was followed, when a mental ward was opened at the Brisbane General Hospital.

O'Doherty's reputation at this period was such that his personal medical services were sought by prominent people; his advice was asked in special circumstances and he was appointed to important official positions. An extract from a press report in June 1875 regarding the illness of Premier Arthur Macalister, reads:

> On Friday he was worse but drove down to Sandgate, and on Saturday morning, just after taking breakfast, he fell to the floor in a

severe epileptic fit. His daughter, who was in an adjoining room, heard the fall, and hastening in, found him in strong convulsions. Dr O'Doherty was telegraphed for, and got down about an hour and a-half after the occurrence . . . .. Last evening he was progressing favourably.

In December 1875, the 660 ton immigrant vessel, *Gauntlet*, arrived in Moreton Bay from London. When the ship's surgeon-superintendent, Dr Hearne, advised Dr Henry Challinor, the health officer for the port, that there had been twelve deaths from typhoid fever among the 270 passengers during the voyage and some cases still existed on board, the ship was quarantined. The passengers were transferred to Peel Island, which was being used for such purposes in addition to Dunwich on Stradbroke Island.

On hearing adverse reports of conditions at Peel Island, the agents for the vessel, J. & G. Harris, took the rather unusual step of engaging Dr O'Doherty to make a special report on the matter. O'Doherty went to the scene with Dr Hobbs, the government health officer — the clash over the reception house had not yet occurred. He examined the ship, spoke to Mr Hamilton, the quarantine superintendent at Dunwich and discussed the affair with Dr Hearne, the *Gauntlet's* surgeon-superintendent. As regulations prohibited O'Doherty from inspecting the quarantine station on Peel Island, he admitted that his subsequent report, written in his usual forthright language, may have contained some minor inaccuracies but he maintained that his account of a number of deficiencies in the management of the passengers on Peel Island was substantially correct. The major defect lay in the absence of a resident superintendent on Peel Island. Dr Hearne, who was instructed to go to the island to care for the patients, was endeavouring to supervise all activities. O'Doherty alleged that for this reason there was no strict isolation of patients, and uncontrolled communication between the sick and the well was frequent. Single male passengers were accommodated in tents, which they were obliged to erect themselves, and while single women were housed in wooden premises, they were provided with blankets but no beds. There was no jetty at which the boats could land passengers and the men waded ashore carrying the women and children.

O'Doherty's report was forwarded to the government and later published in the press. The government took quick action to remedy the deficiencies. A doctor, a resident superintendent, and two assistants were despatched to Peel Island almost immediately and endeavours were made to send nursing staff also. The official report of the Board of Immigration on the incident substantiated O'Doherty's account of the former deficiencies.

In 1876 the *Government Gazette* again announced that O'Doherty had been appointed a member of the Medical Board of Queensland. This time he accepted membership. The appointment was followed the next year by his summons to the Legislative Council, already mentioned, and in 1878 his name was added to the list of trustees of the Brisbane Museum, which he had initiated in 1870 by persuading parliament to vote a small sum of money for its foundation. After occupying temporary premises, the museum would soon move into accommodation specially built for it in William Street, later to be occupied by the Public Library. In the same year O'Doherty accepted the position of consultant surgeon to the Hospital for Sick Children opened in cottages in Leichhardt Street, Spring Hill, through the efforts of Mrs Mary McConnell.

In March 1877 the Irish doctor's advice was again sought to solve a quarantine problem. This time it was the government which asked for help. Sir Arthur Kennedy, accompanied by his daughter, Georgina, and her companion, Miss Banks, had arrived in Moreton Bay from Hong Kong in the steamer, *Brisbane*, to take up the position of governor of Queensland. When John Douglas, the new premier of the colony, and some senior cabinet ministers had gone down the river to greet the new governor, they saw to their horror as they drew near, that the yellow quarantine flag was flying from the *Brisbane*'s mast. Health officer, Henry Challinor, on learning that a Chinese passenger, suffering from smallpox, had been put ashore at Curtis Island two days before, had placed the vessel in quarantine.

An embarrassed premier spoke to the new governor over the ship's side. Sir Arthur said he understood quarantine precautions were necessary at times, but that in this particular circumstance there was no concern for alarm. He clearly expected Douglas to take special action. The premier returned up the river and called a hasty cabinet meeting. It was decided to appoint a medical commission consisting of Drs O'Doherty, Bancroft and Cannan to find a solution to the problem.

The *Brisbane Courier* attacked this decision in a scathing editorial in its issue the next morning:

> A Governor or a Governor's servants are, for anything we have heard to the contrary, just as capable of conveying infection as less distinguished individuals and therefore, if Sir Arthur Kennedy and his suite are exempted from the quarantine we shall have the questionable satisfaction of knowing that immigrants of less importance have been frequently imprisoned on Peel Island without cause, or else that a necessary law is to be put aside in this case with the concurrence of the Ministry, and for the convenience of the gentleman, who is to become Her Majesty's respresentative . . . . Had not Sir Arthur Kennedy been on board the *Brisbane* no Medical Commission would have been thought of, and the law would have been carried out as it has always been hitherto.

However, when the medical commission visited the ship and made its examination it agreed with Dr Challinor, despite the fears expressed by the *Brisbane Courier*. A quarantine period of sixteen days was set for all aboard the *Brisbane*, including Sir Arthur Kennedy and his party, from the time the Chinese passenger was put ashore at Curtis Island. The passengers were transferred to Peel Island but the governor spent the quarantine period cruising and fishing in Moreton Bay on the river steamer, *Kate*, which had been hastily prepared for the task.

On the day that the quarantine was due to end, a large crowd gathered at Petrie Bight to welcome the new governor at a special ceremony. They waited for several hours in vain. Health officer Challinor had again caused trouble. When that diligent officer boarded the *Kate* to examine the governor and the ladies, before lifting quarantine, he advised them that, according to instructions in the quarantine regulations, he was obliged to examine their chests for any sign of the disease. Sir Arthur Kennedy was quite willing to submit to this inspection but Miss Kennedy and Miss Banks were quite adamant in their refusal to suffer such an indignity. In this attitude they were supported by the governor. Dr Challinor, still faithfully following the regulations, refused to release the *Kate* and her occupants from quarantine, and telegraphed his decision to poor Premier Douglas.

The premier again called on his medical commission who, with all the cabinet, once more went down the bay and tried to persuade Challinor to alter his decision. This he steadfastly refused to do. It was O'Doherty who broke the impasse. He said that the health officer had acted consistently in accordance with the letter of his instructions. It would be unwise in the present case to set a bad precedent, but he thought that the rule might be safely relaxed a little as the ladies were blooming with health, and if they would expose their wrists he thought this would be sufficient. His colleagues, Drs Cannan and Bancroft, concurred with his suggestion as did also the premier and his ministers, who, of course, were most anxious for a solution. No trace of smallpox was found on the wrists of the ladies who had readily accepted the modified inspection and the yellow flag was hauled down from the *Kate*, much to the disgust of Henry Challinor, who later placed his protest in writing. The crowd waiting at Petrie Bight to greet the governor gave a loud cheer as they saw the *Kate* round a bend in the river four hours later than they had anticipated. (There was some basis for O'Doherty's examination of the wrists. Perhaps, unwittingly, he was anticipating the future. In later years, when examination for suspected smallpox was still required, quarantine officers inspected the forearms only. The skin eruptions of the disease are most prevalent on the extremities.)

There was one occasion when it appears that O'Doherty may have allowed his loyalty to his co-religionists to influence his medical judgment. The point at issue was whether or not an illness which had appeared in November 1877 among the pupils and Sisters of Mercy at All Hallows Convent, and from which a day pupil had died, was typhoid fever. If it were indeed typhoid fever, an inference would be made that the cause was in the convent itself and this would be a slur on the sisters, with a possible adverse effect on the enrolment for the coming year, particularly in the boarding section of the school. At the time there were fifty-two day pupils and twenty-three boarders enrolled.

During this period bacteriology was a decade or so away from being developed as a branch of medicine, and there were thus no laboratory tests available to confirm or deny the diagnosis, or to determine whether or not food, water or cesspools were contaminated. The diagnosis was made from the doctor's deduction from the history, symptoms and signs in the patient.

When the Local Board of Health was informed that typhoid fever had occurred at the convent — the information certainly had not come from Drs O'Doherty or Mullen, the convent's physicians — it decided that an inspection should be made by the mayor, the chairman, and Drs John Thomson and Richard Rendle, members of the board. When this inspection team arrived at the convent, Drs O'Doherty and Mullen were already present, having been invited by the sisters, but the board members insisted that they be unaccompanied. From a press report there appeared that nothing had been amiss at the convent.

But the matter did not rest there. A public debate through the press evolved. Drs Thomson and Rendle maintained that the cases were typhoid fever — a diagnosis strongly denied by Drs O'Doherty and Mullen. Sectarian differences may have been fanning the flames but there were other factors involved. Dr Thomson was a Local Board of Health member and O'Doherty very prominent in Central Board of Health affairs. The two boards had always been at loggerheads. Thomson was the Brisbane Hospital's house surgeon while O'Doherty and Mullen were visiting surgeons. There was no love lost between the house surgeon and the visiting surgeons. Then, Dr Hobbs, the government medical officer, still smarting over the drubbing he had received in the reception house affair, which had been initiated by O'Doherty's evidence at the magisterial inquiry, joined forces with Thomson and Rendle.

In addition to private discussions the battle was fought with letters to the *Brisbane Courier*. As well as medical opinions the epistles contained personal slurs of which Hobbs' barbs were the most acrimonious:

> The action of Dr O'Doherty in endeavouring to misdirect the public on this subject is inexplicable, seeing that he is a member of the Central Board of Health. The health of the public is more important than that of the convent school. Nero fiddled while Rome was burning and here we find Dr O'Doherty denying the existence of typhoid fever at the convent and endeavouring to prove it was some other harmless fever although reports furnished to the Registrar General contradict this to his face. Instead of opposing the action of the medical members of the Local Board of Health, and writing slightingly of their qualifications for the performance of the duties devolving upon them, it would be far better lending a helping hand, seeing that they labour for the public good and the preservation of human life.

With the school closed — the bishop had wisely suggested an early summer vacation — there were no further cases, and with no fresh cases at the school in the new year, the debate in the press lapsed. However, there were several cases of typhoid fever admitted to the Brisbane Hospital and the registrar-general's reports revealed that typhoid fever continued to feature as the cause of death on numerous death certificates, but, perhaps, as O'Doherty maintained, the patients among the sisters and the pupils at the convent had suffered from some other diseases.

In common with many Irishmen, O'Doherty loved to drink from the cup which cheers. Invited to speak at the inaugural meeting of the Catholic Total Abstinence Society in 1876, he said:

> When at home, at Blackrock, I went to hear Father Mathew lecture on temperance, and the reverend gentleman was very nearly catching me, but he did not. I went on the platform, and it was only by sneaking behind the others that I escaped being put on my knees and made to sign the pledge. Doctors have a great deal to go through, and are placed in positions when a little of the poisoned water, as it is called, is anything but poison .... I feel convinced

that total abstinence is generally commendable. [Father Mathew was famous in Ireland for his work in the temperance field.]

Around 8 p.m. on a Saturday night in May 1878, an uncovered spring-cart driven by a farmer and escorted by friends on horseback, arrived at the Brisbane Hospital. On a mattress on the floor of the cart lay a young man, Alexander Youill, who had been severely wounded in the left leg by an accidental shotgun blast near Nerang, 56 miles (90 kilometres) south of Brisbane over twenty-four hours before. John Thomson, the house surgeon, on examining Youill, found him in a weak condition from loss of blood and the long journey over the rough roads between the farmhouse at Nerang and Brisbane. His leg was so damaged that amputation was the only procedure that could be contemplated.

Thomson's instructions in such circumstances were to consult the visiting surgeon on call. Mounting his horse — there were still no telephones in Brisbane — he rode into the city to consult Dr O'Doherty, the visiting surgeon on call, whom he found at his residence in George Street, hosting a dinner party. O'Doherty instructed Thomson to arrange a consultation of the four visiting surgeons for 10 p.m. Dr Mullen arrived at the hospital at 10 p.m. but Drs O'Doherty and Cannan — Cannan had been a guest at the dinner party — reached the hospital at 11.30. O'Doherty had made two house calls on the way but no doubt the dinner delayed him also. The fourth visiting surgeon, Joseph Bancroft, was absent from Brisbane.

At the consultation the decision to amputate was unanimous and O'Doherty gave instructions to prepare the patient and the operating theatre. Then came a bombshell. Dr Thomson told O'Doherty that he was not in a fit state to operate. The usually genial Irishman exploded. Here was the young house surgeon, who had opposed him over the All Hallows fever cases, now suggesting that he was too drunk to operate, and, unfortunately, his old friend, John Mullen, agreed with Thomson. Then began several hours wrangling. O'Doherty demanded that Thomson ride into the city again and request the consulting surgeon, Hugh Bell, and the hospital committee to come to the hospital to adjudicate. Thomson refused, arguing that Dr Bell seldom came to the hospital, the committee chairman was out of town and the other members were most unlikely to come out at that time of night. At one stage, O'Doherty walked up and down on the hospital verandah, explaining later that he did so in case he was accused of having gone to sleep off his debauch. At 1 a.m. Dr Cannan left the hospital in a cab to go home. At 2.30 a.m. Thomson decided to obey O'Doherty's instructions and rode into the city in order to try to induce Dr Bell to come to the hospital. When the house surgeon had not returned at 4 a.m. O'Doherty decided to walk to his home in George Street. On the way he met Thomson going back to the hospital. A short verbal exchange took place, and O'Doherty continued trudging on his way home. At 6 a.m. Dr Mullen amputated Youill's leg with Dr Bell assisting. After initial satisfactory progress the patient died four days after the operation.

The case, which was fully reported in the press, attracted much attention in medical and political circles, with John Douglas, the premier, demanding a report from the hospital committee chairman. The committee discussed the matter at two special meetings to which Drs Mullen and Thomson, but not Dr O'Doherty, were invited. A report of the second meeting, published in the press, contained, *inter alia*, the following statement: "Other causes, which in the opinion of the committee, it is not necessary here to record, and for which neither Dr Thomson nor Dr Mullen were in any way responsible, then delayed the operation." O'Doherty was condemned by implication.

The Irish doctor wrote a letter of refutation to the *Brisbane Courier*. He accused the committee of star chamber tactics in trying him in his absence and claimed it had shown great animus in hitting him below the belt. He referred to Thomson's claim that he was not fit to operate and said that he "indignantly repelled such an accusation, and denied the right of the house surgeon to sit in judgment on him". He pointed out that, in the seventeen years he had served the Ipswich and Brisbane hospitals, he had performed almost every operation known in surgery, and was quite willing to abide by the verdict of the public as to whether he had done his work creditably or not. At a subsequent magisterial inquiry, Drs Thomson and Mullen were emphatic in their assertions that the delay in operating had not caused the death. They believed the poor condition of the patient brought on by the wound itself, the loss of blood and the exhausting journey from Nerang were the contributing factors. The only adverse statement from the bench was an admonition to the farmer, who had carelessly hung a loaded gun on a nail of the verandah wall from which it fell to the floor and exploded, inflicting the serious wound on Youill, who had been dancing with the farmer's daughter at the time.

In 1878, a dispute flared between Bishop O'Quinn and the Sisters of St Joseph whom he had invited to Queensland nine years before. The main bone of contention lay in the control of the order. Mother Mary McKillop, who had founded this Australian congregation in Adelaide, believed that the seat of government should be in that city. The bishop was adamant that the control should rest with him. The sisters' cause was strongly supported by Denis O'Donovan, erudite scholar and Queensland parliamentary librarian. From O'Donovan's action there emerged a long, bitter dispute between the two strong-willed men. Finally the bishop publicly refused O'Donovan sacramental communion. (By 1880 the order had withdrawn from Queensland.)

O'Donovan retaliated by writing regularly to the press under the pseudonym of *Umbra*, attacking the bishop, and began a voluminous correspondence with Archbishop Vaughan in Sydney in which he spun a subtle web of intrigue around O'Quinn and simultaneously abused his supporters. O'Doherty thus became the subject of many derogatory remarks in O'Donovan's letters. In 1878 he referred to "O'Doherty, who has lately incurred public censure for drunkenness in the performance of his duties". Later he wrote of "O'Doherty, the Bishop's physician, by no means noted for his morality", and again, "One of the partners in this swindle is Dr O'Doherty".

The Irish medico was still very much a public man. In

November 1877, he was one of a number of prominent citizens, who formed a committee to welcome to Queensland the Australian cricket eleven, who defeated a Queensland eighteen by an innings and twenty-three runs at the Eagle Farm racecourse. The Australian team included four players to whom cricket historians still often refer — David Gregory (captain), Charles Bannerman (batsman), John Blackham (wicketkeeper), and Ernie Spofforth ("demon" bowler). A press report of the match stated the "scorers had to leave the field to catch the steamer before making up Spofforth's average".

In the second half of the 1870s O'Doherty became a club man. In December 1876, he convened a meeting with a view to forming a new club in Brisbane "more adapted to the requirements of the professional and mercantile community than the clubs at present in existence in Brisbane". Mr Justice Lilley was elected president of the Brisbane Club — there was no connection with the club of the same name formed at the beginning of the twentieth century — and O'Doherty, a vice-president. Its first premises were situated at the corner of Ann and Wharf Streets but reference to current directories indicates that this club had a short life. O'Doherty's name also adorned the list of members of the Queensland Club and when the Johnsonian Club was founded in 1878, the Irish doctor became a popular member for several years.

CHAPTER 11

Stand Up and Be Counted

In May 1879, the Brisbane Irish community celebrated another centenary — the birth of Thomas Moore — "Ireland's national songwriter". In referring to the arrangements being made for this event the *Brisbane Courier* reported that, "After the entertainment in the School of Arts a supper will take place at the Royal Hotel, and, as Dr O'Doherty is announced to take the chair, we may safely predict this will not be the least pleasant part of the celebrations, and that the qualities that have made the best of Irishmen the most popular of men will receive thoroughly genial illustration from the chair."

The entertainment at the School of Arts, attended by the governor, Sir Arthur Kennedy, and Bishop O'Quinn, featured selections from Moore's *Irish Melodies* as well as a special ode in honour of the poet, written for the occasion by Mrs Hope Connolly, who, along with Eva, had been one of the band of women writers who contributed to the *Nation* in the days of 1848.

At the dinner, O'Doherty proposed the toast to "The Memory of Tom Moore" in an eloquent speech, displaying his wide knowledge of literature generally and of the life and the works of Moore in particular. He admonished those critics who cavilled at the poet as "a carpet knight and pseudo-patriot" and those who questioned his poetic gifts. The doctor claimed that Moore's songs "were the first that ever drew sympathy from his eyes". He pointed out that, "The poet's pen may surely do as good service in the sacred cause as the sword of the soldier" and asked, "What poet has been truer or more loyal to Ireland than Moore?" He added that, "He believed in the poetry of the last generation, which was clothed in the language that did not require an effort of the brain to understand — the language of Byron, of Moore and of Burns . . .. He claimed that Moore's melodies would live as long as Shakespeare or the English language will live . . .."

Towards the end of 1879 came news from Ireland in which there was cause for concern, not celebration. O'Doherty's native land was threatened by a famine which, if not relieved, would have results as disastrous as that of the famine of 1847. After discussing the matter with some of his countrymen, O'Doherty, now acting alone, placed advertisements in the Christmas Day issues of the *Brisbane Courier* and the *Telegraph* announcing a preliminary meeting at the Town Hall on New Year's Eve at which the formation of an Irish Famine Relief Fund would be discussed. He supported the announcement with a letter setting out the position in Ireland and invoking the aid of his countrymen in the colony. The doctor knew that there were many Irishmen who, like himself, felt so keenly for their fatherland that they supported some Irish causes, which were, at times, frowned upon by others who hailed from the Emerald Isle. He knew also that, generally, the latter group, who looked askance at the celebration of such events as the Daniel O'Connell centenary, donated money for special causes. He thus hoped that all Irishmen in the colony, irrespective of their previous demonstration of nationalism, would contribute to the fund he was sponsoring.

Prior to the New Year Eve's meeting O'Doherty contributed two further letters to the press on the subject. In the first he drew attention to a telegram from Ireland advising that the Duchess of Marlborough, the wife of the lord lieutenant of

Ireland, had appealed to Irish people everywhere for contributions in aid of their poor countrymen at present sorely stricken by the almost complete failure of the harvest. His second letter was accompanied by a rather colourful article from the Dublin *Freeman's Journal* which said that "the great masses of the Irish small farmers have only been kept alive on Indian corn during the last twelve months by the sufferance of shopkeepers" and that conditions "have brought poorer brethren of the western coast to the brim of actual starvation". From both letters it was apparent that at this stage O'Doherty believed that any aid would come chiefly from his own countrymen.

In the meantime, however, the doctor had been heartened by discussion with friends and at least one letter in the press suggesting that the appeal should be by no means restricted to the Irish in the colony. He wrote to Sir Arthur Kennedy, the governor, and Arthur Palmer, premier of Queensland, soliciting their help. Their replies were so encouraging that, at the preliminary meeting, the only steps taken were to form a general committee and a decision made to request the governor to preside at a public meeting a week later — a request to which he readily acquiesced. The Irish-born Kennedy had been a law inspector in County Clare during the great famines of the 1840s, a fact to which he alluded during his opening speech at the meeting. The governor accepted the position of chairman of the general committee which included the Catholic and Anglican bishops, O'Quinn and Hale, Premier Douglas, most cabinet ministers and many more prominent citizens. Former Fenian, John Flood, became secretary. Flood, released by the British government after transportation to Western Australia, came east first to Sydney, and then to Queensland where he engaged in newspaper work.

The Irish famine fund appeal was most successful, with not only the Irish in Queensland, but also the general community contributing generously. Queensland raised £12,000 ($24,000) of which over £11,000 was forwarded from Brisbane to the lord mayor of Dublin and over £700 from Charters Towers where numerous Irishmen were among the miners looking for gold there. The *Brisbane Courier* proudly claimed that on a population basis Queensland had raised more than her sister colonies. The total of £95,000 raised in Australia was far more than the contribution from America.

The committee's work was concluded at a meeting in June 1880, at which Joshua Peter Bell, president of the Legislative Council and administrator of the colony during the absence of the governor overseas, thanked all those who had made the campaign such a success. During his speech, the administrator said that, "He could not help referring to Dr O'Doherty who was the first to bring it before the public. His name had gone forth favourably in connection with the fund throughout the colonies and Great Britain. If ever a member to represent Australia in the English Parliament were to be elected, and Dr O'Doherty were to be selected, he thought Australia would not be unfittingly represented. The doctor might have views that he was peculiarly fitted to represent Ireland in the House of Commons."

At a special function a few days later O'Doherty, on behalf of the committee, presented an illuminated address to John Flood for his services as secretary of the fund.

When the 1878 parliamentary session came to an end, the bill to amend the Health Act, drafted by O'Doherty and introduced by the premier, had not been passed and therefore lapsed. Despite this further disappointment, O'Doherty led the Central Board of Health campaign to improve the public health of Brisbane as vigorously as before. Early in 1879 the Irish doctor and Thomas Finney submitted to the board a comprehensive report on the working of the earth-closet system under the Local Board of Health during the previous five years. The local board had made efforts to extend the system in its area of jurisdiction, but these had been haphazard. In Fortitude Valley, where there was great need for reform, there had been no attempt at all to have the inhabitants adopt the system and in other parts of the city there had been no effort to enforce the complete adoption necessary to make it successful. O'Doherty and Finney recommended that the Central Board "take earnest counsel with the Local Board and the Municipal

Council, and if necessary with the Government to have such a reform instituted in such a way as will render the system a blessing instead of a curse to the community". The premier accepted the recommendation of consultation and the city's sanitation and drainage were debated rather bitterly over the next few weeks at the conference table and in the press. As was the custom at the time, members of both boards mixed scientific comment with derogatory remarks concerning their opposite numbers. Alfred Hubbard, chairman of the Local Board, claimed that, "The sudden interest manifested by the Central Board is as remarkable as their previous indifference. What they exist for would puzzle a lawyer to tell."

O'Doherty replied with, "These are the dog days and Mr Hubbard's rabid distemper has clearly got the better of his memory as well as his judgment." Then Dr Joseph Bancroft (Local Board) chimed in and according to Dr Hugh Bell (Central Board) in the first part of his letter, "reflections were cast manifesting a spirit that one regrets to see — unworthy of anyone, especially a scientific man".

The premier suggested a new amending bill be drawn up to meet various difficulties that emerged during the conference and press debates, and O'Doherty introduced a further bill in September 1879. In his initiating speech he said, "The sanitary system should be gone into and made a complete one . . .. It was not sufficient for the Local Board of Health under the Municipal Council to send a few carts here and there through the city; nor that in three-fourths or four-fifths of the city there was no application of the system. At present nobody was absolutely compelled to have recourse to it. He might have his residence subjected to the cleansing system; his neighbour next door might be permitted to do as he liked."

Due to the time taken in the preparation of the bill, parliament did not process the legislation before the end of the session, and all O'Doherty could do was to implore the members to study it carefully during the recess and hope he would have the opportunity to reintroduce it during the next session. But, alas, no action was taken in the next session. The deaths from infectious diseases in an not uncommon display of periodicity showed a reduction. New fever wards built at the Brisbane Hospital were not immediately used. This was sufficient for a legislature notably apathetic towards health measures to forget about O'Doherty's health bill.

But the reduction in infectious diseases was only a lull before the storm. The highest death rate from such causes in the colony's history was recorded in the years to follow. During 1883 there were 1,000 deaths in Queensland from the filth diseases of typhoid fever, dysentery, diarrhoea and enteritis, the cause of which was inadequate sanitation. The Brisbane Hospital opened its new fever wards and they were soon overflowing with typhoid fever and dysentery patients. In the first months of 1884 the deaths in Brisbane from these diseases doubled and the legislators became scared. Panic succeeded where O'Doherty and his colleagues had failed. A new Health Act was passed giving the Central Board of Health greater powers, and the municipal and shire councils, and not local boards, the responsibility of implementing its provisions.

The hostility which often followed the autocratic actions of Bishop O'Quinn reached a flashpoint towards the end of 1879 and the beginning of 1880. Denis O'Donovan, the lay ringleader of the anti-O'Quinn faction, not only had continued his support for the Sisters of St Joseph, much to the Bishop's ire, but also criticised the prelate's financial administration of the diocese and the policy of the Catholic newspaper, the *Australian*. Ill feeling also existed among some of the priests, one of whom, writing under a pseudonym, told the editor of the *Brisbane Courier* that, "I believe they all secretly sympathise with 'Umbra' [O'Donovan's pseudonym] and other writers on the same side, and pray that he may be successful in the good work which he has undertaken." The writer of the letter was hotly attacked by four Brisbane priests in the next issue of the paper.

Bishop O'Quinn clearly needed support and his "chief apologist", as usual, rose to the occasion. O'Doherty organised a committee to prepare a eulogistic address to the Bishop which would be presented at a suitable time and canvassed co-religionists for their signatures to the document.

The opening of a new building at the Christian Brothers School on Gregory Terrace on 13 January 1880 seemed an appropriate occasion at which to present the address and O'Doherty was asked to perform this task. In introductory remarks he said that, "He was honoured by being requested to be the spokesman of the people on this occasion — a request he need scarcely tell them he responded to with pride as well as pleasure. He heartily wished he was gifted with a 'tongue of fire' to do the justice to the theme which it deserved. As it was, he could only assure His Lordship of his entire belief that every word of the address he would read today, expressive of the respect and veneration of the people, would be but the echo of the general sentiment of the colony, Protestant as well as Catholic." The 750 signatures to the address included, besides O'Doherty, other prominent laymen as John Murtagh Macrossan, minister for Works and Mines and later premier, Andrew Joseph Thynne and Thomas Henry Fitzgerald. An extract reads as follows:

> It may be unusual on our part, who are in a manner more intimately connected with the head of this diocese and are thus always under your eye, to add our humble and dutiful testimony to what our brethren have so spontaneously done in other parts; but our excuse is that we have observed of late, with deep pain and indignation, that covert attacks have been made to assail your Lordship that we have now, as always, the most unshaken confidence in your prudence as a Bishop, and the firmest faith in the mild unspoiled purity of your life, and that while God gives us life we shall each and all, in public and in private vindicate your honour against all calumny.

O'Donovan attacked the manner in which the signatures to the address had been collected. He wrote both to the press and to Archbishop Vaughan in Sydney. His letter to the archbishop included the following:

> The letters in the press . . . reflected principally not on the Bishop but on the committee who obtained the signatures to an address to the Bishop by improper means . . . . Except some remark of this kind the whole correspondence bore on the unworthy means adopted by the address-committee to deceive the people into signing it and the miserable result of 744 signatures (many of them no

doubt duplicates) notwithstanding that it was a declaration in favour of Catholic education as well as in favour of the Bishop, notwithstanding the threats of the clergy from the altars, notwithstanding the fact that many of those who signed it (even the very leader Dr O'Doherty) are so far from believing what the Bishop has done for education that they send their own children to non-Catholic schools. [Although enrolled with the Christian Brothers in 1875, Kevin O'Doherty Jun. after returning from a long absence due to travel spent a few months at the Brisbane Grammar School.]

Despite O'Donovan's attempts to denigrate O'Doherty along with other O'Quinn supporters the Irish doctor retained his position as leader of the Catholic laity. Twelve months after the events at the Christian Brothers School an almost identical function took place at All Hallows School on Bowen Terrace. On 2 January 1881 Bishop O'Quinn laid a foundation stone for a school building. O'Doherty, on behalf of the Catholic community, read and presented another address to the bishop praising his work in education and eulogising his standing among all denominations in the colony. Two weeks later, it was again O'Doherty who took the *Brisbane Courier* to task for omitting the names of two All Hallows School students from the list of Queenslanders, who had been successful in the Sydney University matriculation examination.

A few months later a meeting was held in St Stephen's schoolroom to arrange details of a function at which O'Quinn would be honoured for the attainment of the twenty-second anniversary of his consecration as Bishop of Brisbane. Reverend Fouhy, who chaired the meeting, said that certain circumstances demanded special congratulations connected with his Lordship's recent restoration to perfect health from a very severe and trying illness — which restoration could be attributed to the skill of Dr O'Doherty.

The bishop's restoration to health was shortlived. A relapse occurred and this time the skills of Dr O'Doherty were of no avail and O'Quinn died on 18 August 1881. O'Doherty was one of a number of pallbearers, who shouldered the coffin in relays, as the funeral procession left St Stephen's Cathedral, traversed city streets and returned for the burial in a vault in St Stephen's itself. One month later a special memorial service was attended by a congregation which the press estimated numbered 3,000 people.

Shortly after the bishop's death O'Doherty made public his relationship to him in these words:

> I loved him personally for three and twenty years . . . and during a great portion of that time I loved him as few men loved another. There were points of sympathy between us — reminiscences of other times and other scenes — community of friends in far-off lands — similarity of tastes acquired amid surroundings very different from those of life in Queensland — which drew us much and closely together when I first came to this city, and which, now that he is gone, make me mourn him with a grief that only the most soul-united friends can feel, and which no greatness of intellect, no fascination of manner, could inspire if not allied with some of the noblest attributes of heart. Are not the qualities of such a man sufficiently great and sufficiently numerous to furnish matter for the most exalted encomiums? And is it wise in the interest of religion, to provoke discussion on those features of his administration on which it must be permitted at least to hold different opinions? Those who think as I do on these matters helped to swell processions that streamed through his house last Thursday to pay the last tribute of respect to their dead bishop . . .. Are these men to be dragged once more by ill-advised allusions into a controversy which can have no practical interest at present . . . . Let us join cordially in doing honour to the more beautiful and lovable traits in the character of our loved chief pastor about which we are all agreed; and let us forget the frailties, the imperfections, the errors from which he, no more than any other creature born in sin, was not entirely preserved. Let us hope and believe that his intentions purified even the most questionable of his acts, and let his memory be handed down to our children surrounded with the united love and veneration of the whole of that people over whose spiritual interests he ruled so long. In whatever is done . . . to record in a lasting manner the remarkable episcopate and the many high qualities of the first Bishop of Brisbane, I will most heartily join as far as my means will permit me; and I think I may safely say that there is not a Catholic in the diocese who will not do the same.

O'Doherty's leadership role in Catholic affairs did not change with the bishop's passing. He chaired the memorial committee which recommended that O'Quinn be honoured by a statue and a "Benevolent Asylum for the reception and succour of unfortunate and distressed women throughout the colony". The doctor also chaired a committee which organised a reception for the Right Reverend Robert Dunne, bishop-elect, and at a reception in March 1882 an address of welcome and congratulations to the new bishop was signed: "K. I. O'Doherty, For the Catholics of Brisbane". In the three following years his services were eagerly sought for the position of chairman at St Patrick's Day celebrations.

When T.H. Fitzgerald signed the address which was presented to Bishop O'Quinn at the Christian Brothers School in January 1880, he had only recently returned from North Queensland where he decided that the Johnstone River district was suitable for the establishment of a new sugar-growing venture. Henry Fitzgerald had entered the Queensland parliament at the same time as O'Doherty, later becoming treasurer in the Lilley government but had resigned to pioneer sugar-growing in the Mackay area.

After Fitzgerald had failed to find financial support for the new project through the expected channels, Bishop O'Quinn persuaded Florence O'Reilly, a wealthy spinster living at All Hallows convent, to provide the necessary funds and a number of blocks of land at Johnstone River, each 1,280 acres (256 hectares) were selected in the name of a number of Sisters of Mercy. These would be developed along with Fitzgerald's own land in a plantation which was given the name of Innisfail. Fitzgerald also arranged for a block to be selected for his old friend O'Doherty which would be developed separately.

By April 1880, Fitzgerald was ready to leave Brisbane and twelve white men and twenty-two Kanakas with the necessary equipment embarked on the *Corea* for Johnstone River. Early in the following year O'Doherty sent his youngest son, Kevin, aged twenty years, to commence work on his selection. It is hard to imagine the young man's feelings as he supervised the clearing of the thick scrub which covered all the new land with the help of one or two white men and the main labour force coming from Chinese or Kanakas. Mail and fresh supplies came infrequently by sea from Cardwell further south and fever often reduced the work force to deplorable helplessness. The riddle of the "coastal fevers" was not solved until well into the twentieth century but malaria, scrub typhus and leptospirosis (Weil's disease) were probably all at work in young O'Doherty's period, taking heavy toll of those who had joined the venture.

A few months later, Dr O'Doherty with the owners of two neighbouring blocks, R.H. Ryan and G.W. Gray, formed the Queensland Sugar Company to develop their combined areas, to which they gave the name, Inishowen, after the area in Ireland where the O'Doherty clan had its origins. A *Brisbane Courier* article of January 1883, reporting the progress at the Johnstone River included the following: "Inishowen (Dr O'Doherty). Mr A. Owen Jones, manager, has over 150 acres cleared, 100 acres of which is under cane. Buildings and river frontages are being pushed vigorously ahead. The mill [manufactured in France] is expected in July next. It will have the latest improvements, and no doubt this estate will prove a splendid investment if properly managed; 120 Kanakas and twelve Europeans are employed."

To the west of the Johnstone River district lay scrub-covered mountain ranges, which bounded a plateau where pastoralists were settling around Atherton and where tin had been discovered at Herberton. Supplies were being taken to this tableland by packhorses and mules, but there were discussions at government level of a proposed railway to make access easier. Three centres fought fiercely for selection as the coastal starting point of the proposed line — Port Douglas, Cairns and Johnstone River with its harbour of Mourilyn. In June 1883, O'Doherty, Fitzgerald and others with interests at Johnstone River waited on the minister for Works, Albert Norton, to push their claims for a railway from Herberton to Mourilyn. O'Doherty told the minister that, "The mere fact that Christie Palmerston [well-known North Queensland prospector and explorer] had travelled from the Johnstone River to Herberton in eight or nine days, cutting his way through dense scrub, proved the route must be an easy one." Archibald Meston, chairman of the Cairns Divisional Board, in opposing O'Doherty's claim, said that, "The rear of the Mourilyan discussion was brought up by our stately friend, Dr O'Doherty, as a sort of invincible guard or 84-ton gun, intended just to put a conclusive and irremediable finish on the engagement. He was proudly triumphant in a knowledge of a fact that Christie Palmerston went from Johnstone to Herberton in nine days. Dear artless and unsophisticated senatorial Aesculapean! If Palmerston required nine days to travel 45 miles, he only travelled five miles a day, and must have met very rough country indeed...."

In June 1884, the governor, Sir Anthony Musgrave, and the premier, Samuel Griffith, during a visit to North Queensland, inspected the three rival centres vying for the railway starting point. At Johnstone River the vice-regal party was met by Dr O'Doherty, who had made a special but separate trip to push that centre's claims. All the lobbying of O'Doherty and his friends was in vain, as Cairns was selected for the terminus.

In addition to tin at Herberton, alluvial gold was discovered at Johnstone River in December 1884. O'Doherty and James McSharry took out a mineral lease at Herberton, and one report suggests O'Doherty secured enough land on the lower Johnstone goldfield to monopolise possible sites for a town, but research revealed no evidence to confirm this. Unfortunately for the doctor his speculations came to nought. Despite the paper prediction of favourable results for the sugar plantation, the project failed. In 1889, William Canny, manager at Inishowen, told a royal commission into the ailing sugar industry that, "Mr Gray, managing director of the company, had told him that unless there was a good crushing in the coming season, the plantation would have to be closed as it was not paying". Falling sugar prices, drought and the cane grub had resulted in very poor returns on the £80,000 that the partners had invested in Inishowen. In 1891 the expensive French mill crushed its last cane. The goldfield petered out and any possible plan O'Doherty may have had for a town was no more than a dream. No record can be found of any fortune being made from the tin venture at Herberton.

As a result of his association with the Johnstone River sugar-growing, O'Doherty changed his attitude towards the use of Kanakas in the industry. Not long after Fitzgerald left

Brisbane with his Kanakas he spoke on the practice in parliament. Hansard carries this report:

> He had introduced a Bill in the other Chamber to repeal the Polynesian Act, but he had lived long enough to rejoice that the proposal he had made had not been acceded to. He had been led to move for the repeal of the Act at that time because of the odium which had been brought upon the colony from the depredation and atrocities that had been perpetrated in the South Sea Islands by those who attempted to kidnap and carry the Islanders by force . . . . It was very desirable that the employment of the Polynesians in the pearl fisheries should run on undisturbed . . . . It was of the utmost importance — not merely that the sugar industry but the other industries — the growth of tea, coffee and spices — should have every encouragement.

Four years later, after Kanakas had been used at Inishowen, he had retained his changed attitude when he said that, "If people would only take the trouble to ascertain the civilising results of the employment of the islanders in Queensland they would find that in the colony, as well as in the islands themselves, the results had been most beneficial to the islanders."

For the first two decades after Queensland became a separate colony, the Medical Board was empowered to register not only doctors but pharmacists as well. Chafing under the control by a board consisting solely of medical practitioners, the pharmacists took steps in 1880 to throw off this yoke. At a meeting in October of that year, chaired by the well-known Moses Ward, it was decided to form a Pharmaceutical Society of Queensland of which Edward Taylor became the first president and Fletcher Yeo, the secretary. The society's first aim was to persuade the government to introduce legislation, which would create a separate pharmacy board to control the registration of pharmacists and to conduct a course of study and examinations, by which eligibility for such registration would be determined.

The medical profession led by the majority of the Medical Board members vigorously opposed the idea that the pharmacists should contol their own destiny. However the pharmacists found an ally among the doctors — O'Doherty. The

Irish doctor, having served an apprenticeship to a Dublin apothecary at the beginning of his medical course, was not only favourably disposed towards the pharmacists' proposals but also had the courage to express publicly a view contrary to that held by the rest of his profession and to champion the cause in parliament. In introducing a bill which met the aims of the Pharmaceutical Society he said that, "He knew of instances of men being admitted as pharmacists who ought in no way be permitted to practise, and that the object of the bill was to provide the public with some more efficient guarantee than had hitherto existed, that they would be provided with proper drugs, and that they would have the prescriptions of medical men properly compounded." But the doctors had lobbied successfully and the bill lapsed.

Introduced again in 1882, a select committee was appointed to examine the proposed legislation. The inquiry was an airing of the views of the two professions put forward by their leaders. Dr Joseph Bancroft, chairman of the Medical Board, claimed that, "As a body the pharmacists of Brisbane are ill-informed and unable to carry out the management of a Board of Pharmacy." This opinion had also been conveyed to members of both Houses of parliament in a letter signed by all members of the Medical Board except O'Doherty. Finally the bill was passed in 1884 despite the efforts of the doctors to block it. Speaking in the final debate, O'Doherty was reported as saying that, "At the present time the most villainous and deadly compounds were being dispensed by persons who probably didn't understand the dangerous nature of drugs in their charge. He never had occasion to take any of his own prescriptions, but he did not know the day he would have to — it might be tomorrow — and it would be very unpleasant if an incompetent chemist gave him an overdose of some poisonous drug by mistake. He disapproved of those medical men who dispensed their own prescriptions, thus 'taking the bread' of honest druggists."

The last comment not surprisingly angered some of his medical colleagues and it prompted Dr Richard Rendle, a prominent practitioner, who had opposed the legislation, to write to the *Brisbane Courier* saying that "Dr O'Doherty is not willing to give anyone credit that in dispensing his own prescriptions he does so in order to protect both patient and doctor from risk of error but implies it is done for pelf." A patient then replied by saying, "Dr Rendle indulges, I observe, in a little crow over his big medical brother, the genial Dr O'Doherty, a man whose many good deeds done in his professional capacity will, I venture to predict, be gratefully remembered and enthusiastically spoken of in that by-and-by which is the future of doctors as of other poor mortals."

In the early 1880s doctors in Queensland were all general practitioners and in the country areas particularly, due to the lack of external help, were obliged to tackle every kind of medical problem which presented. In Brisbane, however, there were some — and O'Doherty was one — who had special skills with the scalpel. As has always been the case, these surgeons attained a high reputation in the community, and many of their collegues were quite prepared to transfer to them patients needing surgery. The following report which appeared in the *Brisbane Courier* of 27 November 1880 reveals how O'Doherty stood in this regard:

> We were shocked to find, on enquiry yesterday morning that the injuries sustained by Mr Albert Drury's son were of a nature which necessitated amputation of both his feet. The heel of one foot, and the other leg from the calf downwards, were lacerated in such a frightful manner that Drs Concannon and Cannan decided that the only hope of saving the little fellow's life was to submit him to this dreadful operation and on Dr O'Doherty's arrival from Sandgate, whither he had been to visit a patient, the amputation was effected.

As was the practice during this period O'Doherty operated in his frock coat without surgical gloves, using chloroform anaesthesia. Unfortunately, like other surgeons of this era, he lost many patients from sepsis. Antibiotics were decades away and even Joseph Lister's carbolic spray introduced in operating theatres in Britain in 1867 had not reached Brisbane. The Irishman's claim during the fracas over the delay in amputating Alexander Youill's leg in 1878, that he had performed almost every operation known, was no idle boast.

Unfortunately no medical journal contains accounts of his work, as he never bothered to put pen to paper on the subject. However, two accounts of later dates may be taken as authentic opinions of his surgery. The *Australian Medical Gazette* of 1905, in an obituary, included the following:

> In his prime he was known as a dashing and original surgeon and used to get good results from two operations which he claimed as his own but never published. One of these was the removal of the head of the femur [thigh bone] in intra-capsular fractures in order to improve the usefulness of the limb; the other was a method of exploring the back of the ankle-joint . . .. He had some success with ovariotomy as many as thirty years ago.

Sandford Jackson, eminent surgeon and medical historian, wrote in 1926 that before he came to Brisbane in 1882, the only successful ovariotomy in that city had been performed by O'Doherty. Ovariotomy — removal of ovarian cysts — was generally the first operation performed wherever surgeons were beginning to enter the abdomen. Thus, around 1880, O'Doherty performed the first abdominal operation to be carried out in Queensland.

Despite his lone stand against the remainder of the profession during the introduction of pharmacy legislation, in 1882 the Irish doctor was elected president of the revived Queensland Medical Society. In his inaugural address O'Doherty recommended one committee for the management of the Brisbane Hospital, the Children's Hospital and the Lock Hospital, a return to the appointment of doctors as coroners and the use of Brisbane Hospital as a preliminary medical school. He also recounted some advice that a distinguished Dublin physician had given to a new graduate from the Royal College of Surgeons:

> I perceive you are highly elated at your success and doubtless imagine you are about forthwith to rise to the top of the tree and distance your competitors in the race for a discerning public. Now, take the advice of an old man, and if you attain to the position you aspire, to study less to secure the favour of the public than the goodwill of your professional brethren. Make their interests your own. At all times seek their advice, and assistance, and, credit me, you will find this, the golden key to success in your career.

The *Brisbane Courier*, misunderstanding O'Doherty's advocacy that doctors should not curry favour with the public to mean neglecting the welfare of patients generally, admonished him for repeating the advice of the Dublin physician. He was also criticised for suggesting a wide-ranging hospital committee and for his desire to see the medical profession provide coroners but received a modicum of praise for recommending a preliminary medical school at the hospital. Like its predecessor of 1871, the second medical society had a short existence. It has been suggested that the absence of scientific meetings and divisions over ethics, medical politics and hospital management caused its demise. However, the interest must have been no more than lukewarm at any time as of twenty-seven members only nine paid their subscriptions.

Dr Sandford Jackson came to Queensland in 1882 to take up duties as assistant house surgeon at the Brisbane Hospital at the same time as Leighton Kesteven commenced as house surgeon. Kesteven was in trouble almost from the first day. He was accused of furnishing his residence with hospital beds and helping himself to the spirits in the hospital dispensary. Then three visiting surgeons, O'Doherty, Bancroft and Thomson, complained bitterly to the hospital committee that Kesteven made arrangements to consult with them regarding seriously ill patients and was then absent from the hospital at the appointed time. Worse still, he initiated treatment without consulting them. This was indeed a blow to their dignity. The wrangling continued for several months until Kesteven was dismissed and Jackson was promoted to the senior position. Meanwhile, in January 1883, O'Doherty resigned his position of visiting surgeon. He was now fifty-nine years of age and had served in an honorary capacity as visiting surgeon at the Ipswich and Brisbane Hospitals for twenty years. His private practice, parliamentary duties, church and Irish affairs still occupied much of his time. At the meeting at which his resignation was reluctantly accepted, he claimed that a radical change in the management of the hospital was needed, and repeated his opinion that the house surgeon should be the executive of the visiting staff.

By 1880 most of Queensland had been settled by Europeans although some areas were sparsely populated. Pastoralists, gold-miners and sugar planters had pushed into the tropical north of the colony. It was the first time that white man anywhere in the world had undertaken manual labour in the tropics. This new venture was accompanied by predictions of physical and even moral degradation for the whites involved, and English experts held that under the tropical sun the sheep, if they could survive in the Queensland north, would soon grow hair instead of wool.

O'Doherty, with his sugar plantation which employed mostly Kanakas, was one of the many who believed that white men could not survive unscathed after working in the tropics. A record of a speech in parliament in 1884 reads:

> The Hon. K.I. O'Doherty ... again asserted that no white man could venture into the scrub without sacrificing himself. He would go further and say that white men would venture to work there with their energy which was remarkable. He had seen them sweating under that tremendous heat, and though they did their work, what was the result? There was not a place where they did that work where there was not fire-water, and he would say from his experience as a physician that the mortality from the necessity of imbibing the most vile liquor that could be sold in any part of the world, arose from the manly efforts they made to accomplish what was an impossibility. Without those stimulants they would not stand the work, and the consequence of indulgence was that three-fourths of them were laid in an early grave. Take those men into the scrub and ask them to go and do the work they were called on in order to make way for cultivation, and he unhesitatingly said that three-fourths would come out with utterly broken constitutions or would leave their bones in the scrub.

Two important events in the O'Doherty family life took place in 1882. The two elder sons, William and Edward, made a triumphant return to Brisbane after successfully completing their studies overseas, and a month later the family moved into a new home in Ann Street which father Kevin had commissioned to be built for them. After graduating with honours in dentistry in Philadelphia, William went to Dublin where, obtaining further dental qualifications at the Royal College of Surgeons, he commenced practice with his uncle, also William. However, rheumatism forced him to leave Ireland and somewhat blunted the joy of his return. Edward, having obtained degrees in surgery, medicine and obstetrics, came back as ship's surgeon on the BISN steamer, *Zamora*.

The new house, named "Frascati", after the district at Blackrock where Kevin's mother lived in her later years, was a stately, two-storied stone residence of fourteen rooms, with three consulting rooms on the ground floor, of which Kevin and Edward occupied two in their combined medical practice. In the third consulting room William commenced his dental practice. Later "Frascati" became the nurses' home for St Martin's Hospital, built next door to St John's Anglican Cathedral. (The first section of the cathedral was consecrated in 1910. St Martin's Hospital was opened in 1921.) Spencer Browne, in his *Journalist's Memories*, commented on an early function at the new O'Doherty residence in these words:

> At the *Frascati* house-warming, Dr O'Doherty was congratulated on having four sons to worthily uphold his name. I well remember the old man's words to an enthusiastic toasting of his health, in which he referred to the boys. He said, "Well they are here today bright and cheery, but they are in God's hands and we do not know what the future holds for them." I was pretty young, and we were often a wild lot; but the words of old Dr O'Doherty seemed to clutch my heart with an icy hand. Was it Celtic premonition?

For many years the Brisbane daily press published very full reports of the news from the British Isles. In the late 1870s and early 1880s the readers of the *Brisbane Courier* and the *Telegraph* were given detailed accounts of events in Ireland. They read of the new leader of the Irish political party — the Protestant Charles Stewart Parnell, an Irish landlord, noted for his nationalism; they read, too, of the Irish Land League, formed by former Fenian, Michael Davitt, to fight for the peasants against exorbitant rentals, evictions and oppressive landlordism. They learnt how the pressure of social ostracism and the refusal of services to Captain Boycott, an agent for the absent landlord of a Mayo estate, added the word, "boycott", to the English vocabulary. There were accounts also of alleged agrarian violence by the Land Leaguers.

In October 1881, Parnell was imprisoned in Kilmainham jail under the Coercion Act, without a charge being made, but was later released when Gladstone, the English prime minister, promised coercion would be dropped and the problem of rent arrears examined. In turn Parnell agreed that agitation would cease. The Land Leaguers claimed a victory when Gladstone introduced a Land Act giving tenants legal assessment of fair rents and prohibiting arbitrary eviction. The Land League was suppressed but replaced with the Irish National League and the Irish leader pushed on with his objective of Home Rule for Ireland — self-government within the British empire.

The Brisbane dailies received their news from agencies in England and thus printed the British version of events in Ireland — a pro-British, anti-Irish view which also emerged in the numerous editorials on the Irish question which appeared in those journals. The *Brisbane Courier* in 1880 spoke of "widespread disaffection, lawless violence, rumours of intended risings and secret preparation for rebellion" which the editor considered the logical outcome of "Parnell's incendiary harangues". However, the same paper admitted the "flagrant injustice which all Englishmen might look back upon with shame". The *Telegraph* believed that there would be "no guarantee of peace to Ireland in Home Rule" and that there was "no alternative but compulsory subjugation." The anti-Irish feeling reached new heights after the murder in 1882 of the chief secretary for Ireland, Lord Cavendish and the under-secretary, T.H. Burke — the Phoenix Park murders in which Parnell was not involved.

The Brisbane Irish, particularly the Catholic Irish, distrusted the news articles and editorials in the daily press and looked to the weekly Catholic paper, the *Australian*, for the "correct" version of the Irish question. The *Australian* printed extracts from the Irish papers, which, although some weeks old, gave its readers different versions from those which appeared in the daily press. In its editorials it expressed such views as: "In short, there is general consensus [on the continent] that British government in Ireland is neither more nor less than the rule of force and oppression" and that "notwithstanding the claims of the landlords and the Tory press, all impartial and well-informed men must concede the agitation has been carried on with very little violence".

It was in this climate that a Brisbane branch of the Irish Land league was formed in January 1881 with the sole purpose of raising funds to send to Ireland to aid the Parnell party. Elected chairman, O'Doherty commented on the absence of other leading Irishmen, who were apparently fearful of the consequences their presence would have either on their status in the community or on their business. In his opening speech the doctor referred to his own rebel days of 1848 and outlined Parnell's career as well as the objects of the Land League in Ireland. A resolution was passed to send an address to Parnell informing him that, "We in the distant land deem it a sacred duty to take part with our countrymen at home and abroad, and not merely to sympathise with you but, as far as our numbers and means permit, to contribute to the success of your labours."

Each of the Brisbane dailies published an editorial on the formation of the Brisbane branch. The *Brisbane Courier* was kind to O'Doherty, saying that, "The doctor's presence was, we are satisfied, dictated by a strong sense of duty, and with one or two exceptions, he made, for him, to such an audience and on such a subject, a studiously moderate speech" but reminded him that, "If they [Parnell and his followers] need sympathy at present, then sympathy is given to shooting landlords and bailiffs, maiming cattle, burning hayricks, poisoning coverts and establishing both in town and country, the worst despotism on earth — the despotism of the mob." The *Telegraph* bared its teeth in the following condemnation:

> The chairman, like an old warhorse, snorting and prancing with delight at the sound of battle, seemed to revel felicitously with memories of past rebellion. Now after all his offences have been condoned, confidence and honour placed on him, he comes forth to a public platform to give his countenance to the outrages, cruelties, assassinations, perpetrated under the auspices of the Land League. Other Irish gentlemen, of influence and position, refused to sanction by their presence the illadvised proceedings on Monday night. The formation here of a branch of the Land League is an

affront to all loyal subjects and a positive source of social mischief. It is a pernicious effort to encourage in the breasts of Irishmen the sentiments of disloyalty.

At a subsequent meeting of the Brisbane branch at which Bishop O'Quinn presided, it was announced that the Brisbane collections of £176 had nearly reached the target of £200 and the Queensland total amounted to over £750.

From August 1881 there came to Australia a number of Irish representatives to give the Irish viewpoint and gather further funds. In January 1883 the Redmond brothers, John and William, landed in Adelaide and then went to Sydney. Their arrival coincided with the trial of men charged with the murders of Lord Cavendish and T.H. Burke, at which allegations were made that Land Leaguers were involved with the assassinations. The Redmonds received a hostile reception in the press with Henry Parkes, notable New South Wales politician, clamouring for their expulsion. They came to Queensland in March where their reception was still hostile. John Redmond spoke to 2,000 people at a welcoming picnic at Goodna where O'Doherty presented an address to the visitor. Later John Redmond addressed further meetings at St James' school and at the Theatre Royal. During the Redmonds' visit O'Doherty did not stand quite alone. While he chaired the meeting at the Theatre Royal, John Macrossan, minister for Works and Mines, presided at the functions at the St James' School at which Patrick O'Sullivan, MLA for Ipswich, was also present. The Brisbane press was not as vitriolic as on other occasions, with the *Brisbane Courier* only raising doubts as to whether Ireland would be satisfied with Home Rule.

The Redmonds' visit to Brisbane coincided with a camp of the Queensland Volunteer Forces at Lytton. O'Doherty, who was surgeon major to the Forces, took John Redmond to view the camp, and there was "general alarm within the lines" and the raising of eyebrows in the officers' mess. It was also during the visit that a Brisbane branch of the Irish National League was formed, with O'Doherty transferring as president from the dissolved Land League to the same position in the new organisation, with John Macrossan becoming vice-president.

In November 1883, at the suggestion of John Redmond, arrangements were made to hold an Irish national convention at St Patrick's Hall, Melbourne to which delegates from all Irish National League branches in Australia and New Zealand were invited and all other kindred bodies were represented with a view to uniting all Irish organisations in the two countries, as well as forming a permanent body to which Ireland could look for moral and practical support. Some difficulty was experienced in finding an appropriate chairman for the convention who, ideally, would have come from Melbourne. However, when the Redmonds arrived there, leading Irishmen declined to associate with their campaign. Sir Bryan O'Loghlen, well-known in Ireland and a former premier of Victoria, refused all invitations to attend the Redmond meetings and Frank Gavan Duffy, fearful that his law practice would be jeopardised if he supported the campaign, was equivocal when he spoke at a Redmond meeting. The organisers approached O'Doherty who accepted immediately, and, with Macrossan, was nominated as a Queensland delegate. The *Brisbane Courier* condemned the intended action:

> Right-thinking and common-sense people of all classes will be sorry to see public men of such large experience and considerable influence in affairs as Dr O'Doherty and Mr Macrossan permitting themselves to be jockeyed to the front as delegates for Queensland to the convention of the Irish National League shortly to be held in Melbourne. It is, we think, to be regretted that any such league has been formed in the colonies; to be regretted because of the asserted connection of it with secret societies in Ireland and America and the measure of blame which must be shared by it in the outrages committed by them.

The *Melbourne Argus*, in commenting on O'Doherty's intention, said that, "He occupies a position of Irish leader in Queensland analagous to that which Sir C.G. Duffy so long occupied in this colony." The Brisbane *Telegraph* considered the best method of dealing with the convention was to ignore it altogether.

O'Doherty in his opening address at the convention spoke of his part in the 1848 rebellion, expressed his expectation of

Home Rule for Ireland, and, at the same time, pledged loyalty to the British throne. Included in the resolutions passed by the gathering were pledges of support towards the Home Rule campaign, approval for Parnell's policies and a decision to form a federal council of the Irish National League in Australasia with O'Doherty as the first president.

The *Brisbane Courier* again condemned O'Doherty and added that, "We repudiate on behalf of the vast majority of Queenslanders all sympathy with the convention in Melbourne. It is a disloyal assemblage aimed against our Queen and country." In the midst of the continuous criticism and the reluctance of other leading Irishmen in Australia to be involved, O'Doherty had again stood up and been counted.

CHAPTER 12

Triumph then Tragedy

In 1885 O'Doherty was to receive his reward for his unswerving loyalty for the Irish cause and his strong support for the Redmonds during their time in Australia. He announced that he was planning a visit to his native land, leaving his son, Edward, to manage their medical practice in Brisbane. Although there are no records to confirm it, there was apparently a promise of a seat for an Irish electorate in the House of Commons, should the occasion arise. Gladstone, England's prime minister, had been in power since 1880 and a general election was expected late in 1885.

Hints of what O'Doherty hoped to achieve appeared in press comment and in his own statements before he left Australia in April. The *Australian* reported that, "Mr Redmond has seen during his visit how his [O'Doherty's] people revere and esteem him here; and to Mr Parnell and the great party he leads, the doctor's patriotic antecedents are such to ensure him, did he accept it, a seat in the British Parliament for an Irish constituency." On his way through Melbourne O'Doherty attended an address by Mr Blake, member for the Irish electorate of Waterford, who like many before him, had come to keep the Irish flag flying in Australia. When asked to speak at the conclusion of the address, the doctor said that, "He would have no scruples about going in heart and soul with Parnell . . . . Nothing would give him greater pleasure when he returned to Ireland than, in his old age, to throw his aid into a cause with such a backbone."

For several months after his arrival in Ireland, O'Doherty rode the crest of a wave. Soon after his arrival he had an interview with Parnell, and subsequent events show that at this meeting O'Doherty was assured of a safe seat in the House of Commons, provided he was willing to take the pledge binding all members of the Irish parliamentary party to sit, act and vote together. It was a pledge that O'Doherty willingly took.

Next, the medical staff of St Vincent's Hospital, where he had served as an honorary surgeon in the late 1850s, entertained him at an outing to Glendalough in the picturesque County Wicklow. O'Doherty's son Kevin, who had left Australia in February 1885 for Ireland on the *Quetta* with the intention of studying medicine in Dublin, shared his father's pleasure on this day.

O'Doherty's arrival in Ireland had been hailed by Michael Davitt, the founder of the Land League and one of Parnell's chief lieutenants, with a letter in the Dublin *Freeman's Journal* in which he suggested the city fathers should bestow on the doctor the freedom of the city. It was a suggestion with which the Dublin corporation agreed, and the ceremony was arranged for 1 September. The official party occupying the stage included Michael Davitt, the Redmond brothers, O'Doherty's son and several other members of the Irish parliamentary party and aldermen. The lord mayor invited the "returned exile" to sign the roll of honorary freemen and then presented him with the certificate of freedom together with a casket of bog-oak, set with Irish stones and surmounted with an Irish wolf-dog, in which the certificate could be stored. In the evening the lord mayor entertained Parnell and O'Doherty at a banquet, at which the doctor responded to the toast of the "Sea-Divided Gael".

While O'Doherty was receiving a hero's welcome in Ireland

back in Queensland the *Brisbane Courier* was waging a vendetta against him. The news of the bestowal of the freedom of the city of Dublin was greeted with a column and a half of sarcasm, in which a broadside was fired at Ireland and the doctor was belittled:

> Doctor O'Doherty is, so to speak, "starring it" in the Emerald Isle, or the Isle of the Saints or the "most distressed country" as it is variously known . . . and Mr Parnell has been pleased to give the doctor his political *imprimatur*, and the halls of the tyrant — which is Irish for the House of Commons — will yet resound with the soul-stirring eloquence of this survivor of the glorious men of '48.
>
> He has "honoured" a popular photographer with several sittings for his photograph . . . and last but not least, has had with much pomp and circumstance and oratory, the freedom of the city of Dublin bestowed on him . . . . He, having been a citizen for five minutes, and having made a speech, had done his duty as a citizen, and the bog-oak casket, "set with Irish stones and surmounted with a carved wolf-dog" will attest to future generations — the proudest proof — that Dr O'Doherty had done what Ireland, doubtless like England, expects every man to do — his duty . . . .
>
> So that all things considered, he is reaping not unpleasant remarks for the little indiscretions of his hot youth when he was full of imagination and his genial heart overflowing with romance.

In June 1885 Gladstone's Liberal government was defeated on the floor of the House of Commons and the prime minister resigned. Lord Salisbury formed a conservative government, and in the ensuing months all parties began to prepare for the general election planned for late November. The Irish parliamentary party held a series of conventions at which their candidates were selected. O'Doherty's star rose still higher at the County Meath convention on 8 October for which fifty priests and one hundred and eight delegates met at Navan. He was selected as the party's candidate for North Meath, a decision which John Dillon announced to a crowd in the market square from a window in Kelly's hotel.

O'Doherty was in the limelight again, when a fortnight later he lectured to a large audience in the Round Room of the Rotunda Maternity Hospital, the subject being, "The Irish in Australia as a Branch of a Sea-divided Gael". Shortly afterwards he learnt that he would be unopposed in the forthcoming election. With his seat in the Commons now assured, he was granted permission to make a short visit to Brisbane to attend to business affairs. Before he left Australia he was unsure of his future but now with the prospect of spending some time as representative for North Meath, he wished to attend to pressing financial matters. Before he left England as surgeon-superintendent of the *Duke of Westminster*, Arthur Hemmant, a former agent-general for Queensland, "gave a lunch in Dr O'Doherty's honour, whereat several representative colonists assisted".

News of the declaration of the poll announcing O'Doherty as member for North Meath reached Brisbane in early December, while he was still on the high seas. The Catholic *Australian* was delighted but the *Brisbane Courier* continued to attack O'Doherty with these words:

> Who knows but he may prove to be the very hero of whom a loved and loving prophetess, not unknown to him, saw visions and dreamt dreams many years ago. The alien senate may hang on his eloquence. It, he may convert — not to the creeds of his youth, for the creeds and aims of the Young Ireland party of 1848 are now as obsolete as the aboriginal Tasmanian — but to the *divide et impera* policy of the persistent and unfervid Parnell. The alien senate will haply wonder that such a good thing as our Doctor should come out of the Australian Gallilee — and — but let us quote the Cassandra utterance of the poet prophetess we alluded to above;-
> *And forward bends the listening world, as to their eager ken*
> *From that dark and mystic land appears the man of men.* [From Eva's poem, "The People's Chief".]

The *Duke of Westminster* came to Queensland via Torres Strait and O'Doherty learnt the official election results at Cooktown in North Queensland. As the vessel steamed south the Brisbane Irish community announced a reception for the doctor when the vessel arrived in Moreton Bay. The river steamer, *Kate*, had been hired to take friends and supporters to meet the overseas ship, the band would play, luncheon would be served and welcoming speeches delivered. The *Brisbane Courier* could not resist firing yet another shot at O'Doherty:

> It is proposed to give Dr O'Doherty a reception on his arrival here . . . . Dr O'Doherty, the surgeon-superintendent of the *Duke of*

Westminster, will be heartily welcome to most of us. But the Parnellite member for Meath is a functionary for whose office we have little respect. He, who used to be the free member of a free Parliament, has given himself over as a talking and voting machine into the hands of a party in the British Parliament, whose chief characteristic is almost insane hatred of Britain and of the British, who have condoned and profited by crimes and outrages of the vilest kind, and who have again and again shown their indifference — except as a source of money contributions — for the colonial Empire of our Sovereign.

There are no details available of the personal business which brought O'Doherty back to Brisbane. There were three areas which may possibly have needed attention — the medical practice, the Queensland Sugar Company and a probable mortgage on "Frascati". He had left Edward in charge of the practice and he now decided to withdraw from the practice himself — hardly an issue which needed a special voyage from Ireland. Records of the Queensland Sugar Company reveal that O'Doherty still held sixty shares, each with a paper value of £100, at the end of 1886. If the doctor had wished to dispose of these, the business could quite easily have been conducted by mail. The most likely reason seems to have been a need to discuss with his bank manager his financial position. From the time the Brisbane Land League was formed in 1881, the *Brisbane Courier* and the *Telegraph* had severely and continuously criticised the doctor for his vigorous support for the Irish cause. As a result his medical practice suffered and it was probably the difficulty he was experiencing in maintaining payments on the family home, "Frascati", and other commitments, which forced him to make the hurried visit to Brisbane.

In addition to the reception on the day of O'Doherty's arrival, his supporters arranged a public banquet in his honour at the Town Hall on 20 January over which Chief Justice Sir Charles Lilley presided. A few days before the banquet the *Brisbane Courier* warned that, "People who propose to take part in the projected O'Doherty banquet should make up their minds what they mean by it or they may find themselves hereafter in a very unpleasant position . . . . If it can be said in

England that here, in the capital of an important colony like Queensland, Doctor O'Doherty was banquetted in his capacity as an Irish MP, the statement will be used to make English people believe that we Queenslanders sympathise with the anti-England faction led in the House of Commons by Mr Parnell."

Despite the *Courier*'s warning, over 300 attended the banquet but all cabinet ministers and most other members of parliament absented themselves, and, apart from the Honourable E.B. Forrest, MLC, and P. O'Sullivan, MLA, the only prominent citizen present was Sir Charles Lilley. The member for North Meath was thus boycotted by his former colleagues and the leading citizens of Brisbane.

The *Brisbane Courier* was delighted and said that, "The banquet given to Dr O'Doherty last night afforded a complete demonstration of our contention that this country does not sympathise with the Parnellite party." The journal commented further on the absence of legislators and community leaders and added that, "It is necessary to point out in the clearest and unmistakable manner the nature of last night's demonstration, so that neither in this colony or elsewhere shall there be any pretext for attaching to it a political significance which it does not possess."

The *Telegraph*, however, while acknowledging the significance of the absence of the Brisbane establishment, said:

> It was quite excusable that there should be gratulation at Dr O'Doherty's election to the Imperial Parliament. It is gratifying to know that the gratulation was devoid of defiance. If Dr O'Doherty purposes to uphold in its integrity the union of the three kingdoms, whilst seeking only self-government for Ireland and if he seek these ends by peaceful and constitutional means we believe he will be followed to the old country by the kindly sentiments if not the good wishes of some whose caution kept them from the entertainment held last evening in his honour.

Four days later O'Doherty left Brisbane on his return to England. At both Sydney and Melbourne he was entertained by the Irish community. Among 200 who attended the banquet at St Patrick's Hall, Melbourne were Sir Bryan O'Loghlen and Frank Gavan Duffy, the two prominent Irishmen, who had declined to become involved in the Irish National Convention in 1883 during the Redmonds' visit. Perhaps now they were influenced by the very recent cablegrams from England, which contained messages that Gladstone was in favour of Home Rule for Ireland — messages which heralded some respectability for that movement in Australia.

When O'Doherty arrived back in London, parliament had been in session several weeks and he hurried to the House of Commons. It was one of the proudest days of his life when, as a new member, he was presented to the Speaker. He then began to learn of the political developments that had taken place during his absence. In the 1885 general election the Liberals were returned with 335 seats and balanced exactly the Conservatives with 249 seats and the Irish Nationalists with 86 should Parnell choose to vote with the Conservatives. Lord Salisbury continued in power and the Queen opened parliament on 21 January. Parnell's policy was to use the balance of power to support whichever major party was more likely to introduce legislation which would benefit Ireland. When he learnt that Lord Salisbury opposed granting Ireland Home Rule, but Gladstone believed such action would be the solution to the Irish question, the Irish leader directed his party to vote with the Liberals on a minor legislative measure and thus defeat the Conservatives. Lord Salisbury resigned and Gladstone formed a government. When O'Doherty took his seat in the Commons a Home Rule bill was being drafted.

Gladstone introduced the bill (the Government of Ireland bill) on 8 April. Its main provision was a bicameral Irish parliament which would deal with all except prescribed subjects such as defence, foreign affairs and international trade. The bill would mean that the Irish members would no longer have seats in the British parliament. O'Doherty spoke in the second reading debate on 4 June. He had this to say:

> I have an exceptional claim to speak in this debate from the fact that I have travelled all the way from the other end of the world — from the Colony of Queensland — with the special object, commis-

sioned in fact, to deliver myself on the particular question which is now before the House . . . I may state with tolerable certainty that the record which I will lay before the House of the effect of the struggle for Home Rule in Australia and of the results which have accrued from it, ought to act as a guide to the statesmen of this country in endeavouring to solve the great problem of Irish autonomy . . . .. The whole of the Australian colonies received this benefit of Home Rule in its fullest extent . . ... In no single case of these six colonies has there been the slightest difficulty since the privilege of self-government was conferred upon them.

Not all of Gladstone's party supported him in his decision to introduce self-government for Ireland. Two factions — the Whigs led by the Marquess of Hartington and Joseph Chamberlain's Radicals — opposed the measure, and when the crucial vote was taken in the small hours of 8 June, they voted against the bill which was defeated by thirty votes. Gladstone resigned and another general election ensued.

The defeat of the Home Rule bill marked a turning point in O'Doherty's life. From then on the fates were to be cruel. In a long letter he advised the Irish National party that he was declining to be re-nominated giving "imperative family reasons" for the decision. In later years his daughter, Gertrude, advised a Brisbane paper that the "imperative family reasons" were financial difficulties. The problems he had endeavoured to solve during his visit to Brisbane could only have worsened, for he received no remuneration for his parliamentary duties. There was a fund from which some members of the Irish National party received help but O'Doherty was not one of these. A study of the Irish parliamentary party cash book for the period reveals only one entry involving the doctor. He had received £150 in advance in anticipation of an electoral contest in North Meath, but, when he was unopposed he refunded the money.

It was O'Doherty's life style together with the antipathy of the *Brisbane Courier* and the *Telegraph*, particularly the former, which were responsible for the fall in his bank balance. There were always servants in the house and the doctor was driven on his rounds by his coachman. The dinner party which preceded the confrontation at the hospital in May 1878, when he was accused of being too drunk to operate, was one of many he held. O'Doherty gave generously to his church and other organisations. Two sons were educated overseas and various members of the family were often travelling on the high seas.

When the *Brisbane Courier* attacked O'Doherty for his vigorous support for the Irish cause the editor was always careful to state that he held the doctor in high esteem as a citizen. However, the constant criticism of his Irish nationalism drove many former patients away, and was a major contributing factor in producing the unhappy circumstances in which he now found himself.

O'Doherty returned to Brisbane from Ireland in September 1886. It was a quiet homecoming — no band, no public banquet. From discussion with his doctor son, Edward, he realised he would have great difficulty in retrieving his former practice. Edward, too, had lost patients — *the sins of the father*. Kevin decided to leave Brisbane for a while and made arrangements to go to Sydney to take over the practice of Dr Morris of 53 Castlereagh Street, who was going to Europe for fifteen months. In November he applied for a position of honorary surgeon at St Vincent's Hospital. None of the selection committee knew the applicant well, but when one member said O'Doherty seemed genial and gentlemanly, he was appointed.

In Sydney he was welcomed by the congregation of St Mary's Cathedral and the Irish community. In a speech at a meeting of the Cathedral Building Fund in January 1887, he told his listeners that his first glimpse of the cathedral had been in 1849 from the deck of the *Mount Stewart Elphinstone* which had brought him and his friend John Martin to Australia as political prisoners. On 17 March he responded to the toast, "The Day We Celebrate", which had been proposed by Judge Fawcett at the Sydney St Patrick's Day banquet. Then the Sydney Irish community decided that the doctor should be given a testimonial. One of the letters received with a donation suggested that the testimonial was mooted because, "Dr O'Doherty, in good report and bad report has never been ashamed of his church or his country and, supported by his gifted wife, he has ever rendered his influential aid in advancing the interests of our holy religion in Australia; and for his native land, I need scarcely say, in his youthful days he passed through fire and water." It also seems probable that the testimonial organisers had in mind the doctor's reduced circumstances. Late in July some of the subscribers met at Kickham's Occidental Hotel at Wynyard Square to present O'Doherty with the first instalment in the shape of a purse of 250 sovereigns.

In August 1887 O'Doherty was appointed government medical officer at Croydon, North Queensland, at a salary of £50 per annum and the right of private practice. After pastoral workers in the Croydon district had noticed evidence of gold over a few years, a rush began early in 1886 and by the time of O'Doherty's appointment the goldfield was in full swing. To reach Croydon it was necessary to travel to Port Douglas by ship, and then follow the sea voyage with a coach trip of several days over very rough roads, or continue by ship around the tip of Cape York down into the Gulf of Carpentaria to Normanton, following with a shorter overland trip. Later in 1891 a railway connected Normanton to Croydon. The goldfield was in dry, sandy country and later miner's phthisis took heavy toll. This, with diseases due to poor sanitation generally existent in the early years on gold fields, made Croydon an unhealthy spot. In 1889, the *Australasian Medical Gazette* reported that, "The death rate is so abnormally high in Croydon that the life assurance companies have instructed their agents to issue no more policies."

Why then did O'Doherty at the age of sixty-four years elect to go to this frontier mining town? Had the magnetism of gold once again made his pulse beat faster? Had his hopes been raised at the thought of a favourable speculation which would solve all his financial problems? These seem to be the only answers.

In his position of government medical officer, O'Doherty conducted many autopsies and gave evidence in several coronial inquiries. In one case, the *Croydon Mining News* saw fit to criticise the opinion of the doctor and the police magistrate who both considered that a child had died of neglect. The editor, probably reflecting the tenor of social attitudes in the mining town, said:

> According to the evidence of the father the child was attended with arrowroot, cornflower and other infantile luxuries supplemented with powders and syrups of squills in the way of medicine. This did not satisfy Dr O'Doherty who affirmed medical aid would have saved the child's life. It does not satisfy the P.M. who preached a homily on the heinousness of parents to allow their kids to expire without the aid and assistance of medical men . . . . If people, in obeying nature's laws, become the parents of sickly, puling infants and refuse to rush about like lunatics to keep them out of heaven, we fail to comprehend why the law should compel them to do so.

At another inquiry Dr O'Doherty stated he had been called to a confinement but the baby had been born before his arrival. He attended the mother for a few days, but as she was making satisfactory progress, he was advised his services were no longer required. A few days later the woman became deranged and her husband called a chemist who said that, as the woman was dying, a doctor's services would be of no use. Dr O'Doherty performed a postmortem and then issued a certificate on which he declared that death was caused by, "Sudden access of puerperal mania from an attack of milk fever and the absence of any medical care during the attack arising from the ignorance of the attendants".

During the inquiry the husband, a cordial manufacturer, stated, "I called Dr O'Doherty on the Wednesday. He seemed to be the worse for liquor. He seemed to be a little excited and seemed to stagger coming up the stairs." Dr O'Doherty called four witnesses, two hotel proprietors with whom he stayed, an unregistered medical practitioner and a pharmacist's assistant, who either refuted any evidence of the doctor's intoxication on the day in question or generally during his period in Croydon.

In other medical practice O'Doherty visited patients at the Croydon Hospital which in one issue of the *Mining News* called tenders for: — Wines, Spirits, etc. — Brandy (Hennessey***) per case, Whisky (***) per case, Guinness' Stout, per case and Foster's Ale per case. On one occasion with two other doctors he examined at the watch-house a Chinese, suspected of suffering from leprosy. His two colleagues supported O'Doherty's opinion that the patient was indeed suffering from the disease. However, the police magistrate examined the lesions with his walking stick, and decided that it was not a case of leprosy and the Chinaman was allowed to go free.

O'Doherty returned to Brisbane in 1889 with no sign of having made a fortune. In fact subsequent events showed that his resources were still low. A few of his friends, who welcomed him back, apparently believed this was to be the case. They presented him with a horse, a saddle, bridle and a purse of sovereigns and expressed pleasure at seeing the "genial old doctor once more amongst them". There is no evidence of any mining venture in which O'Doherty was involved while he was at Croydon. Amongst the O'Doherty memorabilia is a Gold Fields Homestead lease in his name for 1888, but such leases were granted to residents on goldfields as well as to holders of miner's licences.

While O'Doherty was away in Croydon the family circumstances worsened. "Frascati" had to be vacated and Edward and William found other premises. The consulting rooms in which Kevin had proudly commenced practice in partnership with his son were now occupied by Dr James Campbell. Then in 1889 Edward was declared bankrupt. The colony's economic position was not favourable for restoring fortunes, family or otherwise. There had been considerable expansion in the 1880s during a boom period but towards the end of the decade there was a serious downturn. Unemployment soared and there were empty business premises and dwellings in the city and the suburbs. At the end of 1891 a soup kitchen was opened in Brisbane to feed the destitute. To add to Brisbane's troubles there were two major floodings in 1890 and 1893 respectively, inundating homes in the low-lying districts thus bringing further distress to many of the city's citizens.

Although the period was not propitious to rebuild a medical practice O'Doherty set about the task. The frequent changes in his professional address listed in official records reveal the difficulties he experienced. In 1891 he went to Warwick, a large country town in a farming district, 100 miles (160 kilometres) south-west of Brisbane. He returned to the city after a few unprofitable months. In an advertisement announcing one change of address he offered medical advice for five shillings and advice and medicine for seven shillings and sixpence. The doctor, who had once alleged that practitioners who did their own dispensing were taking the bread from the mouths of pharmacists, had now resorted to the same practice to augment his meagre income. Then in 1892 some help came from the government which, overlooking his past support for the Irish cause but remembering how well he had served the colony, appointed him to three part-time positions — secretary to the Central Board of Health, superintendent of the Quarantine Station and surgeon to the Diamantina Orphanage with a total annual remuneration of £302 ($604). It was approximately half the remuneration of the medical superintendent of the Brisbane Hospital and equal to the salary paid a suburban primary school head teacher.

Despite the problems with his practice O'Doherty took a keen interest in other aspects of the medical profession. He was an active contributor at meetings of the Queensland Medical Society, which once again had been revived, demonstrating cases and calling on his vast experience to add valuable comment to many discussions. Along with three colleagues, Drs Cannan, Bell and Margetts, he had the distinction of being elected an honorary member of the Medical Society for his great contribution to the profession over a very long period.

The Queensland Medical Society had foundered before when discussion on other than scientific subjects pervaded the meetings, and it was still uncomfortable when such problems presented. One burning question of this nature was the profession's relationship with friendly societies. To overcome the difficulty of dealing with the subject, the doctors formed a new society — the Queensland Medico-Ethical Society — and elected Dr O'Doherty its president. In his inaugural address O'Doherty said that, "The main purpose of our association is to bring about a strong defensive union between members of the profession." The *Brisbane Courier*, in commenting on the new society, said that it was remarkable that, as a body, the medical profession had previously done so little to protect itself. Under O'Doherty's guidance the society had an active but short life. In 1893, O'Doherty was responsible for the society's circulation of a document to all candidates in a forthcoming election, pointing out the need for action on the establishment of a colonial health department, compulsory notification of infectious disease, the establishment of public abattoirs and regular inspection of dairies. This action brought praise from the *Brisbane Courier* and the *Australasian Medical Gazette*. The Medico-Ethical Society became redundant when in 1894 the Queensland branch of the British Medical Association was formed, and was willing to tackle any problem involving the profession, ethical or otherwise.

But the gods still had many more cruel blows in store for Kevin and Eva. Within the space of ten years they lost through death all four sons and one grand-daughter. Bank manager, Vincent, aged thirty-two years, was the first to go. He was killed when knocked down by a horse-drawn cab while crossing George Street, Brisbane at night on 3 November, 1890. He was survived by a widow and a young son, Louis. Two years later, Eileen Esme, four-year-old daughter of Edward, was buried in Toowong cemetery. Then, William, the eldest son, aged thirty-seven years, died on 9 October 1893 after a protracted illness. On 15 February 1900, Eva's birthday, Kevin junior was buried in the Kalgoorlie cemetery, Western Australia, after dying from pneumonia in his fortieth year.

The fortunes of Dr Edward O'Doherty improved during the second half of the 1890s. He was discharged from his bankruptcy in January 1896. The next year he was elected president of the Queensland branch of the British Medical Association and in 1899, after seventeen years as outpatient physician at the Brisbane Hospital, he was promoted to inpatient physician. But the good fortune ended in 1900. When entering a cab outside his residence in Byrne Terrace, on Wickham Terrace on 4 July he slipped and hit his head on the kerb. He died twelve hours later from a brain haemorrhage. The forty-three-year-old doctor left a widow and a daughter,

Mignon. Of eight children born to Kevin and Eva only their youngest child, Gertrude, was still alive.

During the late 1890s, O'Doherty still occupied consulting rooms and, when able, carried out his part-time duties, with son, Edward, at times acting as locum. Official records give his professional address as 48 Queen Street with Wickham Terrace, his private residence. In 1896 and 1897 he turned his mind to another field. Articles appeared in the press relating to O'Doherty's defrosting process — a method of preserving Australian beef being shipped to England. Meals from meat, which had undergone the process, were served to friends and government officials at the Parliament House dining rooms and the diners claimed that, "The meat was fit for an emperor". With the help of Brownlie Henderson, the government analyst, the method was brought to the stage where the *Government Gazette* of 23 January 1897 announced that an application for a patent had been made for the process in the name of Kevin Izod O'Doherty of Wickham House, Wickham Terrace. Wickham House was a boarding-house of which Miss A. Murphy was the proprietess.

Varying accounts, written and oral, of O'Doherty's alcoholic propensity have been handed down, with little evidence to confirm their contents. Photographs of him in old age reveal no evidence of the ravages of alcoholism. When he was approximately seventy years of age, the government saw fit to appoint him to official part-time positions and the profession elected him president of the Medico-Ethical Society. When he was well into his seventies he worked with the government analyst on his meat preserving process. These facts do not point to a man drinking too much.

On the other hand there is the substantiated case when he was considered by his colleagues as being too drunk to operate after a dinner party. There, of course, may have been other instances not recorded. There was no substantiation of the accusation made by the Croydon patient's husband that the doctor was drunk when he called to attend to his wife. However, the character witnesses, whom O'Doherty called, two hotel-keepers and two associated with the medical profession, who rejected the accusation, may have been biassed in his favour. Like many who have been accused in similar circumstances, O'Doherty reacted strongly.

In summary, O'Doherty certainly "liked his drop"; he was fond of dining and wining well; there was one substantiated case of his having too much to drink to do his work efficiently, but he was not an alcoholic.

Around the turn of the century, Kevin and Eva moved to a rented cottage at Rosalie, bounded by Heussler Terrace, Bayswater and Thomas Streets. During World War I, when there was great antipathy to anything German, this part of Heussler Terrace was renamed Haig Street. The rented cottage was a far cry from Killeen House and Lisdonagh in Ireland and "Frascati" in Ann Street, Brisbane. Here, the old man suffered another misfortune — he went completely blind. The seclusion enforced by the affliction was most distasteful to the former very public man. Official records show the government was still generous and approved his occupation of part-time positions, although there was a reshuffle of positions with a reduction of remuneration to £202 ($404) per annum. Of course, he was now unable to perform the duties, but three doctors, who regarded him with great affection — John Thomson, Espie Dods and John Flynn — acted in his stead while O'Doherty received the much-needed salary. (John Thomson and O'Doherty had settled their differences and were later good friends.) In at least one case — official visitor to the Goodna Asylum (previously Woogaroo) — O'Doherty was listed as occupying the position with Dr Thomson performing the duties in his absence. Finally, on 15 July 1905, at the age of 81, Kevin Izod O'Doherty breathed his last. He was buried in the Toowong cemetery.

Extracts from obituaries read;

> *Brisbane Courier.* His genial nature endeared him to a very wide circle of friends and amongst those who were contemporary with his active years in Queensland his name will long be cherished.
> *The Age* (Brisbane). There was nothing that was not large, and generous and open-minded, in the character of the well-known doctor — in truth it was this wholesome freedom from hypocritical restraint which caused him the troubles of his life.

The *Australasian Medical Gazette*. Personally, he was a warm-hearted, generous, impulsive Irishman, most popular amongst his professional brethren and a favourite in every class of society.

After Kevin's death, for a number of months the only money coming into the cottage at Rosalie was Gertrude's salary as a typiste, which, when she was appointed to the public service in this capacity in June 1906, was £60 ($120) per annum. The straitened circumstances were probably the reason for a move to another rented cottage in Norwood Street, Toowong, a nearby suburb. Then later in 1905, Eva received from Ireland a little over £300 ($600) from an insurance policy on Kevin's life.

She also received an offer of help from Father Hickey in Yorkshire, England, who had suggested a new publication of her poems and who arranged a small testimonial for the aged widow. Eva was extremely grateful for this offer of help and in her reply to Father Hickey she poured out her heart. The Irish in Australia had been very sympathetic in her loss but Kevin's death had been almost ignored in Ireland — only one letter from the Dungarven Town Council was received. She was particularly critical of the Redmonds and John Dillon who had tendered no condolences. From William Redmond, who had been near Brisbane, when Kevin died, she received no message. She thought this was cruel treatment in view of the support Kevin had given the Redmonds' campaign in Australia, when other prominent Irishmen had held back. Eva told Father Hickey that, "It was a very losing game for a professional man, but the doctor was not the sort of person to count the cost."

Eva and Gertrude, with slightly improved financial circumstances, returned to the Rosalie cottage, but the loss of her four sons and then her husband caused Eva much sadness which she revealed in the poem, "Tenebrae", which she wrote in April 1906, at the age of 76 years. Two stanzas read:

Tenebrae

> Night's solemn hour! upon the holy fane,
>   The mystic lights upon the altar burn,
> The voices chanting in a sad refrain,
>   Unceasing seem to mourn —
>   When lo! with sudden smite,
>   Is quenched one shining light,
> One light has vanished from the holy fane.
>
> Thus one by one in gathering fear and gloom
>   The phantom voices murmuring low between,
> Each light goes out with fatal stroke of doom,
> Until upon the scene
>   A dismal darkness falls,
>   A silence that appals,
> The darkness and the silence of the tomb!

The poem was the last in the volume which Father Hickey had persuaded M.H. Gill & Sons, Dublin to publish in 1909 which unfortunately brought meagre returns.

Meanwhile in Australia, a testimonial for Eva had been arranged by the combined Irish communities in the three eastern mainland states and Tasmania. Through benefit concerts and similar functions as well as donations the results were pleasing. A statement to 1 June 1909 revealed that over £1,300 ($2,600) had been raised of which Eva had already received £400 ($800). However, she did not live long enough to receive the full benefits, for after an attack of influenza she died on 21 May 1910, aged 80 years. She was buried alongside her husband and her son, Vincent. An obituary referred to the "poetic fire and graceful verse contributed to the *Nation* in those stirring days of national agitation", and to her early life with Kevin. Later it said she "led a refined and unassuming life in Brisbane, mingling little in society, devoting her spare time to reading and composition".

On 18 January 1912 over 1,500 people — had there not been a tram strike the total would have been higher — gathered at the O'Doherty grave-site to witness the unveiling of a memorial placed over the resting place of Kevin and Eva by the Queensland Irish Association, under the chairmanship of

T.J. O'Shea. "The memorial is a fine imposing Celtic cross hewn from Aberdeen granite and exhibiting the Irish wolf hound, round tower, and sprig of shamrock, together with the late Dr O'Doherty's family coat of arms". On the face of the column supporting the cross the inscription reads:

> SACRED
> To the memory of
> KEVIN IZOD O'DOHERTY
> The Irish patriot
> Died 15 July 1905, aged 81 years
> Whose name will live in Irish history
> And whose memory ever remains enshrined
> In Irish hearts at Home and Abroad
> Also his gifted wife
> EVA OF THE NATION

On the base is inscribed:

> This monument is erected by admirers of the late Dr O'Doherty and his wife as a mark of appreciation of their unsullied patriotism and exulted devotion to the cause of Ireland.

Epilogue

Gertrude O'Doherty continued in her employ in the public service till, late in life, she married Inspector M. O'Sullivan of the Queensland police force. She died in 1949 aged seventy-nine years and bequeathed to her stepdaughter, Mrs A.G. Melhuish, numerous documents relating to the O'Doherty story. Mrs Melhuish and her daughter, Colleen, kindly gave the authors free access to this valuable material. Louis O'Doherty, son of Vincent, was killed in April 1918, fighting in France with the Australian forces. With his death the male line from the union of Kevin and Eva ceased. "Frascati" was purchased by Dr A.B. Carvosso, before it became the nurses' home for the St Martin's Hospital.

After the death of Dr Edward O'Doherty, his widow, a daughter of Major General G.A. French, who once commanded the Queensland Volunteer Forces, went with her daughter, Mignon, to England. Mignon was educated at the Royal School, Bath, and in Paris. She had a long and successful career on the stage and in films. One interesting role which she played was that of Mrs Boyle in the original cast of Agatha Christie's *The Mousetrap*. Mignon married Tom Nesbitt, a fellow actor, and bore two children, Prudence and Thomas.

Prudence Chapman, and Thomas junior's two daughters, Caroline and Vivian, were traced in 1982. The authors spent three wonderful days with Caroline and Vivian, great-great-granddaughters of Kevin and Eva, in New Hampshire, USA. One of Caroline's most precious heirlooms is the engagement ring by which the betrothal of Kevin and Eva was sealed.

References

Abbreviations used in references

ACR	*Australasian Catholic Record*
ADB	*Australian Dictionary of Biography*, Melbourne: Melbourne University Press
Adv	The *Advocate* (Melbourne)
AMG	*Australasian Medical Gazette*
AONSW	Archives Office of New South Wales
Aust	The *Australian* (Brisbane)
BC	*Brisbane Courier*
BT	*Ballarat Times*
CMN	*Croydon Mining News*
CT	*Colonial Times* (Launceston)
DEM	*Dublin Evening Mail*
DEP	*Dublin Evening Post*
DFJ	*Freeman's Journal* (Dublin)
DG	*Daily Guardian* (Brisbane)
DHR	*Dublin Historical Record*
HTC	*Hobart Town Courier*
ILN	*Illustrated London News*
JOL	John Oxley Library (Brisbane)
JQLC	*Journal of the Queensland Legislative Council*
LT	*The Times*, London
MA	*Melbourne Argus*
MBC	*Moreton Bay Courier*
MJA	*Medical Journal of Australia*
ML	Mitchell Library, Sydney

NA	North Australian
PRO	Public Records Office
QES	*Queensland Evangelical Standard*
QGG	*Queensland Government Gazette*
Qlder	*The Queenslander*
QPD	*Queensland Parliamentary Debates*
QSA	Queensland State Archives
QT	*Queensland Times*
QVP	*Queensland Votes and Proceedings*
SFJ	*Freeman's Journal* (Sydney)
SMH	*Sydney Morning Herald*
TA	Tasmanian Archives
Tele	*The Telegraph* (Brisbane)
THRA	Tasmanian Historical Research Association
TIEFA	*The Irish Exile and Freedom's Advocate*
TPD	*The Pilot* (Dublin)

Chapter 1

Green Street Court. T.K. Moylan, The Little Green, *DHR*, 8 (June–Aug. 1946), pp. 81, 135.

Judge Crampton's harangue and O'Doherty's comments. J.G. Hodges, *Proc. Treason Felony Act, Dublin, Aug.–Oct. 1848* (Dublin: A. Thom, 1848), p. 763.

Previous Irish convictions. T.D., A.M. and D.B. Sullivan, *Speeches From The Dock* (Dublin: M.H. Gill & Son, 1953).

The O'Doherty clan. E. MacLysaght, *Irish Families, Their Names and Origins* (Dublin: A. Figgis, 1972) and I. Grehan, Irish Family Series, *Ireland of the Welcomes* (Dublin: Sep.–Oct. 1977), p. 30.

O'Doherty's immediate ancestry. O'Doherty family bible, in the possession of M. Carroll, Kilternan, Co. Dublin, and personal interview, 1980.

Kevin Doherty-Mary Knabbs marriage. *Registry of Deeds*, Kings Inns Law Library, Dublin.

William Doherty's career, *Registry of Attorneys Memorials*, Kings Inns Law Library, Dublin.

William and Anne Doherty's addresses. *Dublin Street Directory*, 1816 to 1841.

Births of Kevin O'Doherty and siblings and wet nursing. O'Doherty family bible.

rds. *St Andrew's Church Yearbook for 1978*.

...s medical course. C.A. Cameron, *The History of the ... College of Surgeons, Ireland* (Dublin: Fannin & Co., ...), p. 796 and certificates in possession of Mrs A.G. ...lhuish (personal interview, 1979).

... Kelly and O'Flaherty families. E. MacLysaght, *Irish Families*.

...va's notebook. In possession of Mrs A.G. Melhuish.

Kelly-Skerrit marriage. *Registry of Deeds*, Kings Inns Law Library, Dublin.

Kelly-O'Flaherty marriage. O'Doherty family bible and Eric Macfhinn, Galway College, personal communication, 1978.

Eva's poems. Brother Allen of Daniel O'Connell College, Dublin (gift to authors of 1909 edition).

Chapter 2

Emancipation and repeal. A. MacIntyre, *The Liberator* (London: Hamish Hamilton, 1965) and G. O'Tuathaigh, *Ireland before the Famine* (Dublin: Gill and MacMillan, 1972).

O'Doherty's childhood impression of O'Connell's return. *BC*, 9 Aug. 1875.

Founding the *Nation* and Young Ireland movement. C.G. Duffy, *Young Ireland* (Melbourne: G. Robertson, 1881); L. O'Brien, *Charles Gavan Duffy* (Dublin: Duffy & Co., 1967); C. Pearl, *The Three Lives of Duffy* (Sydney: Univ. of NSW Press, 1978); T.D., A.M. and D.B. Sullivan, *Speeches From The Dock* (Dublin: Gill & Son, 1913) and A.M. Sullivan, *New Ireland* (London: Washbourne, 1877).

Early issues of the *Nation*. National Library of Ireland, Dublin.

Repeal Bill. *Hansard (Commons)*, 22 (1834), cols. 1155–59, 1203–10, 23 (1834), cols. 67–70, 243–50.

The Famine. A.M. Sullivan, *The Black Forty-Seven* in his *New Ireland*; D. Edwards and D. Williams, *The Great Famine* (New York: Russell & Russell, 1976) and C.W. Smith, *The Great Hunger*, (London: New English Library, 1979).

The five issues of the *Irish Tribune*, contemporary issues of the *Freeman's Journal* (Dublin), and the *Nation* were read in the National Library of Ireland, Dublin.

Chapter 3

Newgate Prison. T. Moylan, The Little Green, *DHR*, 8 (June–Aug. 1946), p. 140 and C.G. Duffy, *Four Years of Irish History* (London: Cassell, Petter, Galpin & Co., 1883), p. 728.

Duffy's transfer to Newgate prison. *DFJ*, 10 July 1848.

Jury packing. *DFJ*, 10 July 1848; *TPD*, 24 July 1848 and *DEM*, 4 Aug. 1848.

Troop movements. *DEM*, 26 July 1848.

Leadup to and Ballingarry skirmish. A.M. Sullivan, *New Ireland* (chapters "Forty-Eight" and "After Scenes") and C.G. Woodham-Smith, *The Great Hunger* (chapter 16).

P.J. Smyth memoirs. Ms 4758, National Library of Ireland, Dublin.

O'Doherty's trials. J.H. Hodges, *Proc. Treason Felony Act, Aug.–Oct. 1848* (Dublin: A. Thom, 1848).

Press comments on trials. *DFJ*, 23 Aug. 1848; *LT*, 22 Aug. 1848; *DEP*, 22 Aug. 1848 and *TPD*, 25 Aug. 1848.

Smith O'Brien's sentence. *TPD*, 18 Oct. 1848.

Smith O'Brien — a martyr. *ILN*, 14 Oct. 1848.

Approach to O'Doherty to plead guilty. C.J. Duffy, *Four Years of Irish History* and Williams to Martin, Ms 3226, National Library of Ireland.

Kevin and Eva discuss British offer. J.H. Cullen, *Young Ireland in Exile*, (Dublin: 1928).

Count Dalton's effort to save Williams. C.G. Duffy, *Four Years of Irish History* (London: 1883).

Second escape attempt. C.G. Duffy, *Four Years of Irish History* (London: Cassell, Petter, Galpin & Co., 1883) and *TPD*, 18 Oct. 1848.

Richmond prison. P.D. O'Connor, Richmond Bridewell, *DHR*, 25 (Sep. 1972), p. 152.

Events in prison. Martin's journal, PRO, Belfast, D2137/1/44.
O'Doherty's journal. In possession of M. Carroll, Kilternan, Ireland.
Romance in Richmond prison. John Martin to Eva, 6 June 1850, in possession of Mrs A.G. Melhuish.
Eva's ring. In possession of Caroline Nesbitt, New Hampshire, USA.
Departure of O'Doherty and Martin. *MBC*, 27 Oct. 1849.
Walpole's journal. ML, A.2085.
Mount Stewart Elphinstone. C. Bateson, *Convict Ships* (Sydney: A.H. & A.W. Reese, 1959).
Surgeon Moxey's journal, ML, AJCP, Reel 3205, Adm. 101/55.
Irish community meeting. *SMH*, 10 Oct. 1849.
Ship movements. *SMH*, 22 Oct. 1849.

Chapter 4

Denison's attitude. C.H. Currey, Denison, *ADB*, 4, p. 46 and P.A. Howell, *Eldershaw Memorial Lecture*, 1978, THRA.
Grey's memo. PRO, Surrey, England, C.O., 408/32.
Exiles on the wharves. W. Denison, *Varieties of Vice Regal life*, 1:131.
Events on arrival. Martin's journal, PRO, Belfast, D2137/1/44.
O'Doherty's physical description. TA, convict records, 2/363, 1849.
Advice to exiles. *HTC*, 31 Oct. 1849.
Ticket-of-leave regulations. In possession of Mrs A.G. Melhuish.
Description of Oatlands. J.S. Weeding, *The History of the Lower Midlands* (Launceston: Mary Fisher Bookshop, 1975) and Vera Fisher, *Linking Oatlands with* ... (Hobart: Specialty Press, 1972).
Bishop Willson, Rev. Hall, Rev. Bond. Cardinal Moran, *History of the Catholic Church in Australasia* (Sydney, F. Coffee & Co., 1895).
Martin to Mrs Connell. Nat. Lib. of Aust., ACT, 287/1.

Denison on leniency. PRO, Surrey, England, C.O. 280/249/
22–24.
Mitchel's arrival. *TIEFA*, 13 April 1850.
O'Doherty to Martin re ticket-of-leave. PRO, Belfast,
D2137/1/31.
Williams to Eva re Glendalough. Nat. Lib. of Ireland, M.
10520.
O'Doherty in court. *HTC*, 24 Dec. 1850.
Impression Bay. Ian Brand, *Penal Peninsula* (West Moonah,
Tasmania: Jason Publins, 1978), p. 76.
Magorian's letter. J.H. Cullen, *Young Ireland in Exile* (Dublin:
Talbot Press, 1928), p. 124.
O'Doherty to Martin re roadwork. PRO, Belfast, D2137/1/44.
Denison's reply to Willson. J.J. Cullen, Bishop Willson, *ACR*,
July 1951, 28:3.
Mitchel on O'Doherty. J. Mitchel, *Jail Journal* (Dublin: M.H.
Gill & Son, 1921), p. 254.
St Mary's Hospital. W.E.L.H. Crowther, Dr Bedford and
St Mary's Hospital, *MJA*, 2 (1944), p. 25.
Inquest. *CT*, 20 Aug. 1852.
Sheehy to Sheridan-Moore. ML, AM, 38.
O'Doherty to Martin re employment. PRO, Belfast,
D2137/1/45.
O'Doherty to Martin re £15. PRO, Belfast, D2137/1/50.
Smyth to Martin from Melbourne. PRO, Belfast, D2137/1/59.
Conditional pardon. PRO, Surrey, England, 989, No. 50.

Chapter 5

Testimonial committee meeting, Farmers' Arms. *MA*, 15 June
1854.
Ship movements — *Ariel, Ladybird, Red Jacket, Mermaid. MA*,
14–19 July 1854.
Description of goldfields. G. Serle, *The Golden Age*
(Melbourne: Melb. Univ. Press, 1963) and James Flett, *A
Pictorial History of Victorian Goldfields* (Melbourne: Rigby,
1977).

John O'Shanassy — biography. S.M. Ingham, O'Shanassy, Sir John, *ADB*, 5, p. 378.
Description of Melbourne. William Kelly, *Life in Victoria, 1853 and 1858* (Melbourne: Lowden reprint, 1977) and W.H. Newnham, *Melbourne — Biography of a City* (Melbourne: Hill of Content Pub. Co., revised 1985) and contemporary issues of *MA*.
Testimonial dinner. *MA*, 24 July 1854.
Description of Smith O'Brien gold cup. *MA*, 28 Dec. 1854.
Smith O'Brien and Martin depart on *Norna*. *MA* 28 July 1854.
Smyth to O'Doherty, 28 Feb 1856. Copy in JOL, Brisbane.
Events at Ballarat (general). *BT* and *MA* from August to December 1854.
Letters criticising Dr Carr at coronial inquiry. *BT*, 14, 28 October 1854.
Criticism of Dr Carr in Supreme Court. *MA*, 20 Nov. 1854.
Eureka Stockade. *BT* and *MA*, issues first week of December 1854 and Raffaelo Carboni, *The Eureka Stockade* (Melbourne: Dolphin Books, reprint, 1947).
The *James Baines* — description. Basil Lubbock, *The Colonial Clippers* (Glasgow: Brown & Ferguson, 1948)
The *James Baines* at Melbourne and Captain McDonald. *MA*, 13 Feb., 9, 11 March 1855.
James Baines — passenger list. Provided by PRO, Melbourne.
James Baines, log of 1856 voyage. Provided by the Center for Polar and Scientific Archives, Washington, USA.
Passenger list of *James Baines* ex Melbourne 11 March 1855. PRO, Melbourne.
Alfred Carr to Sir George Grey, 2 July 1855. PRO, Surrey, England, H.O., 12/2/81, ERE 9115.
T. Arthur, Sub-Inspector of Police, Portumna to Inspector-General of Police, Dublin, 9 July 1855. PRO, England, H.O., 12/2/81, ERE 9115.
Duffy's letters re full pardon and congratulations. O'Doherty's papers, JOL, Brisbane.
Date and place of marriage of Kevin and Eva. Family Register, copy in JOL, Brisbane.
Eva's travel document and second marriage certificate (Paris).

Copies, JOL, Brisbane.
La Pitié Hôpital, Paris — description. Provided by administrator, La Saltpetrière Hôpital, Paris in personal interview, 1978.
Eva's letter to Martin re her life in Paris. PRO, Belfast, D2137/1/47.
Duffy's letter to O'Doherty re full pardon. Copy given to authors by Brother Allen, O'Connell College, Dublin, in personal interview, 1978.
Palmerston's statement re pardon in Commons. *Hansard (Commons)*, 3rd series, vol. 142, p. 263.
Proclamation of free pardon. Sir George Grey, to All It May Concern, PRO, Surrey, England, H.O., 12/2/81, ERE 9115.

Chapter 6

William's birth. Family register, copy, JOL, Brisbane.
Examination conditions. C.A. Cameron, *History of Royal College of Surgeons, Ireland* (Dublin: Fannin & Co., 1916).
Graduation certificate. Copy, JOL, Brisbane.
O'Doherty to Martin. PRO, Belfast, D2137/1/49.
Conditions in Ireland; Cullen and Duffy and the Fenians. P.S. O'Hegarty, *A History of Ireland under the Union* (London: Methuen, 1952); Joseph Lee, *The Modernisation of Irish Society — 1848-1918* (Dublin: Gill & Macmillan, 1973) and Y.M. McLay, *James Quinn — First Catholic Bishop of Brisbane* (Graphic Books: Armadale, Vic. Australia, 1979).
Eva to Martin. PRO, Belfast, D2137/1/47 and 1/48.
Martin's reply. In possession of Mrs A.G. Melhuish.
Details of births of Edward and Vincent. Family register, Copy, JOL, Brisbane.
Ocean Chief, passenger list. PRO Melbourne.
Ocean Chief, description of voyage. *MA*, 3 Oct. 1860.
O'Doherty's arrival in Sydney. *SFJ*, 20 October 1860.
Medical practice at Botany St. *SFJ*, 27 Oct. 1860.
Lecture to Young Men's Society. *SFJ*, 7 Nov. 1860.
Eva's poems. *SFJ*, 30 Jan. to 20 Nov. 1861, at intervals of one

to two weeks.
Change of practice to Pitt St. *SFJ*, 4 May 1861.
St Patrick's Day banquet. *SFJ*, 20 March 1861.
Bishop Quinn in Sydney en route to Brisbane. *SFJ*, 8 May 1861.
The *Telegraph* leaves Sydney for Brisbane. *SFJ*, 1 March 1862.
The *Telegraph* voyage to Brisbane. *BC*, 1 March 1862.
O'Doherty registers with Medical Board. Certificate (copy), JOL.
Description of early Ipswich. J.G. Steele, *The Explorers of the Moreton Bay District* (Brisbane: Univ. of Qld Press 1972); L.E. Slaughter, *Ipswich Municipal Centenary* (Ipswich: Ipswich City Council, 1960) and Ipswich Historical Society, personal communication.
River steamers. M.B. Mills & J. Innes, *The Romance of the Bremer* (Ipswich: Ipswich Historical Society, 1982).
O'Doherty commences practice. *QT*, 7 March 1862.
Forbes Terrace description. Ipswich Historical Society — personal communication.
Hospital surgeon. *QT*, 25 April 1862.
McGinty's career. *QT*, 10 Nov. 1862.
Church dispute. *BC*, 10 May, 12 June, 22, 23 July, 4, 5, 13, 21 Aug., 8, 12 Nov. 1862, 19, 23 Jan., 13 May 1863; *NA*, 10 June, 16 Aug. 1862; and *QT*, 16 Jan., 15 May 1863.
Bishop's education campaign. *QT*, 15, 29 Sep., 8 Oct. 1864.
St Patrick's Day banquet. *BC*, 21 March 1863.
O'Connell monument. *QT*, 4, 8 Sep. 1863.
The new railway. *NA*, 26 Feb., 1864; *QT*, 22 Jan. 1864; *BC*, 24 July 1865.
O'Doherty helps at fire. *BC*, 12 Sep. 1863.
Eva at Ipswich. *QT*, 10 July 1863, 28 June 1864.
Births of John and Jeanette. Family register, copy, JOL, Brisbane.

Chapter 7

River steamers. M.B. Mills & B. Innes, *The Romance of the*

Bremer (Ipswich: Ipswich Historical Society, 1982).
Brisbane bridge. *BC*, 8 Aug. 1865.
Early Brisbane. G. Greenwood & J. Laverty, *Brisbane, 1859–1959* (Brisbane: Brisbane City Council, 1959); *Pugh's Almanacs* and files of *BC* and *DG*.
Brisbane architecture. *BC*, 11 May 1864.
Clearing of the streets. *BC*, 27 June 1865 (Ann St), 28 July 1865 (Duncan's Hill and Turbot St).
Drainage and sanitation. *BC*, 26 Aug. 1865.
Appointed surgeon to Brisbane Hospital. Minutes of Brisbane Hospital committee, 28 Feb. 1866, QSA, HOS 1/D7 and *BC*, 1 March 1866.
Hospital at Bowen Hills. R. Patrick, *Horsewhip The Doctor* (Brisbane: Univ. of Qld. Press, 1985), p. 38.
Dr S. Burke. *BC*, 12 Aug. 1867, 21 April 1868.
O'Doherty at Lady Bowen Hospital. Report of Select Committee on Hospitals of the Colony, *QVP*, 1866, p. 1648 and *BC*, 20 Nov. 1867.
Brisbane Volunteer Rifles. *BC*, 2, 8 May 1867.
Fullerton's house (Adderton). *BC*, 8 May 1858.
Sisters of Mercy liquidation fund. *BC*, 23 April, 9 July, 8 Dec. 1866, 7, 25 Sep., 1 Oct 1867 and Mother Bridget Conlon's memoirs, All Hallows archives.
St Vincent's orphanage. Mother Conlon's memoirs.
Building St Stephen's. *BC*, 22 Sep., 28 Oct. 1863, 18 Jan. 1864, 6 May 1867 and Brisbane Archdiocesan archives, collection books, St Stephen's cathedral.
Philosophical Society. *BC*, 28 Aug. 1866.
Winter races. *BC*, 1 June 1867.
Fenians. *BC*, 23 Jan., 26 April, 15 Dec. 1866
O'Doherty campaign and election. *BC*, 6, 15, 17, 26 June, 8 Aug. 1867 and L.A. Bernays, *Sixty Years of Politics in Queensland, 1859–1909* (Brisbane: Govt Printer, 1909).

Chapter 8

O'Doherty — Contagious Diseases Bill speech. *QPD*, 5

(1867), p. 471.
Correspondent, re Contagious Diseases Act. *BC*, 22 Oct. 1867.
Rescindment, Contagious Diseases Act proclamation. *QGG*, 47 (1911), p. 591.
Absence of grammar school, Brisbane. *BC*, 18 Oct. 1867.
Quinn to O'Doherty re trustee. Quinn's letterbook, Brisbane Archdiocesan Archives, 15 Nov. 1867.
O'Doherty gazetted as trustee. *QGG*, 9 (1868), p. 78.
Foundation stone. *BC*, 1, 2 March 1868.
Opening Grammar School. *BC*, 2 Feb. 1869.
Sons enrolled at Cleveland. *Cleveland State School, Souvenir History 1868–1968* (Brisbane: 1968).
Attempted assassination of Prince Alfred. *BC*, 13, 14, 16 March, 6, 29 April 1868 and P. O'Farrell, *The Irish in Australia* (Sydney: Univ. NSW Press, 1987), pp. 209–11.
Gympie goldfield. *BC*, 6, 11, 14, 19, 29 Nov. 1867, 20 Feb., 25 May, 4, 27 July, 4 Aug., 7, 14, 25 Sep., 13 Oct., 18 Nov. 1868; *QPD*, 6 (1868), p. 825.
O'Doherty faces another election. *BC*, 10, 11 July, 25 Aug., 6, 18, 26, 28 Sep. 1868.
Woogaroo Asylum. Bowen to Denison, 17 Jan. 1860, NSW CSIL, 60/444, Minute 15, 963, AONSW; W.A. Brown to Col. Sec., 17 July 1863, COL/A42, 63/1591, QSA; *QVP*, (1868–69), p. 687, *QPD*, 9 (1869), p. 161 and *QGG*, 10 (1869), p. 155.
O'Doherty's Oyster Bill. *QPD* (1871), p. 160.
Move against Lilley. *BC*, 19 Feb. 1870.
O'Doherty's surgical prowess. *BC*, 19, 22 Jan., 9 April 1870.
Governor's medical attendant. *BC*, 3, 23 Jan. 1871.
Lilley's university bill. *QPD*, 11 (1870), p. 173.
Eva on ball committee. *BC*, 22 July 1867.
Ladies' farewell to Lady Bowen, *BC*, 18 Dec. 1867.
Eva Mary's birth and death. Family register, copy JOL, Brisbane.
Move to George and Mary Streets. *BC*, 1 Aug. 1868.
Martin's letters of 1867, 1868. In possession of Mrs A. G. Melhuish.
Medical Board member. *QGG*, 9 (1868), p. 977 and QSA,

A/38177, 1 April, 1869. Brisbane Hospital Committee minutes.

Chapter 9

O'Doherty and museum. *QPD*, 11 (1870), p. 242.
O'Doherty recommends railway commission. *QPD*, 11(1870), p. 171.
Railway commission report. *QVP*, 1871 (first session), p. 675.
Railway commission debate. *QPD*, 12 (1871), p. 201.
Railway public meeting. *BC*, 16 May 1871.
Railway second commission. *QVP*, 1872, p. 1327.
Tenders for barrows and fence. *BC*, 19 Dec. 1872.
Turning first sod of railway. *BC*, 31 Jan. 1873.
First train to Ipswich. *BC*, 15 June 1875.
Tissot criticised. *BC*, 25, 26 July 1871.
O'Doherty's Polynesian labourers' bill. *QPD*, 13 (1871-72), p. 374.
O'Doherty's health bill. *QPD*, 14 (1872), p. 595.
Registrar General's 1872 report. *QVP*, 1873, p. 861.
Opposition to local board of health. *BC*, 31 July, 1, 22 Aug., 10 Sep. 1873.
Palmer-Morehead estrangement. *BC*, 2 June 1873.
O'Doherty retires from parliament. *BC*, 27 Oct. 1873.
O'Doherty and a medical school. *BC*, 16 April, 3 May 1872, 2 May 1876; *Queenslander*, 13 April 1872; *QVP*, 2 (1875), p. 111.
Report of Education Commission of 1874. *QVP*, 2 (1875), p. 437.
Simon Ziemen's murder. *QPD*, 13 (1871-72), p. 292.
Alleged midwife's blunder. *BC*, 30 May 1870.
Cannan's inaugural speech. *BC*, 8 May 1871.
Hospital's town dispensary. *BC*, 26 April 1872.
Hospital finance and new committee. *BC*, 13 Aug., 6, 11, 12, 13, 18 Nov. 1872 and *QGG*, 1873, p. 447.

Warwick riot. *BC*, 26 July 1871.
Hibernian Society. *BC*, 8 Sep. 1871.
The Orange Riot. *BC*, 7, 9, 10 Nov. 1874 and *Tele*, 7 Nov. 1874.
Lilley's education bill. *QPD*, 15 (1873), p. 218.
Public meeting re education bill. *BC*, 24 June 1873.
Non-vested Schools Abolition bill. *QPD*, 16 (1874), p. 394.
O'Doherty declines to sit on education commission. *QVP*, 2 (1875), p. 437 and BC, 25 Sep. 1874.
Education bill of 1875. *QPD*, 18 (1875), p. 525.
Opening, St Stephen's Cathedral. *BC*, 13, 15, 18, 19, May 1874.
Enoggera goldfield. *BC*, 17 Oct. 1872, 10, 13, 24 Feb. 1873.
Pro Bono Publico tin mining company. *BC*, 3 Oct. 1872.
South Monkland Extended Gold Mining Company. *BC*, 22 March, 28 May 1873 and A/21322, QSA.
O'Doherty and football. *BC*, 18 Aug. 1870.
O'Doherty and regatta. *BC*, 20 Aug., 27 Oct. 1873, 25 Aug. 26 Nov. 1874.
O'Doherty sons win school prizes. *BC*, 18 Dec. 1869, 22 Jan. 1872.
Eva at St Stephen's bazaar. *BC*, 17, 23 May 1871.
O'Dohertys leave George St. *BC*, 9 Sep. 1874.
O'Dohertys at Leichhardt St. *Post Office Directory for 1875*.
O'Doherty's letter to Gertrude. In possession of Mrs A.G. Melhuish.

Chapter 10

Daniel O'Connell centenary. *BC*, 16, 19, 21 July, 7, 9, Aug. 1875 and P. O'Farrell, *The Irish in Australia*. (Sydney: Univ. NSW Press, 1987), pp. 216–18.
Sutton's letter. *BC*, 26 July 1875.
Infant mortality rates. Registrar General's reports, *QVP*, 2 (1876), p. 453, and 2 (1877), p. 647.
Local Board of Health report. *BC*, 20 Jan. 1876.
Scientific meeting. *BC*, 29 Aug. 1876.

MLC appointment. *BC*, 5 May 1877 and *Tele*, 5 May 1877.
Amendment to Health Act. *QPD*, 25 (1878), p. 66.
No. 6 Harris Terrace, George St. *BC*, 11 March 1876.
Agent's ad. re Harris Terrace. *BC*, 18 Jan. 1876.
Kevin (jun.) at Christian Brothers School. Personal communication school principal and *BC*, 7 Aug. 1875.
Eva's arrival in San Francisco. *Adv*, 12 Dec. 1876 (quotes *San Francisco Monitor*).
Edward and William, academic progress. *BC*, 20 Feb 1877 and 19 April 1879.
Reception house dispute. *BC*, 21, 23 Oct. 1876; *Tele*, 23 Oct. 1876; *BC*, 2, 9, 21, 24 Aug. 1877: *QES*, 11 Aug. 1877; *QPD*, 22 (1877), p. 179; *QVP* 1 (1877), p. 1235 and *JQLC*, 1 (1877), p. 427
Macalister's illness. *BC*, 28 June 1875.
Gauntlet inquiry. *BC*, 29 Jan., 2, 4, 29 Feb., 6 March 1876 and *QVP*, 2 (1876), p. 1093.
Appointment to Medical Board. *QGG*, 19 (1876), p. 824.
Appointment to museum trustees. *QGG*, 22 (1878), 9 Feb.
Museum building. G. Greenwood and J. Laverty, *Brisbane 1859-1959* (Brisbane: Brisbane City Council, 1959), p. 144.
Appointment to Children's Hospital. *BC*, 18 Oct., 1878.
Sir Arthur Kennedy's quarantine. *BC*, 27, 28 March, 11 April 1877.
All Hallows convent fever. *BC*, 17 Dec. 1877, 10, 11, 12, 18, 19 Jan. 1878.
Catholic Abstinence Society. *BC*, 25 Sep. 1876.
The Youill affair. 30 May, 3, 4, 6, 11, 14 June 1878 and Brisbane Hospital minutes, 29 May 1878, HOS 1/D10, QSA.
O'Quinn and O'Donovan. Y.M. McLay, *James Quinn, First Catholic Bishop of Brisbane* (Armadale, Victoria: Graphic Books, 1979), pp. 51, 192-93, 205-11 and O'Donovan to Vaughan, 5 Nov. 1878, 1 March 1880, 22 Sep. 1881, Sydney Archdiocesan Archives (Brisbane Box).
Australian eleven. *BC*, 3, 5 Nov. 1877.
Brisbane Club. *BC*, 23 Dec. 1876, 27 Jan., 10 Feb. 1877 and *McNaught's Directory, 1878-79*.
Queensland Club membership. Personal communication,

secretary, Queensland Club, 1988.
Johnsonian Club. *BC*, 2 Dec. 1878.

Chapter 11

Thomas Moore. *BC*, 24, 28 May 1879.
Irish famine. *BC*, 25, 31 Dec. 1879, 1, 5, 7, 8, Jan., 2 Feb., 6 Mar., 5, 11, 12, 15 June 1880.
Public health. *BC*, 12, 18, 19, 26, 28, Feb., 7, 14 Mar., 7, 8, April 1879; *QPD*, 28 (1879) p. 411; *Registrar General's Report for 1883, QVP*, 2 (1884), p. 133, and J.H.L. Cumpston and F. McMallum, *The History of Intestinal Diseases in Australia*, C'wealth Health Pubn No. 36, pp. 612–14.
O'Quinn-O'Donovan controversy. *BC*, 10, 12, 13, 14, 17, 19, 21, 22, 23 Jan. 1880 and O'Donovan to Vaughan, 9 Feb. 1880, Sydney Archdiocesan Archives (Brisbane box).
Address to Bishop O'Quinn at Gregory Terrace school. *BC*, 19, Jan. 1880.
All Hallows matriculants. *BC*, 3, 11, 14, 18 Jan. 1881.
O'Quinn's death. *BC*, 13 June, 18, 20 Aug., 6, 8, 10, 21 Sep. 1881.
O'Doherty's relationship to O'Quinn. R. Wynne, Kevin Izod O'Doherty, ACR. Jan. 1950, p. 31.
Reception to Bishop Dunne. *BC*, 15 March 1882.
Johnstone River sugar growing. *BC*, 19 April, 17 May 1880, 21 Sep. 1881, 13 Jan., 1, 2, June, 11 Oct. 1883, 18, 22, 23, 25 April, 23 May, 14, 16 June 1884, 16 Jan. 1885: D. Jones, *Hurricane Lamps and Blue Umbrellas* (Cairns: Bolton Press, 1973), pp. 107, 139, 212, 228, and *QPD*, 31 (1880), p. 154, 40 (1884), p. 89.
Pharmacy bill. *BC*, 27 Oct., 15 Dec. 1880, 23, 25, 28 July 1884; *QPD*, 34 (1881), p. 139; Progress Report of Select Committee of Council on the Pharmacy Bill, *JQLC*, 2 (1884), p. 235 and *QPD*, 40 (1884) p. 14.
O'Doherty's professional activities. *AMG*, 24 (1905), p. 394; E.S. Jackson, An Address, *MJA*, 2 (1926), p. 855; QMS, Minute Book (1), p. 39, AMA House; *BC*, 19, 21 Dec. 1882,

25 Jan. 1883 and *QPD*, 40 (1884), p. 52.
Return of O'Doherty sons. *BC*, 14, 15, 31 July 1882.
Frascati. *BC*, 15 Aug. 1882 and Spencer Browne, *A Journalist's Memories* (Brisbane: Read Press, 1927), p. 107.
Brisbane papers on Ireland. *BC*, 21 Aug. 1880, *Tele*, 6 Jan 1881, *Aust*, 12 Feb. 1881.
Brisbane Land League. *BC*, 1, 2, Feb. 1881, *Tele*, 2 Feb. 1881.
Redmonds in Brisbane. *BC*, 18 Feb, 24, 27, 28, 30 March, 2, 3 April 1883.
The Irish National Convention. *BC*, 10, 13, 15 Oct. 9, 13, 16, 17 Nov. 1883, *MA* (quoted in *BC* 6 Nov. 1883).

Chapter 12

Proposed visit to Ireland. *Tele*, 20 April 1885, *Aust*. 20 April 1885, *Adv*, 9 May 1885.
Parnell interview. *Aust*, 16 Jan. 1886.
Freedom of the city. *Aust*, 22 Aug., 24 Oct. 1885, *BC*, 22 Oct. 1885.
County Meath convention. *DFJ*, 9 Oct. 1885.
Rotunda lecture. *Aust*, 19 Dec. 1885.
Elected unopposed. *Aust*, 5 Dec. 1885, *BC*, 7 Dec. 1885.
Brisbane reception. *Aust*, 9 Jan. 1886, *BC*, 6 Jan. 1886.
Qld Sugar Company. QSA, A/21359.
Banquet. *BC*, 16, 21 Jan. 1886, *Tele*, 21 Jan. 1886, *Aust*, 23 Jan. 1886.
Sydney entertains. *Adv*, 30 Jan 1886.
Melbourne entertains. *Adv*, 6 Feb. 1886.
Speech in Commons. *Hansard (Commons)*, 3rd series, vol. 306, p. 1064, 4 June 1886.
Letter of resignation. *Adv*, 28 Aug. 1886.
Sydney practice. *AMG*, 6 (1886-87)
St Vincent's Hospital appointment. *St Vincent's Hospital Annual Report, 1886* and personal communication from hospital archivist, 1979.
St Mary's Cathedral speech. *Adv*, 22 Jan 1887.
St Patrick's Day speech. *Adv*. 26 March 1887.

O'Doherty testimonial. *Adv*, 6 Aug. 1887.
Croydon GMO appointment. *QGG*, 41 (1887) p. 1081.
Inquest (child). *CMN*, 1 March 1889.
Inquest (confinement). QSA, COL/A532, 88/709.
Tender for liquor. *CMN*, 21 June 1889.
Presentation from friends. *Adv*, 5 Oct. 1889.
Edward's bankruptcy. *QGG*, 46 (1889), p. 154.
Changes of addresses. *Post Office Directories*, 1889 to 1905.
Charges for advice and medicine. *Qlder*, 21 June 1891.
Part-time positions. *QGG*, 57 (1892), p. 911; *Blue Books*, 1893 to 1904 and *Pugh Almanacs*, 1893 to 1905.
Attendance at QMS meetings. *AMG*, 9 (1889–90), pp. 97, 98.
Medico-Ethical Society. *AMG*, 10 (1890–91), p. 53, 12 (1893), p. 166 and *BC*, 23, 24 Dec. 1890.
Deaths of sons. *BC*, 4 Nov. 1890 (Vincent), 9 Oct. 1893 (William) and death certificate, Reg-Gen, Western Australia (Kevin jun.).
Edward, discharged from bankruptcy. *QGG*, 65 (1896), p. 143.
Edward's death. *BC*, 6 July 1900.
Gertrude's salary. *Blue Book*, 1906.
Insurance policy. Gertrude to O'Meara, solicitor, Dublin, 21 Oct. 1905 (in hands of Mrs A.G. Melhuish).
Eva's letter to Father Hickey of 1906. JOL, Brisbane.
Testimonial fund to 1 June 1909. JOL. Brisbane.
Unveiling of monument. *The Age* (Brisbane), 3 Feb. 1912.

Index

Acts and Bills of Parliament
  British
    Coercion Act, 19, 242
    Crime and Outrage Act, 37
    Emancipation Act, 18
    Habeas Corpus Act, 19, 37
    Home Rule Bill, 253-54
    Insurrection Acts, 19
    Land Act, 242
    Martial Law, 19
    Treason Felony Act, 1, 26, 41
  New South Wales
    Treason Felony Act, 164
  Queensland
    Contagious Diseases Act, 159
    Education Bill, 194
    Grammar Schools Act, 131
    Health Acts, 181, 206, 226-27
    Lunacy Acts, 168, 212
    Non-vested Schools Abolition Bill, 195
    Oyster Bill, 169
    Pharmacy Act, 236
    Polynesian Labourers' Act, 180
    Primary Education Act, 133
    State Education Act of 1875, 196
    University Bill, 173
Adams, Charles, 209-11
Alfred, Prince, 162-63
All Hallows Convent, 145-47, 216-18, 230, 232
Anstey, Henry, 67, 70
Anstey, Thomas, 67
Aplin, C. D'Oyley, 176
Arnold, Thomas, 82
Arthur, Governor, 67
Arthur, Thomas, 103
Atkin, Robert, 191

Ballingarry, 38-39
Bancroft, Dr Joseph, 142, 144, 211, 215-16, 227, 236, 239
Banks, Miss, 214, 216
Barton, Dr Frederick, 127
Bateson, Charles, 54
Bedford, Dr E.S., 81
Bell, Dr Hugh, 127, 143, 172, 182, 206, 219-20, 227, 259

Bell, Joshua Peter, 171, 226
Bennett, Catherine, 79, 81
Bentley, Catherine, 95-96
Bentley, James, 95-96
Bernays, Charles, 157
Bernays, Lewis, 161
Blackall, Governor, 162, 171-72
Blackburne, Judge, 46
Blake (Irish MP), 247
Bleay, Solomon, 66
Bond, Father, 66
Bowen, Sir George Ferguson, 144, 147, 151, 161, 167
Bowen, Lieutenant, 59
boycott, 241
Boyne, Battle of, 7
Bramston, John, 190
Brentall, Reverend F., 203
Brisbane Club, 222
Brisbane Courier on O'Doherty
    Irish affairs, and, 243, 245, 249, 250-252
    medical activities, and, 186, 239
    Moore centenary, and, 223
    obituary, 262
    O'Connell centenary, and, 204
    Queensland politics, 155, 157, 166-67, 171, 177, 184, 185, 207
    royal commission on education, and, 196
Brisbane Grammar School, 160-63
Brisbane in 1867, 138-41
Brisbane Municipal Council, 140, 183, 226-27
Brisbane Volunteer Rifle Corps, 144
Brookes, William, 155-56, 161
Brown, William, 118
Browne, Spencer, 125, 241
Bruton, Miss, 40-41
Burke, Dr Stephen, 143
Burke, T.H., 242, 244
Butt, Isaac, 1, 35, 42-44, 46, 48
Byrne, Dr Theo, 144

Cahill, Reverend Dr, 9
Cairns, 233-34
Campbell, Dr James, 258
Cane, Dr, 38
Cani, Dr, 197
Cannan, Dr Kearsey, 168, 182, 186, 188, 215-16, 219-20, 259
Carlyle, Thomas, 71
Carr, Dr Alfred, 95-96, 98-99, 102-3
Carvosso, Dr A.B., 266
"Castle Catholics", 112, 116
Catholic Association, 17
Cavendish, Lord, 242, 244
Central Board of Health, 182, 205-7, 226
Challinor, Dr Henry, 129, 168, 214, 216
Chamberlain, Joseph, 254
Chapman, Prudence (great-granddaughter), 267
Cheyne, Dr John, 10
Chichester, Arthur, 5
Christian Brothers, 208, 229
civil service commission on Woogaroo Asylum, 168
Clarendon, Lord, 31, 37, 46
Clonmel, 45
Cluseret, General, 115
Cobb & Co, 93, 138, 165
Colles, Professor A., 10
Collins, David, 60
Conlan, Mother Bridget, 146, 148
Connell, Mr & Mrs, 70
Connolly, Frank Glynn, 172
Connolly, Mrs Hope, 223
Coote, W., 156, 167
Corrigan, Dr Dominic, 10
Coveney, Mr, 62
Crampton, Judge, 1-5, 48
cricket eleven, Australian, 222
Cromwell, Oliver, 7
Crooke, Dr William, 74
Croydon, 256
Cullen, Cardinal, 112, 117
Cummins, N.M., 23
Curran, Dr John, 42-43

Dalton, Count, 47
Davis, Thomas Osborne, 18, 21-22
Davitt, Michael, 242, 248
Day, William, 185
Denison, Sir William, 60-61, 71, 76, 79

Dillon, John Blake, 18, 36–38, 40
Dods, Dr Espie, 262
Doheny, Michael, 114
Doherty, Anne (mother), 8–9
Doherty, Anne Eliza (sister), 8
Doherty, George (great-grandfather), 6
Doherty, George (uncle), 6, 102, 106–7
Doherty, Jane Annette (sister), 8
Doherty, John, Chief Justice, 46
Doherty, John Timothy (brother), 9, 11, 113
Doherty, Kevin Izod (grandfather), 6, 8
Doherty, William (father), 6, 8
Doherty, William Izod (brother), 8, 11, 113, 116, 240
Donovan, Michael, 11, 44
Douglas, John, 196, 207, 214, 216
Drogheda, 7
Duffy, Sir Charles Gavan
  arrest, 31
  Australia, in, 121, 151, 245
  Eva, and, 71
  famine, and, 24
  the *Nation*, and, 18, 112
  Newgate jail, in, 34–35, 37, 45, 47, 49
  O'Doherty's pardon, and, 104, 108
  Richmond jail, in, 21
Duffy, Frank Gavan (son), 245, 253
Duke of Westminster, 250
Dunne, Bishop Robert, 161, 232
dysentery, 228

Edmondstone, George, 170, 172, 179, 184, 189
Elgee, Jane, 69
Elkington, Dr John, 160
Elm Cottage, 65
emancipation, Catholic, 8, 16–18
Emma, 57, 59, 61, 84
Emmet, Robert, 2
Ennis, Father, 46
Enoggera Gold Mining Company, 198
Eureka Stockade, 94

famine
  (1840), 22–24
  (1879–80), 224–26
Fenianism, 114–15, 151–52, 163–64
Ferguson, Samuel, 35
Finney, Thomas, 226
Fitzgerald, Lord Edward, 7
Fitzgerald, Francis, 46
Fitzgerald, Thomas Henry, 197, 229, 232
Flood, John, 115, 225–26
Flynn, Dr John, 262
Forrest, Dr, 197
Forrest, E.B., 252
Fouhy, Reverend, 230
Frascati (Brisbane), 241, 258, 266
Frascati (Ireland), 9
Fraser, S. (MLA), 167, 170, 172
French, Major-General G.A., 266
Fullerton, Dr George, 127, 145

Galvin, John, 79
Gandon, James, 6
Gauntlet, 213
Gladstone, William Ewart, 242, 247, 249, 253–54
Godfrey, Dr, 187
goldfields
  Ballarat, 94–96
  Canoona, 164
  Croydon, 256
  Enoggera, 198
  Gympie, 165
  Johnstone River, 234
  Peak Downs, 164
Gormley, Miss, 14
Gorry, Christopher, 131, 161
Graham, William (MLC), 211
Grattan, Henry, 8
Graves, Professor Robert, 10
Gray, G.W., 233
Green Street Court, 1, 41
Gregory, Augustus, 198
Grey, Earl, 60
Grey, Sir George, 102, 104, 109
Griffith, Sir Samuel, 195, 234

Hale, Bishop, 225
Hall, Dr Edward, 66
Hall, Reverend, 61

Halloran, Arthur, 156, 172
Hampton, Dr John, 71
Hancock, Dr Robert, 142
Handy, John, 184
Hargreaves, Edward, 164
Harris, George, 147
Hartington, Marquess of, 254
Hassett, Thomas, 210
Hatchell, John, 43
Headford, 13–14
Hearne, Dr, 213
Heath, Captain, 169
Hemmant, Arthur, 250
Hibernian Benefit Society, 192
Hibernian Gold Mining Company, 198
Hickey, Father, 263–64
Hirley, Mrs, 188
Hoban, Denis, 27, 31, 34, 45
Hobbs, Dr William, 127, 139, 172, 182, 209–13, 217
Hodgson, Arthur, 167
home rule, 242, 244, 246, 252–54
Hope, Louis, 180
Horan, Father James, 180
Hospitals
    Brisbane, 142–43, 173, 185, 189–90, 212, 228, 239
    Brisbane Children's, 214
    Coombe's Maternity, 114
    Croydon, 257
    Ipswich, 129
    Lady Bowen, 141, 144, 188
    Meath, 10, 11
    Pitié, 107, 111
    Rotunda Maternity, 249
    St Mark's, 11
    St Martin's, 241
    St Mary's, 81
    St Vincent's (Dublin), 11, 114, 117, 248
    St Vincent's (Sydney), 255
    Saltpetrière, 107
Hotham, Sir Charles, 95
Hubbard, Alfred, 227
Hue and Cry, 37
Hutchison, Peter, 48

Inchiquin, Lord. *See* O'Brien, Sir Lucius
infant mortality, 136, 205
Inishowen
    (Ireland), 5
    (Queensland), 233–34
Irish Confederation, 25–27
Irish Exile and Freedom's Advocate, 72
Irish in Australia, 89, 119–21, 202, 204, 224, 245
Irish Land League
    (Ireland), 241–42
    (Brisbane), 243
Irish National Convention, 245–46
Irish National League
    (Ireland), 241–42
    (Brisbane), 244
Irish population, decrease in, 22
Irish Republican Brotherhood, 114
Irish Tribune, 3–4, 27–31, 35, 41–42, 44
Ivy House, 13
Izod (family name), 9

Jackson, Dr Sandford, 238–39
James Baines, 97–100
Johnsonian Club, 222
Johnstone River, sugar-growing at, 232
jury-packing, 4–5, 36, 43, 48

Kate, 215–16, 250
Kellow, Henry, 125
Kelly, Edward, 13
Kelly, Hyacinth, 13
Kelly, Colonel Thomas, 115
Kempes, crown solicitor, 47
Kennedy, Sir Arthur, 214–16, 223, 225
Kennedy, Miss Georgina, 214, 216
Kenyon, Father, 37–38
Kesteven, Dr Leighton, 239
Kickham, Charles, 114
Killeen House, 14, 40, 110
King, Governor, 59
King, Henry, 191
Kinsella, wet nurse, 9
Knabbs, Mary, 6

Lalor, James Fintan, 25
Lalor, Peter, 25, 95–96
Lang, Reverend John Dunmore, 156, 192

Lannigan, Bishop, 197
La Trobe, Charles Joseph, 88
Lee, Dr Cathcart, 12
leptospirosis, 233
Lewis, E., 167
Lisdonagh, 13-14
Lilley, Sir Charles
    Brisbane Club, and, 222
    Brisbane Grammar School, trustee of, 161
    O'Doherty banquet, presides at, 251
    political career, 167, 170-71, 173, 177, 194
    royal commissions on education, 186, 195
Local Board of Health, Brisbane, 206-7, 217, 226-27
Logan, Patrick, 142
Loney, Captain Henry, 54
Lubbock, Basil, 99
Luby, Thomas Clarke, 114

Macalister, Arthur, 157, 159, 193, 212
McConnell, Mrs Mary, 214
MacCormack, Mrs, 39
Macrossan, John Murtagh, 229, 244-45
McDevitt, E.H., 197
McDonald, Captain Charles, 97-100
McDonnell, Randall, 161, 163, 197
McEncroe, Archdeacon, 113, 118, 121, 126, 146
McEvoy, Anne, 8
McEvoy, Timothy, 8
McGee, Darcy, 36-38
McGinty, Father William, 130-33
McGrath, Patrick, 89
Mackay, Donald, 97
McKeever, Francis, 44, 49
MacKenzie, Robert, 159, 166
McKillop, Mother Mary, 221
Maclysaght, Edward, 10
McManus, Terrance Bellew
    rebellion, role in, 38-40, 45, 50, 53
    Van Diemen's Land, in, 61-62, 64, 75, 78

Macquarie Harbour, 55
McSharry, James, 234
Magorian, Reverend Hugh, 77
malaria, 233
Manchester martyrs, 115
Manning, W., 161
Margetts, Dr, 259
Marlborough, Duchess of, 224
Martin, John
    Eva in Brisbane, writes to, 174
    Melbourne, in, 90-93
    Paris, in, 102, 107, 116
    rebellion, role in, 2, 31, 34-35, 45, 50
    transportation, 53-57
    Van Diemen's Land, in, 68-70, 72, 79, 80-81, 83-85
Martin, Peter, 95
Mathew, Father, 218
Meagher, Thomas Francis
    rebellion, role in, 24, 36-37, 39, 45, 50, 53
    Van Diemen's Land, in, 61-62, 68, 81, 83
Meath convention, 249
medical practitioners, unregistered, 187
Melhuish, Mrs A.G., 266
Melhuish, Colleen, 266
Meston, Archibald, 233
Miles, MLA, 187
Mitchel, John, 2, 23, 25, 26, 72, 83
Monahan, J.J., 1, 41
Moore, Thomas, 223
Moorfields Church, 102
Morehead, Boyd, 184
Mount Stewart Elphinstone, 53-56
Mourilyn, 233
Moxey, Dr George, 57
Mullen, Dr John, 172, 193, 217, 219, 221
Murray, Bishop, 197
Murray, Sir Terence, 119
Musgrave, Sir Anthony, 234
Musny, Dr M. Henry de, 42

Nairn, William, 61
Nant Cottage, 83-84
Nash, James, 165, 197

Nation, 14, 18–21, 25, 112, 223, 265
Negligan, J. Moore, 11
Neptune, 72
Newgate jail, 33–34
Nesbitt, Caroline (great-great-granddaughter), 267
Nesbitt, Vivian (great-great-granddaughter), 267
Nesbitt, Thomas (snr & jnr), 266
Norbury, Lord, 2
Normandy, Marquess of, 178, 197
Norton, Albert, 233

Oatlands, 63, 65–66
O'Brien, Sir Lucius (Lord Inchiquin), 85, 108
O'Brien, Patrick, 89
O'Brien, William Smith
  pardons, 85 (conditional), 109 (full)
  rebellion, role in, 21, 24, 37–39
  ridiculed in press, 40
  Richmond jail, in, 50
  sentence, commutation of, 53
  testimonial dinner, 91–93
  trial, 45–46
  Van Diemen's Land, in, 61, 71–73
Ocean Chief, 118
O'Connell, Daniel, 8, 16–21, 25, 202–5 (centenary)
O'Doherty, Sir Cahir, 5
O'Doherty, Edward (son), 117, 175, 208, 240–41, 255, 258, 260
O'Doherty, Eva
  ancestry, 12–13, 15
  children, birth of, 110, 117–18, 135, 174, 200
  financial difficulties, 263
  in-laws, and, 113, 116
  Ipswich, in, 135
  Ireland, longing for, 122, 174
  Kevin's absence, and, 71
  marriage, 105–6
  mother, dutiful, 173, 200
  O'Connell centenary, and, 205
  overseas travel, 208–9
  Paris, in, 107–8
  poems, 14–15, 22, 30, 80, 121–26, 209, 264
  Sisters of Mercy, and, 147
  testimonial for, 264
  unworldliness, 115
O'Doherty, Gertrude (daughter), 200, 254, 261, 263, 266
O'Doherty, Kevin (son), 118, 175, 208, 232, 248, 260
O'Doherty, Dr Kevin Izod
  alcohol, and, 218–19, 257, 261
  ancestry, 5–6, 8
  arrest, 31
  Brisbane Grammar School, and, 161–63, 175, 200
  common convict, serves as, 76–78
  education, 9–12
  Eva, reunion with, 96–97, 100–102
  Fenianism, and, 115, 153
  financial difficulties, 251, 254, 256, 258
  generosity, 63–64, 100, 147, 149, 162, 196
  gold, and, 89, 143, 165, 198–99, 234, 256
  graduation, 111
  Hibernian Society, and, 191–92
  Ipswich, in, 127–36
  Ireland, in (1885–86), 247–50
  Irish Tribune, and, 27–31
  last years, 262
  marriage, 106
  medical career, 114, 119, 126, 129–30, 141–43, 172, 187, 210, 212–18, 237–39, 256–60. *See also* O'Doherty, Dr Kevin Izod, public health
  medical school, preliminary, and, 173, 185–86
  migration, 113, 117–18
  nationalism, 10, 92, 120–21, 134, 149–51, 204, 243, 245–46
  Newgate jail, in, 34–35
  O'Connell, centenary, and, 202–5
  pardons, 85 (conditional), 108–9 (full)
  Paris, in 102, 107–8
  physical description, 62
  political career, 152–60, 165–72, 176–78, 180–82,

184–85, 189–90, 206–7,
211, 227, 235–36, 240, 253
(Commons)
public health, and, 183, 206,
226
Quinn, support for, 128,
131–33, 145, 228–31
Roman Catholic Church, and,
144, 148, 196
royal commission on education,
and, 195
St Mary's Hospital, at, 81–83
sectarianism, 179, 190–91
sentence, 4
sporting bodies, and, 199, 222
state aid, and, 133, 154–55,
194–95
Sydney, in, (1861), 118,
(1886–87), 255
ticket-of-leave, 63–64, 74,
75–76
transportation, 53–57
trials, 41–45, 48–49
Victoria, in, (1854–55), 87–98
O'Doherty, Louis (grandson), 260,
266
O'Doherty, Mignon
(granddaughter), 261, 266
O'Doherty, Vincent (son), 117,
208, 260
O'Doherty, William (son), 110,
175, 199, 208, 240–41, 258,
260
O'Donohue, Patrick
rebellion, and, 38–39, 45, 50,
53
Van Diemen's Land, in, 61–62,
64, 71, 72–73, 75, 78, 83
O'Donovan, Denis, 221, 229
O'Donovan, Jeremiah (O'Donovan
Rossa), 114
O'Farrell, Henry, 163–64
O'Flaherty, Francis, 14
O'Flaherty, John, 13
O'Flaherty, Martin, 14–15
O'Flaherty, Mary, 13
O'Gorman, Richard, 36
O'Leary, John, 114
O'Loghlen, Sir Bryan, 245, 253
O'Loghlen, Sir Colman, 43, 46
O'Malley, John, 114

O'Neill, Sir Phelim, 7
O'Quinn, Bishop. *See* Quinn,
Bishop James
Orange riot, 192–94
O'Reilly, Florence, 232
O'Reilly, John Boyle, 115
O'Shanassy, Sir John, 89, 91
O'Shea, T.J., 265
O'Sullivan, Inspector M., 266
O'Sullivan, Patrick, 130, 132, 152,
244, 252
O'Tuathaigh, Gearoit, 40

Pacific islanders, 180–81
Palmer, Arthur, 168, 182, 184,
189, 225
Palmerston, Christie, 233–34
Palmerston, Lord, 85, 104, 109
Panton, John, 127–28
Paris Anatomy School, 102
Parkes, Sir Henry, 119, 164, 244
Parnell, Charles Stewart,
241–42, 248, 253
Pasteur, Louis, 182
Peel, Sir Robert, 17, 21, 24
Pennefather, Baron, 41, 43
Petrie, John, 130, 143, 145
Pharmaceutical Society of
Queensland, 235
Philosophical Society, 150
Phoenix Park murders, 242
Pigot, Lord Chief Baron, 41
Pitt, William, 7
Pockley, Captain, 57
Polding, Archbishop John Bede,
126, 130
politics in early Queensland, 153
Port Arthur, 56
Port Douglas, 233
Porteus, Reverend, 193–94
Pring, Ratcliffe, 172, 179
Pritchard, A.B., 155–57, 161
Pro Bono Publico Tin Mining
Company, 198
Pugh, T.D., 155, 167
Pugh, Dr William, 82

*Queensland Evangelical
Standard*, 212
Queensland Hibernian Society,
191–92

Queensland Irish Association, 264
Queensland Medical Society, 188, 238, 259
Queensland Medico-Ethical Society, 259
Queensland Sugar Company, 233, 251
Queensland Turf Club, 150
Queensland Volunteer Forces, 244
Quinn, Bishop James
  All Hallows School, and, 230
  Australia, arrives in, 126
  Christian Brothers' School, and, 230
  death, 230
  famine (1879–80), and, 225
  Johnstone River sugar growing, and, 232
  McGinty, dispute with, 131–33
  memorial, 231
  Moore's centenary, and, 223
  O'Connell centenary, and, 202–5
  O'Donovan, and, 221, 228
  Orange riot, and, 193–94
  St Laurence O'Toole's seminary, and, 117
  St Stephen's Cathedral, and, 148, 197
  Sisters of St Joseph, and, 221
  state aid, and, 133, 195–96
Quinn, Bishop Matthew, 197

Raff, G., 155
railways, 135, 176–79
Rawlins, Frederick, 182
reception house dispute, 209–12
Redmond, John, 244, 248
Redmond, William, 244, 248, 263
Reilly, Devin, 36
Rendle, Dr Richard, 217, 236
repeal movement, 19–21, 24
Richmond jail, 49
river steamers, 127–28, 138
Robinson, George, 67
Rosenstengel, Herr, 204
Ross, 68
Rowlands, Dr Thomas, 129
Royal College of Surgeons, Ireland, 10, 110–11, 208, 240

royal commissions
  education, on, 186, 195
  railway construction in the colony, on, 178
  railway extension — Ipswich to Brisbane, on, 177
  sugar industry, on, 234
  Woogaroo Asylum, on, 211
Ryan, John, 65
Ryan, R.H., 233
Russell, Lord John, 24

St Laurence O'Toole's seminary, 117
St Stephen's Cathedral, 148, 196–97
St Vincent's orphanage, 148
Salisbury, Lord, 249, 253
Scobie, James, 95–96
Scott, Henry, 182
Scott, John, 177–78
scrub typhus, 233
Scully, Reverend, 132
sectarianism, 179, 190–91, 193–94, 203
select committee
  Pharmacy Bill, on, 236
  Woogaroo Asylum, on, 168
Shaw, J.M., 156
Sheares, H. and J., 2
Simpson, Captain H.G., 177, 182
Sisters of Mercy, 145–48, 216, 232
Sisters of St Joseph, 221, 228
Skerrit, Ally, 13
Skerrit, Patrick, 13
smallpox, 181, 207, 214, 216
Smith O'Brien. *See* O'Brien, William Smith
Smyth, Patrick, 41, 83, 85, 89–90, 93
Smythe, T.M., 156
Sorrell, Lake, 69–70
South Monkland Extended Gold Mining Company, 199
Stephens, James, 114–15
Stephens, T.B., 161, 170
Stokes, Dr William, 10, 12
Stonor, Allan, 73
Swift, 61–62

Index

Tasman, Abel, 59
Taylor, Edward, 235
Taylor, James, 167
Telegraph on O'Doherty
   Brisbane banquet, 252
   Irish Land League (Brisbane), 243
   Legislative Council appointment, 207
Telegraph (steamer), 126
Temple, Dr Thomas, 142
Thomson, Dr John, 211, 217, 219, 221, 239, 262
Thorn, George, 127–28
Thynne, Andrew Joseph, 229
Tiffin, Charles, 142
Tissot, Father Paul, 179, 203
tithes, 18
Tone, Wolfe, 7
Torrens, Judge, 1, 48
Townley, Captain, 193
Towns, Robert, 180
Trident, 53
tropics, white man, and, 240
Tufnell, Bishop, 133, 140, 163
typhoid fever, 217, 228

union of England and Ireland, 7–8

Van Diemen's Land, 59
Vaughan, Archbishop, 197, 221, 229

Wall, Dr, 10
Walpole, Reverend, 54–56
Walsh, William Henry, 177, 179–80, 198
Ward, Moses, 189, 235
Wellington, Duke of, 17
Whish, Captain, 180
Whiteford, John, 65, 74
Whiteside, QC, 46
Whitty, Mother, 145
Wilde, Sir William, 11
Williams, Dalton, 19–20, 27, 31, 34, 47, 49, 72, 74
Willson, 67, 74–75, 78
Wise, Captain, 95
Wiseman, Cardinal, 102, 106
Woogaroo Asylum, 168, 186, 211–12

Yeo, Fletcher, 235
Youill, Alexander, 219
Young Irelanders, 20–21, 24–26, 36–40

Ziemen, Simon, 187
Zouche, Dr Isaiah de, 206